Louis Luyt

UNAUTHORISED

UNAUT

Louis Luyt

MAX DU PREEZ

ZEBRA

Published by Zebra Press
an imprint of Struik Publishers
(a division of New Holland Publishing (South Africa) (Pty) Ltd)
PO Box 1144, Cape Town, 8000

First edition 2001

1 3 5 7 9 10 8 6 4 2

Main cover photograph © *Sunday Times*;
insets (left to right) © *Rapport, Independent Newspapers, Rapport, Beeld*;
author photograph © *Kyknet*

PUBLISHING MANAGER: Marlene Fryer
MANAGING EDITOR: Robert Plummer
EDITOR: Martha Evans
COVER DESIGNER: Christian Jaggers
TEXT DESIGNER: Beverley Dodd
TYPESETTER: Monique van den Berg
PICTURE RESEARCHER: Carmen Swanepoel

Reproduction by Hirt & Carter Cape (Pty) Ltd
Printed and bound by CTP Book Printers

ISBN 1-86872-371-2

CONTENTS

Photographs between pages 120 and 121

ACKNOWLEDGEMENTS

Thanks to Zebra's Marlene Fryer, Robert Plummer, Martha Evans and Monique van den Berg for doing much more than publishers normally do; and to all those who were prepared to share their stories and insights with me for this book. Thanks also to my children and friends for their patience during the last two months of writing.

INTRODUCTION

Louis Luyt is a very unusual man.

Those who really love him hated him on occasion; those who really hate him loved him at some point. It is rare for a public figure to generate such extreme emotions of resentment and admiration, loathing and loyalty. His few friends and many enemies agree on only one thing: he has not had a boring life.

The story of Luyt's life is a story of a man with extraordinary ambition, drive and energy, but it is also a story of a dangerously insecure, sometimes paranoid and often callous man. His dramatic self-destruction was almost as spectacular as his remarkable rise from the poorest kid in a dusty Karoo hamlet to a multi-millionaire industrialist, sports administrator and politician.

Perhaps it was simply inevitable. He felt the pain and humiliation of his youth too intensely; his obsession to overcome it was too fierce. The fanciest Lear Jet, a driveway full of expensive limousines, the most imposing mansion in Saxonwold stilled only one part of the barefoot Afrikaner boy's burning anger. The insults from the teachers and the rich kids, the desperate loneliness of the social outcast also demanded power, recognition and fame. Other poor kids accepted their fate and lived ordinary lives. Louis Luyt spent his entire adult life avenging his first sixteen years.

But he did not know how to stop. Just as Afrikaner nationalism, into which he was born, was energised by the humiliation of British colonialism and then drove Afrikaners to humiliate all those around them, Louis the Bullied became Louis the Bully. (In fact, several other interesting parallels between Luyt's life and Afrikaner nationalism through the apartheid years can be drawn.)

In virtually every interview Luyt gave in his earlier years, he stressed that 'loyalty' was the virtue he admired and demanded most. 'Loyalty is number one in life,' he said more than once, and stated that it was his own best attribute. When he started a beer company and took on the might of South African Breweries, he heard that a student had kicked up a fuss in a pub when the barman said they did not stock Luyt Lager. He had the student traced and paid for the rest of his studies.

But when he thought the young man he often called 'my son', Springbok rugby captain François Pienaar, had outmaneouvred him in negotiations for players' contracts, he helped destroy his career and said to his face: 'The line between love and hate is a thin one, and I hate you.' When the man he saw as the chosen one to receive the Luyt mantle one day, his son-in-law Rian Oberholzer, now CEO of the South African Rugby Football Union, crossed him, he banned him and his own daughter from the Luyt home.

Free State rugby personality Steve Strydom bought Luyt a drink at a function a few years ago. Luyt turned to the person next to him and said: 'This little man Strydom is flitting around me now, but many moths have been burned to death in this candle.'

The Luyt ego is, unsurprisingly, notoriously fragile. He desperately wanted to be an honorary senior officer, with uniform and all, in the South African army. According to the Secretary of Information of the John Vorster government, Eschel Rhoodie, a 'blisteringly angry' Luyt 'pestered' him for weeks about the low rank – lieutenant-colonel – the army had offered him and asked him to talk to General Magnus Malan to upgrade him to at least a brigadier, but preferably a general. 'Somehow I could never get myself to call Magnus Malan about this great injustice,' Rhoodie wrote in his book *The Real Information Scandal.* Luyt made an appointment with Rhoodie on the day he received his uniform as lieutenant-colonel. 'When he arrived it appeared he had nothing to talk about, so I assumed he wanted me to see what he looked like in uniform. I thought he looked impressive.' Luyt refused the offer of coffee in the office, and instead invited Rhoodie to a coffee shop in Pretoria. 'Everywhere we walked Luyt complained about the young soldiers and other officers not using a proper salute to him.' (At a later meeting when the two had an argument, Luyt screamed at Rhoodie: 'I don't work for you, I hire people like you!')

Many of those who worked closely with Luyt, like Springbok coach Nick Mallett, captain François Pienaar and manager Jannie Engelbrecht, immediately point to one characteristic when asked about Luyt: 'Extreme mood swings'.

Whether it's due to a deeply suspicious mind or simple ruthlessness, Luyt has a thirty-year history of tapping the phones of friends, foes and associates, and of recruiting weaker people to spy for him on everybody around him. He did it while he was in the fertiliser business and later the beer industry, say his former business associates and adversaries, and he's done it consistently since he got involved in rugby administration. Springbok hooker James Dalton recently admitted to having spied on his team colleagues for Luyt. His vice-president at Transvaal up to 1990, Chris van Coller, says Luyt spied on his own management and players. The Springbok team manager in 1993 and 1994, Jannie Engelbrecht, says the only explanation for Luyt's knowledge of certain incidents on tour can be that he had players spying on their colleagues and tour management.

Luyt's phone-bugging habits eventually landed him in hot water, but it took many years for them to become public. (When a new administrator appointed by Luyt discovered his phone was being tapped, Luyt threatened him in front of all his colleagues: 'Don't try to threaten me, I'll tell your wife about all your phone calls to your girlfriends.')

In November 2000 Luyt invited me to his home in Saxonwold, Johannesburg (it is called Solitaire ...), to discuss the possibility of writing a book on his involvement in rugby. He was making serious allegations against several highly respected Springboks and rugby officials. When I told him he could not say things like that in a book, he told me: 'I can prove it – I have all these guys on tape on all these issues.'

The further I dug into Luyt's life, the more it became clear to me that this was a man who ruled by fear, intimidation and hard cash. Very few people, even his bitterest enemies, were prepared to talk to me on the record about Luyt. They had seen him destroy too many careers, even lives, the past two decades.

No one can fail to admire Luyt's progress from a poor labourer's son to one of South Africa's most successful entrepreneurs – he was nominated Businessman of the Year by the *Sunday Times* in 1968, by *Rapport* in 1969 and by the *Financial Mail* in 1971, and Industrialist of the Year by the *Financial Gazette* in 1970. And he didn't do it the easy way – he took on the fertiliser, beer and newspaper giants. As one of his long-time associates says: '*Louis hou daarvan om die leeu se bal te kielie*' – Louis likes to tickle the lion's testicles. (In the end this trait was the beginning of his undoing: he tickled the wrong lion – Nelson Mandela, whom he forced to appear in court while President of South Africa.)

Nor can anyone deny that Luyt first saved Transvaal rugby from bankruptcy and mediocrity and then went on to be a major force in the unification of rugby after apartheid and reintroduced South African rugby to the world. Without him the 1995 Rugby World Cup would not have been the most successful in history. Perhaps it says a lot about Luyt that it was exactly this, his proudest moment, that he spoiled with a nasty and childish speech at the formal dinner after the World Cup, to the boos of top international players.

Five years later the same rugby establishment that he had saved and made stinking rich spat him out, and he had to retire to the east coast a lonely, embittered figure.

In a piece after Luyt's 'retirement' from rugby in late 2000, senior rugby journalist Dan Retief wrote that rugby will remember Louis Luyt as 'a man who would rather lose than see others win'.

I have always instinctively disliked tyrants and bullies, but Louis Luyt has fascinated me as a human being for many years. I have often wondered what course his life would have taken if he had been a member of the Afrikaner Broederbond, the secret and powerful society that ruled so much of the Afrikaner's political, cultural and economic life. He was never invited because he came from such a poor family, and by the time he was successful, he had too many important enemies. I'm fairly sure he would have gone on to become a cabinet minister, perhaps even prime minister in the place of PW Botha. Luyt and Botha have many traits in common – they're both megalomaniacs, for one – but Luyt is far more intelligent, resourceful and ambitious than Botha ever was.

But the biggest difference between them is that Louis Luyt has never had an ideology of any kind. He did the old South African Defence Force a lot of secret favours while they were fighting in several neighbouring countries and wore the uniform of an honorary lieutenant-colonel proudly. But he also publicly called for coloured and Indian South Africans to be given the vote back in 1969 and sponsored the first official non-racial sports event in 1974. He was the Vorster government's frontman to start their own newspaper with taxpayers' money. But in 1987 he criticised PW Botha for not extending the vote to black South Africans. In 1988 he had talks with the still banned African National Congress in Harare to normalise rugby, but before the first test after readmission to international sport he broke an agreement and played the old anthem, *Die Stem*, at Ellis Park stadium.

Luyt married his wife, Adri, in 1958. They have four children:

Corlia, a Johannesburg lawyer, Lucien, who runs the Luyt family's export grape farm in the Cape, Adri, a caterer who lives overseas, and Louis junior, who worked for his father at Ellis Park.

Luyt is on record that he doesn't read much apart from the occasional spy novel 'like James Bond', and dislikes going on holiday. He listed as his only hobbies 'my job' and fiddling with electronics: 'I build my own amplifiers. It seldom happens that I have to call in a technician when something goes wrong with an electrical appliance at home.'

I was tempted to write Luyt's book for him. But after three meetings I realised that he truly thought his version of events was the only truth, and that he was only interested in glorifying himself and denigrating everyone else. I could not be a part of that.

A few days before I finished writing this book, Luyt learned through a news reporter that I was writing an unauthorised biography on him, and he phoned me. He expressed his surprise that I had declined to help him write his autobiography and instead was writing a book on him without his co-operation. I reminded him of my reasons, and added that it was more my journalistic style to write independently. He tried to draw me out on what I was going to write, and I simply told him I was writing an honest book and that it was not going to be a 'hatchet job on Louis Luyt'.

That was the truth. This is not a hatchet job. I came across quite a few stories about Luyt's personal life while I was researching this book, and decided not to include them. And I asked every person I talked to who bad-mouthed Luyt if they had anything positive to say about him. I told Luyt on the phone that he was not going to like everything said in the book, because he was a very controversial man. He laughed nervously, and said that people tell a lot of lies about him. The real story of what happened in his life, Luyt told me, will be in his own book about his life, which he was already working on. I sincerely told him: I'm looking forward to that, to reading the Luyt story from the inside.

Luyt started giving examples of lies told about him, referring specifically to the Information Scandal and his role in the launch of *The Citizen* and his fertiliser days. I stopped him and said I could not start asking him questions, because that would mean I would have to give him the entire book and ask for his comment on everything. Then we would be back to his original idea of me writing his book for him.

The next day he issued a press statement saying he had heard I was writing a book about him, and he wanted to put it on record that I had not asked him for information or comment. And that was true.

Asked by news reporters about his views of me, Luyt said he had always respected my work. He added: 'I like Max.' I'm not sure whether he will still say that after reading this book. I do hope that he will agree that I was not unfair to him.

I'll say this to Louis, though: you never bored me in the months I spent researching your life. You have done some remarkable things in your life. And I'm not sure I would have been able to say that about many other personalities in South African public life. Trust me: the Britstown boy would have approved of what you have achieved. Perhaps he would have wanted you also to find peace and sweetness now that you've retired.

1

'IT WILL DRIVE ME UNTIL I DIE'

*I hated the rich. I hated the fact that we didn't have any money
... I was ashamed, people shun you when you're poor ... But
what it did to me was to make myself promise that I will make
it one day, and I think it will drive me until I die.*

– Louis Luyt, 1989

Armblankes. Miserable, semi-literate, dirt-poor white Afrikaners.
Five, six decades ago regarded as one of the biggest social problems
in South Africa.

That is what Louis Luyt's parents were called: *armblankes*, poor
whites.

Louis was born on 18 June 1932 in the quiet little *dorp* of
Britstown on the arid Karoo plains. Those were the years of the
Great Depression, a time of great suffering among most South
Africans other than the comfortable middle classes. Louis' father was
a labourer, first on a farm, then on the railways. When they moved
to the neighbouring town of Hanover, Luyt senior ran a small bak-
ery. It did not last long. In Colesberg he had the unenviable job of
driving the nightsoil truck.

Young Louis was used to not owning a pair of shoes. His clothes were always hand-me-downs, threadbare and almost always either too big or too small. He had to get up at three in the morning to stoke the fire in the family's bread oven. He helped deliver meat and bread – always at the back door, because the young Luyt wasn't welcome at the front of the house. In the early evening he was responsible for controlling the water in the irrigation ditch.

Since his first newspaper and magazine interviews in the late 1960s, Luyt has told two stories from his childhood over and over. One incident that really hurt him was when he went to church and sat down with the other congregants, only to be told to go and sit in the gallery – downstairs was for '*ordentlike mense*' (decent people).

But the event that still makes him clench his teeth when he talks about it happened at school. The teacher was young, blonde and beautiful – at least to the young boys in her class. One day she asked for a volunteer to clean the blackboard. Little Louis rushed to the front. But the teacher dismissed him with a laugh and gave the duster to a rich kid with shiny shoes. Louis slunk to the back of the classroom, humiliated to tears.

'This kind of thing had a huge influence on me,' he told the Afrikaans magazine *Huisgenoot* in 1988. 'I can't really call it hatred, but it certainly made me swear to myself that I would one day show these blighters what I can do.' A year later he told *Leadership* magazine: 'I was the greatest communist ever when I was a youngster. I hated the rich. I hated the fact that we didn't have any money. We never had money, not a penny. One feels ashamed all the time, poor and bare feet and so on. Yes, I was ashamed, people shun you when you're poor ... But what it did to me was to make myself promise that I will make it one day, and I think it will drive me until I die. Whenever I do something, I do it for the poor kid.'

Words that would make any psychologist break into a knowing smile: 'I will make it one day' and 'it will drive me until I die'.

But young Louis had one thing going for him: he was a big, strong boy. There was one way in which he could make it, however poor his background – much like young black Americans boxing themselves out of the ghetto. Rugby. It became his obsession. During school break, Louis ran home to help his father – in exchange for free time in the afternoon to go to rugby practice. Nobody noticed his poor kid's clothes on the rugby field. If they didn't respect him in church or the classroom or at social gatherings, they had to respect him if he was the best player in town. And respect was the one thing he craved. Rugby is more than a physical activity – scholars talk about the 'heroic' and 'mythical' dimensions of sport. Rugby became adolescent Louis' passport to social acceptance in the class-ridden and narrow-minded Afrikaner societies of Britstown, Colesberg and Hanover, where he went to school. It was also the only way a boy from the wrong side of the tracks could become someone the girls would look at twice.

Rugby may have held another attraction for Luyt – as a child, and later as an adult, even if it wasn't consciously so. After the symbolic *Eeufees Trek* (Centenary Trek) of 1938, commemorating the Afrikaners' Great Trek into the interior a century earlier, Afrikaner nationalism was blossoming. Being poor was one way to be shunned by your peers; being a 'bad Afrikaner' was another. In the 1940s and 1950s, rugby was already established as the primary sport played by white Afrikaner males. Deep resentment against the British was the main catalyst for Afrikaner nationalism. Rugby was seen as a very English institution, but the Afrikaners could beat them at their own game. It almost became an anti-imperialist tool. (For decades, the biggest rugby derbies were top Afrikaans schools playing top English schools, or the Intervarsities between Pretoria University and Wits University and Stellenbosch University versus Cape Town University.) If you excelled at rugby, you were almost automatically accepted as a 'good Afrikaner'.

Rugby was also young Louis' passport to acceptance by the *volk*.

11

By the time he started making a success of his career as an entrepreneur, rugby had replaced large gatherings at Republic Day and the Day of the Covenant as the primary *volksbyeenkoms* – more about this in Chapter 3, on Luyt's decision to become a rugby supremo after he had made his mark as an industrialist and entrepreneur.

It is probably also worth noting that white Afrikanerdom was, at least during most of Luyt's lifetime, a radically patriarchal and Calvinistic society. Rugby, some believe, became the only legitimate expression of intimacy between Afrikaner males; the only respectable occasion for male bonding. Of course, others would say the secret Afrikaner Broederbond fulfilled that purpose, but then they did not have the privilege of joint showers and the hugging in the locker room, or of the physical intimacy of the scrums and the rucks …

Young Louis had the body – 6 foot 4 inches – and the determination. In 1949, while he was in Matric at Colesberg, he played for Free State's under 19s. Three years later he made the senior Free State side and was a regular between 1952 and 1960. He captained the side between 1956 and 1958. In 1962 he played in an Eastern Transvaal Invitation Fifteen; in 1965 he even ran out for Northern Transvaal. The legendary Godfather of South African rugby, Danie 'Doc' Craven, said about Luyt's rugby potential: 'He was a good jumper and he had the weight, but he too was a victim of playing at a time when we had lock forwards who excelled.' (*The Craven Tapes – Doc Tells All*, by Keith Clayton and Chris Greyvenstein.) In the book *Dok Craven – Agter die Kap van die Byl*, by George Gerber, Craven listed Luyt as a 'Springbok who never got colours'.

Like thousands of other young Afrikaners from poor backgrounds, Luyt went to work for the South African Railways after school: as a clerk in Bloemfontein at six shillings a day. 'It was tough,' he recalled years later. 'After paying board and lodging there was nothing left. I used to wash and iron my own clothes.' But he played rugby during the winter months, and in summer he was a boxer – he made the provincial team in 1950 – and an athlete – he was selected as a shot-puttist for the Free State team in 1957. Rugby remained his ticket to success: in 1952 Gencor's Ted Pavitt offered him a job as sub-accountant at the Welkom gold mines in order to get him to play for the local club. Again Louis threw himself into the job. Two months after he joined, he went underground, got his blasting certificate and eventually qualified as a shift boss.

He more than doubled his salary at the mines, but then he decided he could make much more money in sales. Luyt was making good progress in his quest for recognition and respect: as captain of the Free State rugby team, people recognised him in the streets of Bloemfontein and Welkom and invited him to their braais and parties. The time had come to indulge his second obsession: he wanted lots and lots of money. In 1957 he joined the Caltex oil company as a technical rep. It meant a drop in salary, but Luyt had the right instincts: he knew that the farmers in the Free State adored their rugby captain and would buy his oil products. He worked around the clock, and in his first year as a salesman sold 347 per cent of his quota. That made him Caltex's top salesman. *Scope* magazine asked him in 1970 how he had pulled it off. His reply: 'I worked, that's how. You can forget any of that lucky break stuff. Everything I got I worked damn hard for.'

The closest Luyt got to a lucky break in his younger days was when Fisons Fertilisers, who had heard of this young super-salesman, offered him a job in sales. He knew his clients – farmers – intimately, and he knew that the market was potentially very big. Also, Luyt was fast growing in confidence and he found that the cut and thrust, the fierce competitiveness of the business world really suited his personality.

Fisons assigned him to Nylstroom, one of their worst regions in terms of sales. In an interview in 1977, Luyt told Afrikaans author

Chris Barnard: 'I bought myself a bakkie. And I drove from farm to farm delivering my products to the farmers myself. It worked like a bomb. I remember one year I made 25 000 pounds in salary and commission – three times more than the managing director. I figured that if they can afford to pay me 25 000 pounds, then I'm probably worth ten times more to them.'

This was a source of great satisfaction to Luyt, and a turning point in his life. It was the last time he worked for someone else. He formed Louis Luyt Enterprises, hired fifteen salesmen and took over Fisons' marketing and sales. Luyt was in business, and his bank balance soon showed it. After four successful years, he was beginning to think it was easy.

It wasn't. The big fertiliser companies – Fisons, AECI and Windmill – unexpectedly agreed on a quota system, slicing up the market among them. Luyt had no inkling, it just happened. Suddenly Louis Luyt Enterprises was out of business. He was stuck with fifteen employees, offices and vehicles, and no product to sell. The rich guys had screwed him again. And the Britstown kid wasn't going to take it lying down.

Luyt mustered all his resolve and every penny he could lay his hands on, and started Triomf Fertiliser and Chemical Industries Ltd. (*Triomf* means triumph – it wasn't just a name he pulled out of a hat.) He promptly announced to the world that a new fertiliser manufacturing giant was about to be born. Triomf issued seven million shares at one rand each, and started building a fertiliser plant at Potchefstroom. But the construction work soon had to be stopped, because he sold less than R1 million in shares in the first year. He tried to sell shares to farmers, but they were caught up in the big drought of the mid-1960s. Other potential investors did not believe Luyt could make a success against the competition of the big companies. The fact that he wasn't a member of the Afrikaner Broederbond meant there was no easy access to big Afrikaans capital.

The thirty-three-year-old Luyt was bitter and angry. He tried every single financial institution in the country. 'They weren't even prepared to talk to me,' he says. It seemed that his first really ambitious undertaking was stillborn. Deeply unhappy, he got on the plane to America to look for capital. In contrast to the stuffy business clique in South Africa, the United States was still a land where the brazen, adventurous entrepreneur was seen as the secret to the economy of the future. Within ten days he explained his plans to five of the biggest American companies, and came home with R3,5 million from the Esso Standard Oil Company, who had financed half the shares in Triomf – the shares, apparently, remained in Luyt's name. Luyt now knew he was going to make it big, and promptly bought up a large chunk of the remaining shares himself. The rest of the shares were also sold, mostly to farmers.

'South African businessmen are scared,' he said about this episode in an interview in 1970. 'No, not cautious, scared. I use that word deliberately. They're afraid to take even a small chance. Don't let anybody fool you – getting capital in South Africa is the most difficult thing in the world. Why did I have to go to America? Unless you're a big corporation, they won't look after you, no matter how sound your idea is … There are many able people, working for other companies, who are capable of going out and starting something for themselves. We lack ideas, we lack imagination, we lack confidence. There are so many ways of making money in South Africa that it's hard not to see them.'

Two years after he formed Triomf, in August 1967, his fertiliser plant went into production and produced 100 000 tons of fertiliser in the first year. This made Triomf a profit of R225 000 after tax. Triomf was Luyt's triumph. The big companies had first bragged that Triomf wouldn't get off the ground; when it did, they took bets over a gin and tonic at the country club that it wouldn't last a year.

By 1968 the major fertiliser manufacturers had to swallow their insults. But instead of welcoming this upstart *Boertjie* in their midst, they colluded to crush him and started a crippling price war. All of them suffered serious losses, but Triomf had more loyalty from the primary consumers of fertiliser – the Afrikaans farmers. Still, Triomf lost almost half a million rand in a few months.

When the price war was at its fiercest, Luyt made one of the boldest moves of his life, and one that eventually made him a multi-millionaire: he offered to buy the Esso shares back. Esso was not only nervous about the future of Triomf, but rumour had it at the time that Luyt had them over a barrel about the legal status of their shares. Luyt apparently got the shares back at a ridiculously low price. He was now the largest shareholder by far.

In August of 1968 his competitors in the fertiliser industry called him to a peace conference. They offered him a deal: stop expanding Triomf, and we'll stop cutting the prices. The gin-sipping country club boys of big industry had gambled against Louis Luyt, and lost. They didn't respect his Afrikaans accent, his table manners or his nouveau riche style, but they had to start respecting his chutzpah and his business acumen.

But they hadn't seen the best of Luyt yet. He sold the 50 per cent share he had bought back from the Americans to South African Breweries – at an extremely handsome profit, naturally. 'Triomf was at last a purely South African company, and this is what I had always wanted,' he said later. Soon afterwards, Luyt and SA Breweries sold 40 per cent of Triomf's equity to farmers' co-operatives. It was a brilliant move. More than 85 per cent of all fertiliser used in South Africa was sold through these co-ops. Why would they push any other product if they had such a big interest in Triomf? In 1969, the company's third year in business, Triomf made a healthy profit of R1,5 million after tax under chairman Luyt.

With his first million in the bank, Luyt became restless. He bought his first executive jet and started a jet charter company, a company financing small businesses and entrepreneurs, a building and property company, a sports equipment business and a petroleum products company. Newspapers fell over their feet to nominate him Industrialist of the Year and Businessman of the Year. In 1970 he was on the front pages of the newspapers again: he had insured his life for R25 million, making him the most highly insured man in the world at the time. He boasted in interviews about the symbols of his wealth: an executive Falcon jet, a Cadillac, a Daimler, a Peugeot Sports, one of the grandest houses in Saxonwold, Johannesburg.

A journalist asked Luyt in 1970 why he didn't just buy a boat and spend the rest of his days cruising around the world. 'You know,' he replied, 'I used to think the same thing when I was younger. I was going to make money, then live a life of ease. But it doesn't work that way. I'm enjoying my money – very much. I enjoy work, and I enjoy success. The thing is, how do you measure success? It's the amount of money you make, isn't it? The money is nothing really, but that's your yardstick for success.'

Luyt's biggest triumph was still to come. He had demonstrated Triomf's potential for growth and his own business aggression, and now he went to talk to the biggest fertiliser manufacturer and part of the Anglo American empire, AECI. Big Louis emerged with an even bigger smile: he had talked them into amalgamation with Triomf, with Triomf holding 51 per cent of the shares of the new company. The new Triomf was now the giant of the southern hemisphere, with four huge factories and ambitious expansion plans – like a huge phosphate plant at Richards Bay.

The fertiliser business was beginning to bore Luyt. In the mid-seventies, he took on his former partners in Triomf – SA Breweries – for a stake in the very lucrative South African beer market. He called his beer Luyt Lager. 'This is a good product,' he said at the time. 'It's got my name on it.'

It was a dirty fight, with rumours of industrial espionage and counter-espionage, secret helicopter flights over the Luyt plant, tapped telephones, poaching of key staff, intimidation of retail outlets and court cases. SA Breweries outmaneouvred Luyt at least once: not long after he announced that he was going to launch a new beer, Stallion 54, SA Breweries launched their own new beer – and called it Colt 45.

Eventually, in July 1973, Luyt sold out to industrialist Anton Rupert. Rupert's Oude Meester group had earlier acquired a substantial shareholding in Louis Luyt Breweries, but Luyt and Rupert rarely agreed on how the group should be run. Oude Meester paid Luyt R1,7 million cash for his half-share in Beer and Malt Investments (Pty) Ltd, which held just over 50 per cent of the shares of Louis Luyt Breweries. The other half-share of Beer and Malt Investments belonged to Rupert's company Rembrandt. Luyt later described the sale of his beer interests as 'the biggest mistake of my life'.

Rand Daily Mail reporter Chris Day recalled travelling back with Luyt in his private jet after one of his stormy meetings with Rupert in Stellenbosch. 'In the plane was a Rupert lawyer, working on a contract with which Louis was not satisfied. The lawyer tried to go to the toilet several times, but Louis said the plane needed to reach a certain height before the toilet could be used. After some while the lawyer – his face etched with white lines – was allowed to make his call of nature. Louis turned to me and said: "You've got to show these Cape hot shots that the action is really in the Transvaal."'

2

LOUIS THE PATRIOT

Luyt ... did a lot for South African sportsmen, he helped the army and the Bureau for State Security by putting his aircraft at their disposal, free of charge, and he is a great patriot.

— *Dr Eschel Rhoodie*

By the early 1970s the power players in the National Party government had taken note of this man Luyt. And they thought he could be useful, especially because they had realised he was politically fairly naïve while his 'heart was in the right place'.

Luyt's high profile as a business maverick, and his yearning to be acknowledged by his *volk* and especially its leaders, made him a sitting duck for the clever men in charge of the secret projects of the John Vorster government's Department of Information. There simply wasn't a better frontman for the government's project to launch its own newspaper. Of all Luyt's ambitious projects that failed in the end, this was the one that did not make him lots of money. On the other hand, it did contribute to the belligerent, maverick image that Luyt seems to have cultivated all his adult life. And, bizarrely, he was the only one who in the end survived the 'Information Scandal' seemingly unscathed – the scandal cost virtually every other participant his career, including Prime Minister Vorster and cabinet minister and National Party crown prince Connie Mulder.

At the heart of this seedy chapter in the history of the National Party's rule was the resourceful and energetic Dr Eschel Rhoodie, Secretary of the Department of Information since 1972. He saw it as his mission in life to counter the bad publicity the apartheid government was receiving in the international community and at home, and he believed the end justified the means. His most senior partners in crime were the Minister of Information, Connie Mulder, and the head of the Bureau of State Security (Boss) and the power behind Vorster, General 'Lang Hendrik' van den Bergh. Over a five-year period, they spent some R75 million on secret projects to improve the image of the government abroad.

Rhoodie believed that most of the negative publicity his government was receiving internationally was based on reporting in the progressive daily newspaper the *Rand Daily Mail*, part of the then South African Associated Newspapers (SAAN) group, and its stablemates the *Financial Mail* and the *Sunday Times*. In 1975 he was told that SAAN was in trouble and shares could be picked up fairly cheaply. In August 1975 he met with Mulder, Van den Bergh and two Rhoodie recruits, Les de Villiers and Jan van Zyl Alberts, in his Menlo Park home and decided to 'solve the *Rand Daily Mail* problem' by buying a majority shareholding in SAAN.

Clearly this could not be done in the name of the government. Van den Bergh formally approached Luyt and asked him to be the frontman for the SAAN takeover. Luyt was keen, Vorster approved the project and Rhoodie transferred R2 million into Luyt's bank account. Another R1 million was to come from the former leader of the United Party, the white opposition party, Sir De Villiers Graaff.

On 27 October 1975 Luyt announced a R9 million takeover bid for SAAN. He lodged his offer of R4,50 a share with SAAN's major shareholders, the Abe Bailey family trust and the Argus group. He told a press conference that his bid was supported by two right-wing publishers, the American John McGoff, an old friend of Connie Mulder's, and the German Axel Springer. McGoff and Springer later pulled out of the scheme, citing financial considerations.

The news of a Luyt takeover bid caused consternation among the editors and senior journalists of SAAN as well as among progressive whites sympathetic to the *Rand Daily Mail*. The *Rand Daily Mail* responded in an editorial: 'It seems curious that a shrewd and successful businessman should seek to take over one of the great newspaper empires in South Africa, the South African Associated Newspapers group, at a time when economic recession and spiralling, inflation-fuelled costs are making desperate men of newspaper owners in South Africa and, indeed, the world.

'And the event becomes even more curious when that man turns out to be Mr Louis Luyt, who made his fortune with Triomf Fertiliser.'

The editorial voiced concern about political influence on editorial policy: 'Mr Luyt has claimed that he is acting in his personal capacity, so dissociating the board of Triomf with its bevy of Nationalist politicians from his action. But, wealthy though he is, he will need the financial support of others, and being a Nationalist supporter he is bound to gather people of like persuasion around him … Indeed, Mr Luyt has already shown his colours in regard to Nationalist policy. He is an enthusiastic sponsor of the Committee for Fairness in Sport which has set itself the task of white-washing sport apartheid overseas.

'If Mr Luyt succeeds, we believe that the powerful voices of Main Street, Johannesburg, Burg Street, Cape Town, and possibly Baakens Street, Port Elizabeth, will be muted to become faint English echoes of the Nationalist-run Afrikaans press. In effect this will mean the last dream of Nationalist Afrikanerdom – to control its own English newspapers to sow its propaganda among the English – will have been realised. And a devastating blow will have been dealt to the cause of Press and public freedom in South Africa and a wide range of public expression stilled. And freedom's last bastion, the newspapers of the Argus group and the few remaining independents, will have become highly exposed and vulnerable to final assault.'

Lawrence Gadar, former editor of the *Rand Daily Mail*, said: 'If, by virtue of his connection with the rather mysterious Foreign Affairs Association, he is seeking public influence, then there is even more reason for him to keep his nose out of the SAAN group, which reflects an enlightened outlook that is at last beginning to prevail in South Africa.'

Speaking to an SABC interviewer, Luyt denied any political motives: 'I think my record speaks for itself. I've never been a politician. I've always been a businessman.' 'So there are no political connections at all?' asked the interviewer. 'None whatsoever,' Luyt replied. 'No connection with any political party, no connections with any Press group whatsoever.'

But Luyt was quoted as saying that he would influence editorial policy if he thought it necessary to do so. 'Under close questioning at his Press conference,' reported the *Rand Daily Mail*, 'he conceded that he found more he liked in Nationalist policy than in the politics of other parties – though he disagreed with some of aspects of it – and said he felt the *Rand Daily Mail* should be more Rightwing.

'Although he repeatedly said he did not want to interfere with editorial policies, he left no doubt that he would do so if necessary.'

Luyt's bid was thwarted, however, when the Bailey trust refused to sell its shares.

Rhoodie, Mulder and Van den Bergh immediately launched the alternative plan: to start an English-language daily newspaper in opposition to the *Rand Daily Mail* with state funds, again with Luyt as the frontman. It was estimated that the newspaper would break even in two or three years, and then the plan was to launch a new Sunday newspaper to counter the *Sunday Times* and neutralise the group's progressive Sunday paper specialising in investigative journalism, the *Sunday Express*.

Vorster later denied knowledge of the plans, but Rhoodie maintained until his death that the Prime Minister was fully informed about the whole process from the start and gave it his blessing. He said the first meeting where Vorster gave the go-ahead took place at 12:15 on 3 November 1975 in the Union Buildings. Rhoodie wrote in his controversial book *The Real Information Scandal*, published in 1983: 'There has never ever been the slightest doubt in my mind that Louis Luyt was the Prime Minister's personal nominee for the take-over of SAAN, and to establish a new daily newspaper. Dr Mulder, Jan van Zyl Alberts, Les de Villiers and I all distinctly recall how, after the dinner party at my house in Menlo Park, General Van den Bergh had told us to make use of the services of Luyt for the SAAN take-over, and that this was also Mr Vorster's wish. Obviously the General had also talked with the Prime Minister the day after we decided to approach Mr Vorster. After the General spoke to me in his office and told me to contact Luyt, I telephoned the fertiliser magnate in Johannesburg. He immediately told me he knew what I was calling about, and within an hour he was sitting in my office eager as a beaver.'

The deal was sealed in Luyt's executive jet – where else? – during a flight to a rugby match in Bloemfontein. Rhoodie, Van den Bergh and cabinet minister Piet Koornhof and their wives were present, although Koornhof could not remember later what they had talked about.

At the follow-up meetings between Luyt and Rhoodie the cost of the project was estimated at R10 million. The room was never big enough for both Luyt and Rhoodie's huge egos, and the two clashed from the start, with Rhoodie calling Luyt a 'prima donna' and Luyt insisting he wasn't going to report to Rhoodie. Mulder accepted the estimates of expenditure and, according to Rhoodie, ordered that the money be invested in one pool in a bank where only the interest raised could be used for the newspaper. He stressed that the government had to be able to access the money at any time. Luyt's version was that the money was loaned to him for the project, and the judicial commission of inquiry eventually believed him. In April 1994, Rhoodie said, Luyt adjusted his estimate for capital needed to R12 million, and the full amount was paid to him. Luyt immediately split the money and, instead of paying it into a bank, paid it into the accounts of three of his personal companies. Luyt always insisted that the money was a loan and there was nothing untoward about paying it into his own accounts.

On 2 April 1976 Luyt and Rhoodie signed a document of agreement to restrict Luyt on the use of the R12 million. Part of the agreement was that the editors and journalists of the new newspaper were to sign an editorial charter drawn up by Rhoodie – a charter also signed by senior journalists of Rhoodie's other front-publication, the newsmagazine *To the Point*. The charter stipulated that the newspaper would be 'independent', would reject the 'manipulation of news' and would separate opinion from straight news reports. It also stated that the newspaper 'will uphold the right of all national groups in Southern Africa, irrespective of race, to self-determination and control of their own destinies'. The journalists had to agree not to 'write, say or do anything which endangers the safety of the Republic and its constitutionally elected Government, or promotes dissension between the different national groups'. It also declared the newspaper 'opposed to Communism, Fascism and Marxism as ideologies inimical to just government and prosperity', but in support of 'free enterprise'.

Luyt himself came up with the name of the new newspaper: *The Citizen*. It is a direct translation of the most influential Afrikaans newspaper of the time and the then mouthpiece of the National Party, *Die Burger*, edited by Piet Cillié. In the Chris Barnard interview of February 1977, Luyt said about *The Citizen*: 'I have always had respect for a newspaper such as *Die Burger* and for a man like Piet Cillié. When *Die Burger* says something, people take note. It is my big ideal to get my newspaper to the point where readers would trust it as they trust *Die Burger*.'

The Citizen started publishing in September 1976. It was soon clear that, businesswise, the project wasn't a big success. It didn't attract nearly enough advertising to be profitable; editorially it didn't compete with its rivals; and it didn't have enough buyers and readers. This time, Luyt was involved in a business he didn't know and couldn't manage properly. And Rhoodie didn't want him any longer, especially after he found out that Luyt had deposited the state money in the bank accounts of three of his own companies. Seven months after the newspaper started, in April 1977, Luyt and his accountant, Fourie du Preez, met with Mulder, Rhoodie and Van Zyl Alberts in the Jan Smuts Airport Holiday Inn. Mulder and Rhoodie told Luyt they didn't trust him and told him to get out of the project. According to Rhoodie, Luyt asked to stay on until the end of 1977 'because he did not want to create the impression he was leaving a sinking ship, which would also reflect adversely on his person and status as a businessman'. Luyt's version was that he told Mulder and Rhoodie to go to hell and take their newspaper with them.

Luyt had to pay back the Information Department's R12 million, but he wasn't held responsible for the losses the paper had incurred. He apparently paid only R10 110 00 back, arguing that he had lost R3 002 576 because Standard Bank had raised their rate of interest on a foreign loan to Luyt when his involvement with *The Citizen* became known to them. However, Standard Bank later declared that he had simply lost that amount on a foreign loan because of the devaluation of the rand. Luyt has often boasted that he repaid the R12 million with one cheque. *The Citizen* was sold to Van Zyl Alberts and Hubert Jussen, the owner of *To the Point.*

Rhoodie wrote of Luyt: 'For a self-made millionaire, Louis Luyt has somewhat of a problem with his ego and he had a bad case of know-allism. Because of this he wanted no one to tell him what to do. He resented my interference immensely, and this caused us endless problems in selecting the staff for the newspaper.' Rhoodie said that Luyt had agreed that staff for *The Citizen* would be checked by

Van den Bergh's Bureau for State Security before their appointment. Sometimes Luyt ignored this, and when appointments were found to be 'security risks', Rhoodie had to order Luyt to get rid of them. This annoyed Luyt, until Rhoodie showed him a letter signed by a top employee of *The Citizen* which had been intercepted by the Bureau for State Security, from which it appeared that the man was 'planted' by a British newspaper.

Luyt had some pretty unflattering things to say about Rhoodie too. Still, Rhoodie wrote: 'Despite Luyt's ego I must confess that I like the man, no matter what he said of me. No matter that he has seven television sets in his house. He did a lot for South African sportsmen, he helped the army and the Bureau for State Security by putting his aircraft at their disposal, free of charge, and he is a great patriot. One could fight with him one day and laugh about it the next day. He was fun on a trip and beyond the problem with his ego, he is a likeable person. When he finally had to go on television to lie about the ownership of *The Citizen*, he did not do so for his own image, but to protect the secrecy of the project. He has become a super wealthy and successful businessman, and I hope he has learned to take it as much as he liked to dish it out to others.'

The Citizen's birth in sin was finally made public in November 1978 by Judge Anton Mostert, who was appointed to investigate exchange control violations. The headlines in South Africa's main newspapers on 3 November 1978 told the story. 'Judge drops bomb', read *Die Burger*'s headline. 'Swindle!' said *Beeld*. The *Rand Daily Mail* declared: 'It's all true!' and *The Star*: 'The Cover-up'. *The Citizen* featured a more subdued headline: '*Citizen* is featured in probe'.

Mostert's main findings were later confirmed by a judicial commission of inquiry under Judge Roelof Erasmus. The Information Scandal was cleverly used by PW Botha and his close allies to get rid of John Vorster and Connie Mulder. Luyt, however, was coated in teflon. He did complain, though, that the episode undermined his relationship with the media. 'After the story the English press turned against me after I had been the golden boy of Johannesburg until then,' he said in August 1998. 'I was quoted on things I never said. I lost all confidence in the press.'

Rhoodie was found guilty of fraud involving R63 205 of government money by the Pretoria Supreme Court, but was acquitted on all counts by the Appellate Division. At a press conference afterwards, Rhoodie stated that a 'handful of powerful politicians' had launched a vendetta against him and his family 'primarily to protect their own involvement in the government's secret propaganda war of 1971 to 1978'.

Why was Luyt chosen for the job, and why did he take it? According to Rhoodie, Luyt had said to them he was the 'only Afrikaner moderate whom the banks and the English press knew had enough personal funds' to finance a newspaper. That was probably the main reason: through his previous dealings (mostly secret) with the government and the Defence Force he had shown that the National Party government could trust him. In 1976 and 1977 Luyt sponsored the international Formula 1 Grand Prix at Kayalami, allegedly also as a front for the government. The fact that it was publicly known that he had made a lot of money through Triomf, coupled with his rogue image, made him a very credible figure to use as a front. Through his interviews at the time, it is also clear that Luyt quite fancied the idea of being a media boss – it meant power and social standing, and it made him a player in the political arena, something he clearly still craved.

In February 1979 Luyt told *Die Burger*. 'Why did I get involved? I was in the clouds. The company was doing well, I was doing well and here the guys come and ask my help with the newspaper. How can a man who is a patriot say no to them? You know they said the Prime Minister, Mr BJ Vorster, chose me. How could I do differently?' He told *Leadership* magazine in 1989: 'When one is young, one is inclined to like the limelight and what-have-you. They told me the prime minister wanted me to be the man. At the time I suppose I was taken in by it all. Yes, it was heady stuff.'

Luyt said he was 'crucified' for his loyalty to his country and the people he dealt with during the newspaper episode. He was particularly angry at Mulder and Rhoodie, who, he said, had betrayed him. 'It left me a bitter man. I couldn't believe that people could run away the way they did, and that they would lie the way they did.' It would have been worse, he said, if he hadn't ignored their orders to destroy all records regarding the *Citizen* deal and instead kept a secret set of all documents to prove his version of events.

But Luyt still had Triomf. Triomf lasted twenty years and made Luyt one of the richest men in South Africa. At its peak, it had an annual turnover of more than R7 billion in today's terms.

Even in those days, tapping the telephones of friend and foe was standard procedure with Luyt. Former *Rapport* journalist and now business editor of the *Daily Dispatch*, Eddie Botha, got hold of a transcript of a telephone conversation between Luyt and Piet Uys, a former rugby Springbok. Uys had been a Triomf employee, but at the time of the bugged conversation, he was working for Triomf's opposition in the fertiliser market, Hanhill Industries. Shortly after the conversation, Uys went back to Triomf. Luyt and Uys were discussing the attack on Maputo by the South African Defence Force. According to Botha, the attack took place close to two fertiliser tanks Hanhill had in Maputo. Part of the conversation went like this:

UYS: 'No, the tank still stands, I hear.'
LUYT: 'Yes, but this was the first attack. The second one will ...'
UYS: 'Yes, well, I said I would have to talk nicely with the general so that he does a good job.'
LUYT (laughing): 'The second one [and] the tank is a goner [*in sy moer in*].'

UYS: 'Yes, with the heavy artillery ... the man said he had used light artillery.'

By late 1981 it became clear that trouble was brewing in paradise. With a steep rise in interest rates, Triomf's already huge debt of more than R140 million rose dramatically, while sales did not. Most of the money was owed to Nedbank – a fact that Luyt and, it was said at the time, the managing director of Nedbank, Ron Abrahamsen, concealed from the Nedbank board.

Triomf was beginning to incur huge losses by 1983. Luyt's private company, LLG (for Louis Luyt Group) Investments, took over AECI's stake in Triomf's Richards Bay plant in 1984 for R38 million. A year later, LLG Investments sold the AECI stake to Triomf Ltd for R44 million – an amount lent to Triomf, astonishingly, by the already embattled Nedbank.

This is how the investigative magazine *noseweek* described the negotiations around 'these masterpieces of salesmanship' in its July 1988 edition: 'At the one end of the table sits Dr Louis Luyt PhD (honoris causa), executive chairman of Triomf, and, as such, the custodian of the interests of minority shareholders (it's a public company, listed on the JSE) and of creditors (including Nedbank, of course). At the other end of the table is, well ... Dr Louis Luyt PhD (honoris causa), representing LLG and custodian of the Luyt family's interests. No-no, Big Louis is TOTALLY innocent of any conflict of interest. Don't dare think that for a moment. Also there, sitting at a remote corner of the table, discreetly averting his gaze so as not to witness the rape of his bank, is Rob Abrahamsen, graduate of the Netherlands School of Economics and the Harvard Business School, President of the Institute of Bankers of SA ...'

This was Luyt's greatest talent as a businessman, something future business administration students will probably study: the ability to spin an intricate web so that nobody can decipher what and how much he controls and/or owns; to confuse even the cleverest accountants and business brains; to make deals with otherwise astute businessmen so that later no one could understand why they were so stupid.

With Triomf's bankruptcy looming, Luyt reduced LLG's share in Triomf's parent company, Lanchem, from 80 to 40 per cent, and in 1985 he sold those shares to the Nasionale Mielieprodusente Organisasie (Nampo) for a reported R30 million. It is not known how Nampo survived the loss when Triomf went down.

Triomf collapsed in 1986, shortly after the crash of Triomf (Richards Bay). Triomf owed Nedbank R462 million, and it was reported at the time that it probably didn't succeed in recouping more than R100 million of that. Only a large new investment by Old Mutual and a substantial lifeboat by the Reserve Bank saved Nedbank from collapse.

In November 1997 the former senior Nedbank regional treasury manager, Terry Crawford-Browne, told the session of the Truth and Reconciliation Commission on the role of business during the apartheid years that Nedbank had lent Triomf almost 100 per cent of its capital. He said Luyt had strong political influence. That was how he was able to obtain import protection for his fertiliser business. He said Old Mutual's recapitalising of Nedbank 'bought' the apartheid government eight more years. It prevented a banking and financial crisis which could have brought the National Party government down, Crawford-Browne said.

In an interview in August 1998, Luyt blamed State President PW Botha for the collapse of Triomf: 'Botha's Rubicon speech and the resulting weakening of the rand had the effect of increasing Triomf's foreign loans sevenfold.' Luyt claimed that he personally lost 'well over R70 million', but added with a half-smile: 'But I didn't put all my money in one basket.' He surely didn't. He was by this time far too shrewd for that.

A last word about LLG, the Luyt company that in 1985 owned 40 per cent of the shares in Lanchem worth about R30 million and sold its shares in Triomf (Richards Bay) (Pty) Ltd to Triomf Ltd for R44 million. At the end of 1986, LLG was quietly liquidated – the only shareholder one André Both, who declared that his company owned nothing whatsoever …

Even more difficult than trying to figure out what Luyt owned and controlled, and what not, is trying to establish his academic qualifications, if any. He told *Huisgenoot* magazine in 1972 that he started studying for a BA degee at the University of the Free State in the late 1950s, and later switched to the University of South Africa, where he also later signed up for a BComm and a BSc. 'No, I didn't finish. My business interfered too much. So now I've given up studying.' In 1977 he told the same magazine that he had started with a B Juris degree. In yet another interview with *Huisgenoot* in 1988, he stated that he had an honorary DCom, and a PhD in business administration 'after study at the University of the Free State and in America'. He added that he was working on his LLD at the University of Pretoria.

Leadership magazine reported in 1989 in a piece after an interview with Luyt that he 'earned a law degree through part-time study, as well as an American doctorate in business administration with a dissertation on arbitration. Now, at the age of 57, he is halfway to completing another doctorate.'

In 1994 *Huisgenoot* reported in a feature on Luyt: 'Louis Luyt never completed any university training. He started studying at Free State University, but did not finish. Later he received an honorary doctorate from them. He also has an honorary doctorate from the Columbia Pacific University in California.'

According to a news release of the State of California Department of Consumer Affairs on 13 January 2000, the Marin County Superior Court had ordered the Columbia Pacific University to close permanently. The California Bureau of Postsecondary and Vocational Training had earlier denied an application by the institution for a licence to operate as a private university. It was found that the 'university' had violated various sections of the California Business and Professions Code, and that it 'failed to meet various requirements for issuing PhD degrees'. Michael Abbot of the California Department of Consumer Affairs said: 'When an institution issues a degree to a student who has not received adequate training, knowledge and skills, the student, employers and the general public are harmed.'

It is widely known among senior staff at the Rand Afrikaans University that Luyt lobbied hard for that university to give him a PhD. He donated R180 000 to RAU to build an athletics stadium, as well as setting up some rugby bursaries. It was reported in 1988 that Luyt had donated R1 million to the University of the Free State.

In his curriculum vitae posted on the website of his political party, the Federal Alliance, in 1999, Luyt simply stated under 'Highest Qualifications': 'PhD Business Administration (honoris causa); Drs Jur (LLD exams successfully completed).'

In February 1998, while he was giving evidence in the Pretoria High Court opposing a commission of inquiry into rugby, he was asked by a counsel for the government: 'Don't you have a doctorate in law?' He replied: 'No, I'm still busy with it.'

But not having a doctorate in law never discouraged Luyt from becoming one of South Africa's most prolific litigants.

3

THE VOLK'S RELIGION

[R]ugby as a cultural phenomenon maintained its endearing attraction for Afrikaners. Rugby provided entertainment, it did not carry an overt political message ... and it provided an opportunity for predominantly male camaraderie and time-honoured ritualistic social behaviour. In short it was a volksbyeenkoms, *a closing of the ranks, but without political soul-searching and sombre over-tones.*

– Albert Grundlingh

By 1983 Louis Luyt knew that his Triomf triumph was fading, and that all that remained was to get out of the mess with as much money stashed away as possible. Even in international terms, Luyt was a rich man – at least in property and investments, if not cash flow. His property in Saxonwold was worth a few million; his luxurious beachfront mansion at Ballito Bay was worth more than R25 million; his Porterville grape farm probably also about that; he had several other smaller companies and investments. The Britstown boy had just turned fifty, and even if he never lifted a finger again, he would never go to bed wondering where his next meal was going to come from. Or his next Mercedes Benz.

But he was still smarting at his failed attempt to be more than just a filthy-rich businessman. Money he had, respect outside the harsh world of cut-throat capitalists he did not. Besides, he was getting bored.

Now why not get back into the business that got him out of the backwater in the first place? He had achieved adulation and respectability through rugby once before, hadn't he?

Luyt was still harbouring deep-seated resentments about being excluded from the elite of his own Afrikaner tribe at this stage. He was rejected as a boy by fellow Afrikaners; he wasn't allowed in the inner circle of his ethnic group. It's not that he didn't try. His two big business enterprises were close to Afrikaner culture: mostly Afrikaner farmers used fertiliser; beer is very much part of Afrikaner male culture. He tried to ingratiate himself with the Afrikaner leadership in the Vorster government by doing them secret favours and even fronting for them with *The Citizen*. He wanted to be loved and respected by his own people.

But they didn't invite him to become a member of the secretive and powerful Afrikaner Broederbond. You couldn't join the Broederbond, you had to be nominated by a Broeder and then weighed up by committees. If you were deemed worthy, you were invited to join. Very few, if any, of those invited declined. But the Broederbond was an elitist organisation. Luyt came from a family of *armblankes* and had no academic qualifications. He wasn't the kind of guy invited to the exclusive circle. It is not known whether he was asked to join during his forties, when he had established himself as a top entrepreneur, and then declined the offer. It is unlikely that he would have refused, and it is probably equally unlikely that he was ever asked: he had too many enemies by that time.

Luyt told *The Star* in August 1994: 'Why am I like I am? I think it's because I've always had to fight for myself ... That could be the problem of my life. I had to fight for everything I ever got ... I wasn't a favourite. I wasn't a Broeder, I didn't belong to any organisations. That's bullshit. I've always been my own master.'

Peculiarly, the one way to the heart of Afrikanerdom without being a senior Broeder was rugby. And this was only true because of the man who had ruled over rugby like a monarch for decades, Dr Danie Craven, who wasn't a Broeder either. Craven wasn't a Broeder because he was 'a Jan Smuts man' and came from a family of 'Sappe' – the white political party (the United Party, formerly the South African Party – SAP), which took South Africa into the Second World War on the side of Britain while the Afrikaner-dominated National Party had pro-Germany sentiments. But Craven was an institution at the heart of Afrikanerdom and of rugby in those years, Stellenbosch University; he was a rugby genius; and he quickly learnt how to coexist peacefully with the Broederbond.

Craven once told the story of how Prime Minister Hendrik Verwoerd had put pressure on him because Craven was trying to change the country's sports policies. When the pressure got too much, he asked the rector of the University of Stellenbosch, Professor HB Thom, to help. Thom picked up the phone, dialled a number and said '*Hendrik, is dit jy?*' (Is that you?). He told Verwoerd to leave Craven alone, which Verwoerd did. Thom, Craven knew, was the chairman of the Broederbond at the time.

The Broeders dominated the South African Rugby Board until very recently. Among the senior Broeders on the Board were Fritz Eloff, Johan Claassen, Steve Strydom, Kobus Louw, Boetie Malan, Jannie le Roux and Avril Malan.

In an authorised biography on Craven, *Doc – The Life of Danie Craven*, Paul Dobson wrote: 'The Broederbond formulated South Africa's sports policy. They were the ones who began to make the changes in 1971. When Craven was elected to the presidency of the South African Rugby Board, he did not know about the Broeder involvement in his election as he was not a member. Nor did he know about the man they called a *skakel*, a connection or switch and in rugby terms a halfback. A *skakel* was a non-Broeder put into an important position where the Broeders decided to exert influence. If he was a success, he would be manipulated. If he failed, there was no damage to a Broeder.'

According to Luyt's associates at the time, he had already decided that he wanted Craven's job in the mid-1980s, when Craven was still firmly in control of South African rugby.

Luyt himself has on occasion called rugby a form of *volksgodsdiens*, an Afrikaner religion. Between 1938, with the symbolic *Eeufees Trek*, and the late 1960s, Afrikaner nationalism manifested itself mainly through huge gatherings and celebrations at the Day of the Covenant on 16 December and later Republic Day on 31 May. But by the early 1970s the temporary political unity in Afrikanerdom was shattered and the mass celebrations became less popular.

In the book on rugby and Afrikaner nationalism, *Beyond the Tryline*, Stellenbosch historian Albert Grundlingh writes: 'Whereas *volksfeeste* had become decidedly anachronistic for large sections of Afrikanerdom, rugby as a cultural phenomenon maintained its endearing attraction for Afrikaners. Rugby provided entertainment, it did not carry an overt political message – at a time when many Afrikaners welcomed a respite from unrelenting political pressure – and it provided an opportunity for predominantly male camaraderie and time-honoured ritualistic social behaviour. In short it was a *volksbyeenkoms*, a closing of the ranks, but without political soul-searching and sombre over-tones.'

In fact, rugby became the substitute for *volksbyeenkomste*, with the added advantage that the only divisions among the *volk* at the rugby stadium were club or provincial loyalties rather than ideological differences. It was the one place where Afrikaners of all political persuasions and loyalties could still get together and be Afrikaners. When all these things are considered, it is no wonder that rugby was the one sport that had serious problems transforming after the advent of democracy in 1994. When Prime Minister John Vorster relented and allowed Maori rugby players to tour South Africa in 1971, it became a major debate which boosted the breakaway of the right-wing Herstige Nasionale Party. The opening up of the Craven Week schools rugby tournament to all races in the early 1980s gave momentum to the second wave of right-wing splits, this time by the Conservative Party.

Grundlingh has an interesting take on why rugby, rather than soccer or baseball or cricket, became the Afrikaner's favourite sport. Apart from the theory mentioned earlier that it was used as an anti-imperialist tool because it was originally an upper-class English game, Grundlingh says the very nature of the game appealed to the evolving self-image of nationalist Afrikaners: 'Implicit in rugby is a certain duality. On the one hand, it can be seen as a collective sport of combat which emphasises stamina, strength, speed and courage; symbolically, the rugged aspects of the game could easily be equated with a resurgent and rampant Afrikaner nationalism. At the same time, despite being a rough affair, it was considered a gentleman's game and an excellent way of inculcating moral discipline in future leaders.'

Rugby heroes were more than sporting heroes. Bennie Osler, Hannes Brewis, Lofty Nel, Tiny Naudé, Hennie Muller, Tjol Lategan, Ryk van Schoor, HO de Villiers, Jan Ellis, Salty du Rand, Tom van Vollenhoven, Frik du Preez, Mof Myburgh, Jannie Engelbrecht and Boland Coetzee were true national icons in the days before Naas Botha, Morné du Plessis, Danie Gerber, Carel du Plessis and François Pienaar. Mannetjies Roux was more than a rugby hero – when he kicked a demonstrator against apartheid sport on the backside after a match at Coventry in 1969, he became a national symbol of Afrikaner pride. The Springbok captain in the 1960s, Dawie de Villiers, became a cabinet minister. Frederik van Zyl Slabbert was regarded as a liberal and a left-winger – he was the leader of the white opposition party in Parliament – but he was always held in high esteem as a '*goeie Afrikaner*', at least partly because he played rugby for Stellenbosch University and Western Province.

A senior rugby administrator of those years and at the time a good friend of Luyt's told me: 'It took me just two or three years to see through Louis. His star as an industrialist had waned, but not his hunger for fame and money. He didn't get involved in rugby because he loved the game. He did it for Louis Luyt and Louis Luyt only. He was clever enough to sense that the game was about to become professional, and that with increased television interest there were millions to be made. His ego and his bank balance – that is why Louis turned to rugby.'

Whatever his motivation, rugby was the world Luyt chose for his next bid for power, money and influence. And there was an obvious first soft target: the Transvaal Rugby Football Union (TRFU). But it was also appropriate for Luyt to go to Transvaal: the Western Cape was the stronghold of old Cape Afrikaner families; Northern Transvaal (Pretoria) was the home of the Afrikaner administrative classes; the Free State was mostly rural and agricultural. Transvaal (Greater Johannesburg) was the rugby home of new Afrikaner money, of the new entrepreneurial classes. And Luyt personified exactly that.

But Transvaal rugby was in serious trouble in the early 1980s. The union was run by an autocratic, feisty old *korrelkop* Broeder, Jannie le Roux, who had treated Transvaal rugby as a personal fiefdom for more than a decade. The Transvaal team was consistently the weakest provincial side, and players and administrators were deeply demoralised and unhappy. Almost typical of the old-style Afrikaner leaders of that time, Le Roux decided that the best cure for the disease would be to build a monumental new stadium at Ellis Park. He did this with the help – and no security whatsoever – of the Afrikaner-dominated bank Volkskas. Towards the end of 1984, the TRFU was bankrupt with interest payments of up to R6,5 million per year.

A very nervous board of Volkskas Bank, the Broederbond and the National Party leadership in Transvaal wanted Le Roux to be replaced. On 1 September 1984 Volkskas gave the union four days to pay their debt to the bank. According to Craven's biographer, Paul Dobson, who called Le Roux a 'direct man despite a certain wayward-ness of conduct', the TRFU president's 'lapses became more obvious and not even the Broederbond wanted him any longer. In fact he was once in trouble with the Broederbond for a "lack of interest".'

Transvaal rugby was a plum ripe to be picked by Luyt. Thirteen of the sixteen clubs affiliated to the union rebelled in late August 1984, demanding the resignation of the entire union hierarchy, including Le Roux. With a little bit of help from his friends and a lot of lobbying, promises and threats, Luyt eventually ousted Le Roux on 3 September and took over the presidency in a caretaker capac-ity until the union's annual meeting at the end of November.

The rebellious clubs were wary at first, suspecting that Luyt's takeover was just a ploy. Luyt reacted angrily: 'I'm no one's puppet and certainly not Le Roux's puppet. He's out. Out.' He promised a new, better administration and said of the clubs' demands: 'I want the same things they want. I agree the clubs should have more say in the union, that they should be able to oust people who don't do their jobs properly.'

But, according to *The Star*, 'Luyt's election as president of the TRFU has not filled the clubs with glee … The rebels will not say so in as many words, but they fear that Mr Luyt may be fashioned in the same mould as his predecessor. Indeed, the new president was elected by many of Mr le Roux's supporters and the clubs' major grievances – that the vice-presidents rule the TRFU – remains.'

The rebel clubs were unimpressed with Luyt, and staged a walk-out at his first meeting. Luyt responded: 'Those of us who wish to serve rugby must follow the correct procedures. Then we can listen to all of those who are dissatisfied. We can not go on like this. Certain people must leave their super-egos behind. We must rebuild Transvaal rugby.'

On 4 September, *The Star* reported, 'A R42 million legal action was halted and players from the 13 senior rebel clubs were asked to stand by for practice sessions and team selection this afternoon. A peace pact to put the brakes on a Supreme Court clash was reached between Mr Louis Luyt and Mr Johan Claasen, general manager of the corporate division of Volkskas Bank.' The bank said in a statement: 'As a result of developments in the TRFU and because of the possibility that rugby could benefit, Volkskas has decided to temporarily halt its legal action.'

Former Springbok and Transvaal player Ockie Oosthuizen gives a behind-the-scenes account of Luyt's takeover. Oosthuizen was the Transvaal captain in 1984. He says he was shocked when he moved to Transvaal from Northern Transvaal to see the poor administration, financial problems and constant rumours about nepotism at Ellis Park. He took it upon himself to do something about it, and soon had the support of most of the players.

But Jannie le Roux quickly saw him as a threat. After a strategy meeting Le Roux held with other management members at his house on the Vaal River, it was decided to isolate Oosthuizen. The next day at a team practice, the coach, Affies du Toit, lined up the team and said those who found it difficult to play for Transvaal under present management should take one step forward. Oosthuizen did that, and he was joined by Dries Maritz. Du Toit then told Oosthuizen: 'Take your boots and go.'

'I regarded myself as suspended from that moment on,' Oosthuizen told me. 'But this had the result that Volkskas, most of the Transvaal clubs and some individuals on the executive committee started increasing the pressure to get things at Transvaal fixed.'

Oosthuizen then received an unexpected call from Louis Luyt, whom he had never met or spoken to before. Luyt told him that they had to meet, because Oosthuizen was the leader among the players and he, Luyt, had a plan to solve all Transvaal's problems. Luyt had no connection with rugby at that point, apart from an honorary position at Diggers club.

'We agreed to meet at the Airport Sun. Louis arrived in his long black chauffeur-driven Mercedes with a few cronies. Louis was to the point. He said he had the infrastructure and enough money to get the Transvaal Rugby Union back on track, but he could not do it without me. I said: Louis, I'll go along, but only if you can state categorically that the administration and finances at Transvaal will be strong and sound, and if you are going to look after the players. In typical Luyt fashion he said: "You've got it."'

But Luyt had a problem with the Transvaal executive committee, who were suspicious that he was acting on behalf of Le Roux and did not want to see Luyt. Oosthuizen then agreed to facilitate a meeting with committee members Jannie Ferreira, Mickey Gerber and Avril Malan at the Rand Afrikaans University immediately afterwards. When they arrived, the members did not want to see Luyt, but Oosthuizen pleaded with them, and they went to sit around a table.

'They were quite hostile to Luyt,' says Oosthuizen. 'Gerber told him to his face they did not trust him and would never accept him, because he was just in bed with Jannie le Roux. Louis was very persuasive. "I'm on my knees before you," he said, and promised to issue a public statement that he wasn't a Le Roux man. I saw these guys change before my eyes, and by the end of the meeting it was clear Luyt was going to take over. He was a bloody good strategist. He had them in the palm of his hand. These same men became his most loyal henchmen in later years.'

Oosthuizen says he and Luyt were 'best friends' after that – 'Louis even lent me his black Mercedes Benz sports.' But it didn't last long.

Towards the end of the season, Oosthuizen had a late-night phone call from Luyt. Luyt said he was worried that it appeared from some financial statements that, contrary to the rules on amateurism, Oosthuizen was receiving money. Oosthuizen later found out that Luyt, who at that stage was still not an elected TRFU official, had a few associates with him when he made the call, and had put the call on speaker phone. Oosthuizen strenuously denied receiving payment, and said if Luyt really believed it, they could discuss it later during the day.

Oosthuizen arrived at his home after work a few days later to find a very nervous TRFU official, Gerhard de Haas, at his door. He had just come to drop off a letter, De Haas said. Oosthuizen took the letter and walked into his house, just in time to hear on the TV news bulletin that he had been suspended for transgressing the Rugby Board's amateur code and had two weeks to appeal. The same accusation was stated in the letter. 'It was a hell of a shock,' says Oosthuizen. 'It was complete nonsense. I never received money for playing rugby. In Western Province, players were already getting R700 a match.'

It later turned out that the ammunition Luyt wanted to use against Oosthuizen was a subsidised home loan Oosthuizen was receiving from RAU. On the last day he had to appeal against the suspension, Oosthuizen and his lawyer appeared before a disciplinary committee at Ellis Park. 'When we walked in, Luyt rushed towards me and said: "I hope you have told your little lawyer that you are going to see your arse today."' But the hearing had no choice but to conclude that Oosthuizen was not guilty on the charge. Oosthuizen announced his retirement from rugby soon afterwards, although he was only twenty-nine years old and one of the country's top players.

'I was instrumental in getting Louis the job as president of Transvaal. He used me to gain power. Without me and my influence with the executive committee and the thirteen rebellious Transvaal clubs he would not have made it. But once he was there, he had to get rid of me because I was too strong; I had too much influence.

'I was merely the first of Luyt's victims. This style of operating runs like a golden thread right through his career as rugby administrator, right up to the end,' Oosthuizen told me. 'He is an utterly ruthless man.'

(Ten years later Luyt and Oosthuizen nearly came to blows in the foyer of a hotel in Christchurch. Oosthuizen was the leader of a supporters' group to the Springboks' tour to New Zealand, and Luyt attacked him in public about being 'negative' about South African rugby. Oosthuizen told him to go to hell.)

At the end of November, Luyt was elected president of the union at the annual meeting with a new executive committee. *The Star* reported on 30 November: 'Dr Louis Luyt was a popular figure at last night's meeting with a laid-back style of leadership. Instead of shouting down members in the style of his predecessor, Jannie le Roux, Dr Luyt gave all a chance to air their views.'

Luyt immediately set out to turn the TRFU and Ellis Park into profitable businesses. His first job was to strip the Le Roux family of their exclusive rights to sell liquor at Ellis Park and to cancel the family's marketing contract. The Le Roux family was out; the Luyt family was in.

Luyt next persuaded the Johannesburg City Council to give the Ellis Park land to Volkskas on a ninety-nine-year lease agreement, and then got First National Bank to loan the TRFU R30 million to buy Ellis Park from Volkskas. Luyt himself said that when the TRFU took over Ellis Park in 1986, the total debt was R53 million. He started paying top players to go over to Transvaal, although he only admitted to this more than ten years later. Despite the still strict rules of amateur rugby, Transvaal players received cars, subsidised housing and money paid into trust funds. And soon Transvaal was again becoming a very competitive provincial side.

There has never been any doubt that Luyt achieved a near miracle by turning Transvaal rugby around so quickly and dramatically. During the first few years of his reign, he was adored by players, clubs, administrators and fans as the saviour of Transvaal.

Luyt was ready to host – and make a good profit out of – the All Blacks who were going to tour South Africa in 1985. But not long before they were due to arrive in South Africa, two New Zealand lawyers, Phil Recordan and Pat Finnigan, took the New Zealand Rugby Union to court. The union was in breach of their own constitution by undertaking the tour to South Africa, they told Judge JP Casey, because the constitution stipulated they had to act in the best interests of New Zealand rugby. The judge agreed and the tour was cancelled. Most of the players wanted to come to South Africa anyway, but their plans didn't materialise.

The cancellation of the All Black tour was regarded as a disaster for rugby in South Africa by the South African Rugby Board and white rugby fans. Danie Craven was devastated, and said South African rugby would never be the same without the All Blacks.

Louis Luyt to the rescue. He secured a sponsorship from Yellow Pages and in 1986 brought the exact same All Black side selected to tour South Africa, bar two players with personal problems, to South Africa for a tour – as the Cavaliers. It is still not known how much money Luyt paid the New Zealand players and management to come on the 'rebel' tour, and how it was paid to them. The rumour was that they were paid in Hawaii and Hong Kong, but nothing was ever proved. Luyt and another businessman and former rugby player, Jan Pickard, even showed the International Rugby Board the audited accounts of the whole project to prove that players were not paid.

In South Africa the Cavaliers were seen as the All Blacks in all but name. The South African Rugby Board gave them an official welcome like they would have given to a proper international team, and all South African players chosen for the national team became full Springboks. The Cavalier players insisted formally they were not in South Africa as All Blacks, but they did perform the traditional All Black *haka* ritual before their matches. On their return, the players received a gentle slap on the wrist: a one-match suspension.

The next year Luyt was again involved in bringing a rebel tour to South Africa, the South Pacific Barbarians, with a sponsorship from First National Bank. They were mainly from Fiji, but included a few Tongans and Western Samoans. But this time the International Rugby Board demanded an undertaking that no more rebel tours would be allowed, or South Africa would be kicked out of the IRB.

The TRFU and Ellis Park did well out of the two tours, and Luyt's standing in the rugby fraternity grew. In April 1987 he reached another milestone on his way to the rugby throne – he was elected to the management of the South African Rugby Board and appointed a member of the financial committee. I love it when a plan comes together, he must have thought.

The rebel tours were condemned by the international community, by the liberation movement, the African National Congress, the internal movement opposed to apartheid, the United Democratic Front, and by progressive whites. Luyt was unrepentant: he did it for rugby and for South Africa, he maintained. (It could be argued that he did it for the money, because he and Ellis Park made a good profit out of it.)

But just as Luyt was being billed as some kind of right-wing reactionary, he announced in 1987 that he could no longer support the ruling National Party. He said he had stuck his neck out to support State President PW Botha before the important referendum on constitutional changes, but only because he understood that the Tricameral Parliament, which accommodated Coloured and Indian South Africans in separate houses of Parliament, would be the beginning of a process to bring black South Africans into central decision-making. It was time for a fourth chamber of Parliament for blacks, Luyt said, even if the then still banned ANC were elected.

The next day the progressive *Cape Times* stated in an editorial: 'It is a long, long way in politics from playing trusted stalking-horse for the government in clandestine newspaper publishing to voting for the Progressive Federal Party, but it seems likely to happen in the case of Mr Louis Luyt … If the expanse of political landscape traversed is a bit breathtaking, the move certainly brings fresh air to South African politics … Mr Luyt's move will not be greeted with enthusiasm by an ageing, grim, played-out Nationalist leadership which is looking more Russian by the day.' The newspaper continued:

'The country has been brought to the rim of disaster by the Botha government. The economy is unresponsive and gripped by an unacceptable level of inflation. Nearly two people are dying every day in "unrest". The press has been savagely bludgeoned. The West has turned its face from this land, and is applying sanctions. Fear and foreboding have replaced the people's hopes. There is lots of construction work ahead, and it needs a rainbow coalition of all South Africans to do it. Welcome, Louis Luyt.'

Luyt never appeared to be a political animal. In fact, a very senior white politician who had close dealings with him told me: 'Louis' political naïvete sometimes astounded me. He never really understood the dynamics of white politics, and had no clue about black politics. His only ideological understanding was that all people should be capitalists and secretly want to be. He treated politics like he did his business environment. But sometimes he had an uncanny sense of timing, and with his bulldozing attitude of "let's just do this thing right now" he sometimes did things right. His shift in the late 1980s wasn't an ideological shift or a change of heart at all. He simply thought that PW Botha was bad for business, and he wanted South African rugby back in the international arena so rugby and his own fortunes at Ellis Park could benefit.'

In July 1987 Frederik van Zyl Slabbert, who had walked out of Parliament to form the Institute for a Democratic Alternative for South Africa (Idasa) with his fellow PFP-parliamentarian Alex Boraine, took a group of about sixty white South African intellectuals and opinion formers to Dakar, Senegal, to meet with Thabo Mbeki and other leaders of the ANC, which was then still banned. It was a meeting of great symbolic importance at the time and helped stimulate the atmosphere for negotiations which commenced within two years of the 'Dakar Safari', as the highly controversial initiative was called.

Tommy Bedford, a brilliant Springbok and Natal loose forward in the late 1960s and early 1970s, was one of the delegates on the Idasa side, as was André Odendaal, a UDF activist and a very talented cricketer, who refused to play in the white sporting structures. (He is presently the director of the Robben Island Museum.) The other accomplished sportsman on the safari was, of course, Slabbert himself. The main aim of the initiative was to break the deadlock existing at that time in South Africa and to help find ways of defusing the conflict and moving the country towards democracy. I remember (I was an Idasa guest also) that Slabbert, Bedford, Odendaal and several others had conversations with ANC leaders about using the normalisation of sport as a tool to normalise society. The ANC was very receptive.

Bedford, on his return to South Africa, persuaded Danie Craven and the South African Rugby Board to make contact with the ANC. Luyt, not at all reluctantly, was delegated to handle the matter, and through Slabbert he established contact with the ANC. He had a first preliminary meeting with the ANC in London, and a second, on 26 May 1988, in Frankfurt. Luyt was excited about the ANC reaction, and sent a full report to the Minister of Foreign Affairs, Pik Botha. But when Pik Botha went to see PW Botha with the report, the State President exploded in anger at the mere thought that Luyt could have had talks with the 'terrorist, communist' ANC.

Luyt was undeterred – he disliked PW intensely, anyway. He then organised a proper, official meeting between the South African Rugby Board, the non-racial South African Rugby Union, and the ANC leadership. The meeting took place on 15 and 16 October 1988 in the Sheraton Hotel in Harare, Zimbabwe. Luyt and Danie Craven represented the South African Rugby Board, Ebrahim Patel represented the South African Rugby Union, and Thabo Mbeki, Steve Tshwete and Alfred Nzo represented the ANC. It was agreed that there could be no real progress until after the Rugby Board and the Rugby Union, the latter representing mostly black players, had merged into one rugby body. A declaration of intent was agreed upon by the three groups, and Patel read it out after the meeting.

Luyt and Craven arrived back in South Africa to face a barrage of criticism. The Minister of Education who was responsible for sport, one FW de Klerk, stoked the fires of protest. He told a public meeting in Lichtenburg on 17 October 1988: 'It is shocking that the president of one of South Africa's national sports bypasses the government and turns to a terrorist organisation which is engaged in terror attacks on innocent civilians every day.' He said his information was that the talks were conducted without the blessing of the Rugby Board. 'I have to warn sports people not to allow themselves to be used by the ANC to further the ANC's aims. The implications of talks with the ANC are far reaching and create particular risks for those who participate in them.'

Craven called De Klerk's speech 'irresponsible' and said: 'It is clear that he wants the Rugby Board to split. But if a split has to happen, let it happen.'

A few days later, PW Botha told a National Party meeting in Benoni that he had 'impeccable proof' that the ANC, 'a gang of terrorists', viewed sport as 'an important terrain where they could perpetrate their subtle subversion'. He said he knew that ANC leaders had said they wanted to use rugby 'to sow divisions in the ranks of responsible South Africans'. He warned Craven and Luyt: 'Don't allow the revolutionaries to make cheap propaganda out of sport.'

Craven's deputy on the Rugby Board, Professor Fritz Eloff, told *Die Burger* that he distanced himself completely from the Harare talks. 'I support dialogue, but this is about the ANC. I don't talk to terrorists. The ANC has nothing to do with rugby.'

Besides Eloff, three other members of the Rugby Board's executive voiced their disapproval of the talks with the ANC: Jan Pickard, Ronnie Bauser and Steve Strydom. The senior rugby administrators of the South African Police clubs attacked Luyt and Craven using strong language. In November, the Rugby Board issued a statement saying it would not have dealings with political parties such as the ANC again.

But it was not all condemnation. A veteran rugby coach, administrator and referee from the southern Cape, Flip Olivier, represented the opinion of many rugby fans when he stated: 'If Dr Craven and Dr Luyt tried to break the country's sports isolation, they deserve praise and they should not be denigrated for it. Prominent leaders of the National Party often admit that "mistakes had been made in the past", and I accept that among these mistakes was the sports policy which was unacceptable to the international community. A mistake that had led to our sportsmen and women becoming the polecats of the world. Dr Craven and Dr Luyt should then rather be supported when they want to do something for our sports people. I have experienced the frustrations of being excluded from international rugby with our young people and I believe we owe it to our rugby players to look for ways out of the deadlock outside of politics. And if some of the people you have to make contact with in the process belong to the ANC, then so what?'

The Southeast Transvaal Rugby Union decided to send a message to the Rugby Board in support of talks with other sports administrators. The union's honorary president, Paul Broodryk, said South African rugby's road back to international acceptance was through Africa, and therefore the talks had to be supported.

De Klerk ordered Craven to a meeting in his office, but Craven refused. De Klerk reportedly even threatened to withdraw the passports of certain sports administrators. Instead, the minister had a meeting with the executive of the Rugby Board. Luyt was the object of De Klerk's wrath, and he had no backing from the other members of the executive committee. 'I was fiercely roasted, but I refused to succumb,' Luyt said later. (At a speech after his inauguration as President of a democratic South Africa on 10 May 1994, Nelson Mandela praised Craven and Luyt for their initiative.)

On 7 October 1988 the executive committee of the South African Rugby Board issued a statement fully supporting Craven and Luyt's Harare talks, declaring that the way back into international sport was through Africa. Steve Strydom even apologised for his earlier criticism of the initiative. After the meeting Craven launched a strongly worded attack on the Broederbond, on the Group Areas Act and on other forms of apartheid.

Botha's and De Klerk's anger at Luyt and Craven for 'talking to the terrorists' was, of course, extreme hypocrisy. At the time of the Harare meeting between Luyt, Craven and the ANC, the National Party government had already started talking to Nelson Mandela in prison as well as to the external ANC leadership. But they called everybody else inside the country who had such contacts 'useful idiots' of the communists who were betraying their own people.

The declaration of intent signed in Harare between the Rugby Board, SARU and the ANC remained just a declaration. The anti-apartheid South African Council on Sport (Sacos) and SARU met the Rugby Board's hard-ball approach with an equally uncompromising approach. In the end it was Steve Tshwete, a keen rugby player in the Eastern Cape in his youth and later one of the forces behind the rugby club of Robben Island where he was a prisoner, who helped the transition along. Tshwete got on well with Luyt – at least in the beginning.

The amalgamation eventually happened on 20 March 1992, and the new body was called the South African Rugby Football Union (SARFU). SARFU would have two presidents: Danie Craven and Ebrahim Patel. Craven would be executive president until March 1993; Patel for the year after that; and in March 1994 a new president would be elected. That was the job Luyt wanted, and that was the job Luyt was to get in March 1994.

It was shortly before his official Harare meeting with the ANC in late 1988 that I met Luyt for the first time. After the Dakar Safari, my frustration with the South African newspapers reached a critical point. I sincerely believed – probably naïvely so – that if white South Africans really knew what the apartheid government was doing in their name, if they really understood the extent of black anger, and if they realised that the leadership of the black majority – especially those in the UDF and ANC – were responsible, moderate and intensely patriotic fellow South Africans, they would change their minds about supporting apartheid. I didn't think the newspapers, especially the Afrikaans-language ones, were giving their readers a good picture of the South African reality. I expressed my frustration to a few friends lying next to a pool in the sweltering heat at the hotel in Ouagadougou, Burkina Faso, towards the end of the Dakar trip. I was challenged by Beyers Naudé, a former Broeder dominee who became an anti-apartheid stalwart, Pallo Jordan, an ANC leader who later became a cabinet minister, and Van Zyl Slabbert 'to do something about it'.

In 1988 I gathered a few trusted friends and founded a weekly Afrikaans newspaper with a strong stance against apartheid, and called it *Vrye Weekblad* (free or independent weekly). I dragged Slabbert in as chairman of the newspaper's board. But we had no money apart from what I could scrape together selling everything I had, including cashing in all insurance and annuity policies. Even the more progressive white businesses thought we were crazy left-wingers, and there was an organised boycott of any advertising in *Vrye Weekblad* by major Afrikaans companies. The National Party leadership called me a traitor, a hater of the Afrikaner, a threat to the security of the state and a communist. (Thirteen years later the ANC, now in government, also called me a traitor and a threat to the security of the state when I criticised the President ...)

Slabbert suggested we approach Luyt for an investment – after all, he had become a critic of the Botha government and of apartheid, he was talking to the ANC, and he clearly had a lot of money. Slabbert and I were ushered in to Luyt's vast, wood-panelled office at Ellis Park. I remember thinking that he had a much larger physique than I thought. I expected him to be an abrasive, aggressive man, but he was actually very charming. Charming in a regal kind of way – he really had the air of a head of state or commander of an empire about him. He listened to what we had to say, vaguely expressed his support for the venture, and said he would consider our request and come back to us. I was not surprised when we never received one cent from Luyt. He was shrewd enough to know that an alternative, slightly anarchistic newspaper couldn't be a good investment, at least not financially speaking.

Luyt clearly found his brief flirtation with politics fascinating. He was deeply annoyed with PW Botha's and FW de Klerk's authoritarian attitude towards him after his contact with the ANC, and yet he enjoyed the goodwill he got from the ANC and other black leaders inside the country and the positive publicity he received from many newspapers in South Africa – his first in many years. In fact, Luyt thought he was quite good at this game. He was frustrated at the continued isolation of South African sport and the effect sanctions were having on the economy. So he decided to get involved a little more.

In 1988, the white opposition to the National Party, apart from the right-wing Conservative Party, was split between three groups. The strongest was the Progressive Federal Party, a liberal party mostly supported by English-speakers and big business, with Zach de Beer as leader. Then there were two smaller groups led by former senior Nats: the Independent Party of Denis Worrall and the National Democratic Movement of Wynand Malan. Worrall's group was seen as the home of more conservative people who were opposed to the government's apartheid policies, and Malan's group was believed to have had the support of a good number of progressive Afrikaans-speakers.

A month after his meeting with the ANC in Harare, Luyt declared that a divided opposition to the National Party government meant a weak opposition. He believed that the National Party was bad for South Africa, and should be defeated at the polls. As he recalled later: 'I called Zach and Denis and Wynand and said, Look, you're so fragmented, why the devil don't you get together? And there is also a fourth element: people like me. I don't vote for any of you but I'm unhappy and there are many like me. In the end, we all want to do one thing and that is to get South Africa back into the international community again, wealthy again, acceptable.'

He asked the three leaders to meet at Solitaire, his Saxonwold mansion, for talks on 18 November 1988. According to Luyt, he warned them as they came through his front door: 'Listen, once you come in here, you can't go back without a deal. Otherwise you're dead.' The three agreed to work towards unity, and met again in December. This time a fourth 'non-aligned' group, represented by the elder brother of FW de Klerk, philosopher and former newspaper editor Willem de Klerk, also attended. Another former editor and prominent political commentator, Harald Pakendorf, attended the meetings as a facilitator and advisor.

Luyt and the four leaders emerged from the meeting with an announcement that they had decided to form a new party and had appointed a committee to prepare a constitution for the party and decide about the leadership and the launching congress. Luyt said the new party would be committed to real democracy, would strive to free South Africa of all forms of apartheid, and would protect cultural, language and religious rights. He said the government's constitutional dispensation was built on the principle of statutarily defined race groups and was morally untenable.

The new party, called the Democratic Party, was launched early in 1989. De Beer, Worrall and Malan were joint leaders. Luyt didn't like this and remarked shortly after the launch: 'I don't like this troika idea. It's nonsense. You have to have a strong man, a leader, and that's it. But if that's the way to take the first step, let's do it that way. But it certainly cannot go on forever. I won't tolerate it, the voters won't tolerate it. You can't have a troika; it's almost like Russia.'

Vintage Luyt. He reportedly tried very hard to persuade Van Zyl Slabbert – the former leader of the Progressive Federal Party who had resigned from Parliament – to make himself available for the new Democratic Party leadership. Slabbert had a strong image and a strong personality, he said. But Slabbert was not interested. Luyt was always in favour of strong leadership. In an interview early in 1988, he said: 'It is my philosophy that a company is lost without a man with personality. Just look at [Hugh] Hefner, [Anton] Rupert, [Raymond] Ackerman.' But when faced with a strong leader, Luyt always rejected their authority, as he did with PW Botha and FW de Klerk, with Craven as head of South African rugby, and with Steve Tshwete who became Minister of Sport in 1994, as well as his successor, Ngconde Balfour.

After the formation of the Democratic Party, Luyt was asked whether he saw himself becoming an active politician. 'It is not fair to mix rugby and politics,' he told a newspaper editor. 'If I decide to follow a political path, I will have to say farewell to rugby.' Of course, when he decided to become an active politician and the Democratic Party didn't want him, he formed his own political party and declared himself the leader. But that was ten years later ...

4

BUILDING THE EMPIRE

I am a professional. For thirty years I have been a top business-
man. There are few people in this town who can teach me any-
thing about the running of a big business.

— Louis Luyt, 1990

It took Luyt less than four years to stabilise the financial and administrative affairs of Transvaal rugby. But his stated ambition was not
just to save Transvaal rugby from sinking into bankruptcy and rele-
gation. He wanted to make it the richest rugby union in the world,
and in the process increase his own fortunes. Luyt wanted nothing
else than to be the King of South African rugby and a major force in
world rugby. He was to achieve these goals within a decade of seiz-
ing the controls at Ellis Park.

But controversy – and serious questions about business ethics –
soon surfaced again. In 1988 Luyt and the Transvaal Rugby Football
Union took Ellis Park Stadium to the Johannesburg Stock Exchange
(JSE) with a share issue in order to raise R30 million to wipe out the
huge debt. The union had built the stadium in 1982 at a cost of R59
million on land leased from the Johannesburg City Council for ninety-
nine years. In 1984 the lease agreement was ceded to Volkskas, the

principal financier. In 1987 the TRFU bought the lease rights from Volkskas for R26,5 million. This deal was financed by First National Bank.

But investors were scared of Luyt after Triomf had nearly sunk Nedbank in 1986, and Luyt had to buy a third of the shares himself. He also had to underwrite units to the value of R12 million. The merchant bank FirstCorp took up R10 million worth of units.

But a year later Luyt had Ellis Park delisted again. By this time, the shares were trading at 80 cents, down 20 cents from when they were issued. So if Luyt had initially bought R10 million worth of shares, as was reported, he would have lost R2 million with the delisting.

But he did not. Luyt persuaded the TRFU, of which he was the president, to buy out all Ellis Park shareholders, including himself, at 110 cents per share with money lent to the TRFU by Trust Bank. So instead of losing two million, it was reported, he made a million on the 33 per cent shares he had had to buy himself. There were rumours that Luyt made a lot more money than R1 million out of this deal, but nobody could ever prove any of it. An equally important bonus was that this latest transaction allowed Luyt to get rid of all the Ellis Park directors voted on the board by the original shareholders. He did not want them, one of these directors told me, because he could not control them. And Luyt still had very grand plans for Ellis Park.

The JSE was alarmed by the transactions. Rumours of insider trading prior to the announcement of an offer to minorities by the TRFU, the controlling shareholder, were rife in business circles when the price for Ellis Park units rose by 20 cents to R1 on 19 April. The units were suspended the next day, but relisted after the announcement of an offer to buy in and delist the next week. Ockert Goosen, a senior manager of Ellis Park's merchant bankers, FirstCorp, said at the time he was satisfied that no members of the boards of the TRFU or Ellis Park gained personally by the announcement of the offer. The JSE stated that in their opinion a prima facie case of insider trading had been made. They referred all their evidence to the Registrar of Companies.

Luyt denied any wrongdoing and threatened to sue the JSE for defamation. He admitted that Ellis Park shares had been bought on the TRFU's behalf, before the bid was announced, to build up the TRFU's stake. But he insisted that this was not insider trading, because the purchases were not for personal advantage. The *Financial Mail* wrote in May 1988: 'If Luyt is pursued for insider trading, he is likely to prove a tough nut to crack.' At the time, according to the *Financial Mail*, Luyt was writing a thesis on 'alterations of control and the protection of non-controlling shareholders in terms of the Companies Act and the rules of the JSE'.

The TRFU initially had problems paying off the loan, but Luyt persuaded the Democratic Party–controlled Johannesburg City Council to give them a soft loan of R10 million at an interest rate of only 10 per cent. By 1993 the union had, remarkably, wiped out its entire debt. By far the biggest moneyspinner was the rental of executive suites at Ellis Park to businesses, and more were in the process of being built. Luyt also made tens of millions for the union by organising sponsorships and advertising. He had also started renting out Ellis Park for soccer matches.

Luyt's honeymoon with Transvaal players and officials didn't last long, however. The clubs were unhappy because he was buying players from outside Transvaal at the expense of loyal club players. He once even brought in a Free State player right before the Currie Cup final, a player who had never played for a Transvaal club in his life. Remember, those were the days before professional rugby, when this kind of thing was illegal. The feeling was that Luyt was destroying club rugby in Transvaal and that the only club he cared about was the Rand Afrikaans University.

But Luyt was most resented for his constant interference: with the selectors, with the team management, with the players. He once fired the coach, Derek Minnie, and took over the coaching himself.

It was a disaster. He took the team over to Windhoek to play against South West Africa (now Namibia). They lost 9–6. After the game Luyt came into the dressing room and started criticising the team. Jannie Breedt was a bad captain and the players were useless, he said. One of the senior players, John Robbie, snapped at him: '*Ag, fok jou, Louis*' (Oh, fuck you, Louis). It was one of the first times that the Irish-born Robbie had spoken Afrikaans. Nobody had ever said that to Luyt, although surely many had wanted to. It took Robbie months to get back in favour again.

There was a standing joke in Transvaal rugby at the time about Luyt's habit of 'discovering' a player and forcing him into the team. When the player performed badly, he was dropped, and Luyt would say he had lost his speed. Whenever a player was having a bad day, players and officials would joke: 'Uh oh, he's going to lose his speed in the next week.'

More importantly, Luyt's style of financial control was causing discomfort and suspicion among his union's executive. Late in 1989 a dossier was compiled by concerned TRFU officials. It contained allegations that TRFU money was used to paint Luyt's Saxonwold mansion and beef up security in and around the huge property; that all the entertainment and other costs incurred for the formation of the Democratic Party came from TRFU coffers; that Luyt had bought cars for himself and his secretary with union money without the knowledge of other officials and without records being kept. The dossier also contained an allegation that Luyt had billed the union twice for the use of his jet to fly officials to Windhoek, and that he paid his mother-in-law an allowance from union funds – a kind of pension, it was alleged. There were documents suggesting that union money was used for Luyt's holiday mansion in Ballito Bay on the KwaZulu-Natal coast. There was also the case of an unauthorised cheque for R30 000 made out to rugby player Tjaart van der Walt. When confronted with it, Luyt said it was payment for Van der Walt to move to Transvaal and play for the union. But Van der Walt never came to

Transvaal, and when the management insisted that the money was never given back to Transvaal, Luyt's bookkeeper, Willie Kruger, took a cheque out of his drawer and said he had forgotten about it.

This dossier, put together by the manager of the TRFU, Faan Venter, then landed on the desk of Luyt's vice-president, Chris van Coller. Van Coller, then a senior accountant at the firm Price Waterhouse, had been Roodepoort Rugby Club's representative at the union since 1975. Van Coller and Venter went through the dossier together and realised that they were sitting on a potential scandal. They considered taking the allegations and documentation to the police or the Attorney-General so a criminal investigation could take place, but decided to consult with other officials first. They went to discuss the contents of the dossier with Avril Malan, TRFU executive member and brother of the former Minister of Defence, General Magnus Malan.

Malan was adamant: the union could not afford a scandal. They had to deal with it in another way. The plan they agreed upon was to vote Luyt out of office and then clean up the union's books. Van Coller was to challenge Luyt for the position of president of the TRFU at the annual general meeting on 25 February 1990. And then the lobbying started.

Van Coller told the newspaper *Rapport* on 18 February 1990 that he wasn't convinced that all spending reflected in the annual financial statement was in the interests of rugby, and that he refused to sign it with Luyt. But that wasn't his only reason for opposing Luyt, Van Coller said. He was campaigning for stricter control of financial matters; he wanted clubs to benefit more from the union financially; and he believed the president of the union should have a democratic style of management.

Luyt was stunned, and as angry as a wounded buffalo at being challenged. Van Coller later told colleagues that Luyt's wife, Adri, came to talk to him and said she was praying for him and hoped that God would forgive him for doing this thing to her husband.

The challengers made their calculations after extensive lobbying. Sixty of the seventy-two people who could vote committed themselves to voting for Van Coller. There was some doubt about a few of them, because the Van Coller camp knew Luyt had done them special favours. But they were absolutely certain of getting forty-five votes at the very least.

But Luyt had apparently also done some calculations. The normal practice over the years was that the manager of the union would distribute the ballots, collect them and then count them in the presence of the media as observers. Late in the evening of 24 February Luyt phoned the manager, Faan Venter, and told him that he had changed the rules and that Venter would not be in charge of the election. Venter, Van Coller and the others frantically sought legal advice the same night, but it turned out that the union's constitution did not specify how the election should take place. There is nothing you can do, said their lawyers.

And then the meeting was convened on 25 February. One of the officials present told me the story: 'There was a strange atmosphere in the room. There were a few Luyt cronies sitting in the back, and there were more journalists than normal. We sat there as the guys with the vote and we knew this was going to be a turning point in our union's affairs. We knew we were going to vote Luyt out, but at the same time we were slightly nervous, because we had seen his powerful temper and threatening behaviour before. Luyt's smiles were more artificial than before, and we could see that he was tense. Still, I think we all avoided eye contact with him, and the handshakes before the start of the meeting were extremely awkward.

'Then we put our little crosses on our ballot papers, and folded them. Instead of Faan Venter, it was Bill Saunderson who collected the ballots. And then Bill and the auditor present, I think it was Jurie Visagie, left the room to go and count the votes, and the journalists sat where they were. Louis also got up and walked out. We didn't know where he went to. Avril Malan took over the meeting.

'And there we sat waiting in absolute silence, interrupted occasionally by a dry cough or a whisper. Bill came back in, walked up to Avril and whispered in his ear. Then Avril dropped the bombshell: Dr Luyt was re-elected. The Luyt cronies in the back clapped hands, but the rugby guys sat dead still. It's like we could not breathe. We knew something really terrible had just happened, but we sat there as if paralysed.

'After a few moments the guy from Goudstad club asked what the vote count was. Nobody answered him. Then he asked where the ballot papers were. Saunderson said: we have destroyed them. We sat there like corpses. We couldn't believe what had just happened. And most of the guys who voted against Luyt were dead scared about their own future. It was incredible. I have never experienced anything like that in my life.'

(The same man who told me this story predicted that I would find it hard to write this biography. 'People gossip about Luyt,' he said, 'but nobody ever wants to talk about it in the open. You will not get people to talk to you. He either buys people, or bullies them.' In the end quite a few people did talk to me, but most did not want to be quoted on what they said and insisted on total confidentiality.)

The next day the Afrikaans newspaper *Die Burger* reported simply: 'Dr Louis Luyt was re-elected as chairman of the union last night. He defeated Mr Chris van Coller, the union's deputy chairman, with a "fair majority" [*taamlike groot meerderheid*] last night. With that a threatening palace revolution was averted.'

Van Coller immediately resigned from the TRFU, and refused to sign the financial statements before he left. The allegations in the dossier that had started the rebellion were never investigated by the police or tested in a court of law. Luyt declared that he couldn't trust Venter any longer, and fired him. Venter was a broken man, especially after Luyt spread rumours that he had taken illegal commission money. Some of the clubs started a petition against Luyt, but Luyt had his spies in the clubs and isolated those who organised against him. The petition was dropped, as were plans to propose a motion of no confidence in Luyt at a special union meeting. People who were known to have voted against Luyt suddenly found their parking rights at Ellis Park cancelled. Clubs that were open in their opposition to Luyt were made to feel his wrath.

In June, businessman George Rautenbach sought an interdict from the Supreme Court to stop Luyt interfering in a contract between his marketing company and the Nissan car company. Rautenbach had a contract with the TRFU to market Nissans at Ellis Park. Luyt told Judge J Joffe that Rautenbach had supported Van Coller during his challenge in February, and this had led to a 'breach of trust'. Judge Joffe declined to grant an interdict against Luyt.

Luyt told *Rapport* in an interview after his re-election: 'In one year I had reduced the union's debt from R33 million to R21 million. Give me time until 1994 and I'll see to it that we don't owe a cent. How many people can achieve that? The critics don't know that the revenue from the suites at Ellis Park is guaranteed for ten years. The contracts have been signed and every year the rates increase by 15 per cent. And there is a waiting list of 42 businesses that want suites. Ellis Park has more executive suites than all the stadiums in South Africa combined. About 85 per cent of Ellis Park's revenue comes from executive suites. The gate money paid by the rugby public does not even present three per cent of the total revenue. So, even if we don't get a single spectator at Ellis Park, we still make money. There can therefore be no question about financial problems at Ellis Park.'

Luyt's response to objections to the way he was handling the union's finances was that the executive committee had given him full power in 1984 to manage the union's financial affairs. 'Now the same people who gave me that right are complaining. I don't understand it.'

Luyt said he was a bitter man, because when he took over ten million shares in Ellis Park on behalf of the union, he was entitled to commission of R350 000, but declined to take it. He had to borrow R5 million from the bank to buy back Ellis Park shares for the union, he said.

'I am a professional. For thirty years I have been a top business-man. There are few people in this town who can teach me anything about the running of a big business,' he told *Rapport*.

Louis Luyt was still the King of Transvaal rugby.

But his journey to the top of South African rugby was far from smooth. On 1 March 1991 he opposed Fritz Eloff for the position of deputy chairman of the South African Rugby Board at the Board's annual meeting at Newlands. He also stood for a position on the executive committee and on the financial committee.

It was a stormy meeting, dominated by Luyt's presence. According to the *Cape Times* report on the meeting, 'Luyt was his usual aggressive self.' At one stage Danie Craven had to intervene in a verbal battle between Luyt and executive committee member Hennie Erasmus, and he warned Luyt to stop making personal attacks. Luyt did not make it on to the executive of the financial committee, and withdrew from the election for the vice-presidency 'for the sake of friendship'.

Eloff then turned on Luyt: 'You are making a mockery of the position. Your remarks in the press to belittle me and my ability are unbecoming and not in the interests of rugby.' Luyt shouted back: 'It is my union's democratic privilege to nominate me for the position, and I'd like to know where you read about me mocking you.'

Luyt was out in the cold, and very angry about it. A few days later, at a reception at his home, he announced dramatically that he was retiring from all rugby. He said he would stay on at Transvaal until the end of 1991 if he was re-elected in March.

'My decision to quit was not easy,' Luyt said. 'My association with Transvaal were happy years, but my business interests gave me no option but to retire from rugby at the end of this year.' He announced that he was getting back into the beer business. He said he had bought the brewery already and planned to corner about 10 per cent of the market to start off with. Luyt denied emphatically that his defeat at the Rugby Board elections had anything to do with his decision. Nobody bothered to ask him publicly why his business activities would interfere with him being head of Transvaal rugby but not with his position of deputy chairman of South African rugby, the position he had sought only a few days earlier.

But the truth surfaced two weeks later. On 21 March 1991 Luyt was re-elected, this time unopposed, as head of the Transvaal Rugby Football Union. In his acceptance speech he said: 'I don't want to make my retirement speech now. I will do that when I retire at the end of the year.' And then he got to the crux of the matter: 'Those people who humiliated me at the annual meeting of the Rugby Board in Cape Town will remain uneasy. They will be worried until the day I retire.' He added that jealousy of Transvaal rugby had been part of the rugby scene in South Africa for several years. 'Don't be bothered by it. Transvaal is a powerful union that will follow its own path and conduct its affairs in a way that suits it.'

The new beer plans came to nothing. In October Luyt announced that the plans for a new brewery had been shelved because of 'an unfavourable political and economic climate'. And of course he did not quit rugby at the end of 1991 – not for nine more years, in fact, and then not out of choice. It was simply not in Luyt's character to be humiliated and then to walk away. His threat to retire was partly petulance, partly a warning to his opponents in the Rugby Board that they'd better start treating him with respect, because they would need his business skills in South African rugby once rugby was allowed back in the international arena after years of isolation. But there was no way that Luyt would quit rugby less than a year before Springbok rugby's biggest opponents, the New Zealand All Blacks and the Australian Wallabies, were scheduled to tour South Africa. There was much empire building still to do at Ellis Park – and money to be made – and Craven's crown of Rugby Supremo would be waiting in 1994. No, Luyt was not about to go away. In fact, Big Louis was just getting started.

In 1990 the president of the last white government of South Africa, FW de Klerk, unbanned the liberation movement, the African National Congress, and released its most prominent leader, Nelson Mandela, after twenty-seven years in prison. De Klerk's National Party, the ANC and other political groupings started talks about a negotiated settlement almost immediately. By 1992 the ANC leadership was confident that De Klerk and his men could be trusted when they said they were committed to democracy.

The ANC advised international sporting bodies and the anti-apartheid movement worldwide that it was time South Africa was re-admitted to world sport. The International Rugby Board declared after their 1992 annual meeting in London that they recognised the progress made by the South African Rugby Board and hoped that normal relations with other international unions could be resumed soon. It was a huge moment for rugby enthusiasts in South Africa, but also in other rugby countries such as New Zealand, Australia, Britain and France. For years the debate had raged: who were the real champions of world rugby? Without South Africa taking part, nobody could say for sure, and the Rugby World Cup competition wasn't regarded as a proper World Cup without the Springboks. South Africa's return to international rugby was to be a major injection for the sport worldwide.

The first official international rugby test after years of isolation took place at Ellis Park on 15 August 1992 – against the Springboks' major rival, the All Blacks. The ANC and the National and Olympic Sports Congress had a prior agreement with the South African Rugby Football Union (SARFU), as the new amalgamated body was now called, that the national anthem during the years of apartheid, *Die Stem*, would not be played before the test, and that the spectators would be asked to observe a minute's silence out of respect for all the people who were dying in the political violence in the country. Not long before the test forty-four people had died in a political massacre at Boipatong, south of Johannesburg. The minute's silence was a compromise; the original proposal was that the Springboks should play with black armbands.

There were close to 70 000 people in the stadium. An unusual feature was that thousands waved the orange, white and blue flag that had been white South Africa's symbol for many decades. Before that, flags were not a big feature at rugby tests. Something was brewing. The revered green and gold, the Bokke, were back and were up against the mighty All Blacks. According to some reports, parts of the crowd chanted rhythmically: '*Fok die ANC, Fok die ANC*' (Fuck the ANC). Quite a number of people were not exactly sober.

The All Blacks defeated the Springboks 27–24, but the real match was off the field. This was a *volksfees* of a different kind. Or perhaps to many it was the last *volksfees* – a last nostalgic occasion to be defiantly white and Afrikaans, a last desperate farewell by an emasculated people to a way of life and a time when white Afrikaners and their rituals were all-important in the country of braaivleis, rugby, sunny skies and Chevrolet.

Louis Luyt must have sensed the atmosphere, or, more likely, perhaps he harboured exactly the same sentiments. There was no minute of silence. Luyt had *Die Stem* played over the public address system, and tens of thousands of white people belted it out as if it was their last time.

Albert Grundlingh called it 'the last convulsions of a dying order' and 'an act of nationalistic cultural defiance by people who knew that politically the South Africa they had known and supported had all but vanished'.

Other people remembered it differently. François Pienaar, then an up-and-coming young Transvaal player who was to become South African rugby's golden boy under the new era, conceded that it might have been 'politically clumsy', but to him 'it remained an awe-inspiring couple of minutes'. He said: 'I know others saw an unacceptable degree of racial arrogance in the crowd's amazingly powerful singing, but I just saw pride and a sense of relief that the years of isolation were coming to an end. I felt intensely proud to be a South African that day.' But then, Pienaar did have a weakness for old South African symbols. Four years later, despite having become a friend of Nelson Mandela's, he condoned the waving of the old South African flag at a Bloemfontein rugby test instead of supporting his team manager, Morné du Plessis, who condemned it.

The ANC were livid. The message of the behaviour was that the spectators at the test did not give a damn about peace and democracy, they said, and they expressed the hope that it wasn't the majority white attitude. They condemned Luyt as arrogant and said he had clearly tried to destroy the newly found rugby unity all on his own. They also reminded him that it was within their power to put a stop to all international tests. Luyt more or less told them to go to hell.

The joint presidents of SARFU, Danie Craven and Ebrahim Patel, issued a statement condemning the playing of *Die Stem* at Ellis Park. They apologised unconditionally for the offence it may have caused, and undertook that SARFU would keep its promise of no anthem and a minute's silence at the next test against the Wallabies.

The New Zealanders and Australians were deeply embarrassed by the incident. They were happy to come and play rugby, but they did not in any way want to be associated with Luyt's reactionary and provocative behaviour. The president of the Australian Rugby Union, Joe French, said his team was ready to go back home if the ANC wanted them to.

Luyt was unrepentant. SARFU had no constitutional right to make such an agreement with outsiders – the SARFU constitution was on his side, he said. He was also an instant hero among many white Afrikaners. He boasted that his office couldn't handle all the telephone calls and faxes of congratulation coming in. A shield with the

South African coat of arms made by a former foreign minister in the cabinet of Hendrik Verwoerd, Eric Louw, was donated to Luyt by Louw's son to honour him for his 'brave deed'.

Luyt's argument was disingenuous: why was it acceptable for the African hymn *Nkosi Sikelel' iAfrika* to be played at soccer matches, but unacceptable to play *Die Stem* at rugby matches, he asked. He challenged SARFU management to discipline him – 'then we'll see who wins'.

Luyt went further and mobilised some of the Transvaal clubs behind him on the issue. André Botha, chairman of the club Germiston-Simmer, said his club had the support of fourteen senior Transvaal clubs to break from SARFU and form a new independent rugby union. He said he had informed SARFU that they would break all ties with it if SARFU was going to 'continue to be dictated to' by the ANC.

'We as rugby people cannot allow the ANC to take away the right of every real South African to sing their national anthem at test rugby through blackmail,' Botha said.

This was so obviously a lot of nonsense. These clubs knew, as did Luyt, that an 'independent' union would be dead in the water. Nobody would play against it, and its players would never be able to become Springboks. More importantly to Luyt, it would have been a financial disaster. It was pure posturing to bolster Luyt's obstreperous stance. Luyt said he would persuade the clubs that breaking away was not worth it – 'we should rather get rid of the problem people in SARFU.'

There was immense pressure inside the ANC to have the rest of the test matches cancelled. But Nelson Mandela's view was that such a step could further alienate white South Africans, already very insecure about their future, and bolster the right wing. His priority, he said, was to take white South Africans along the path of negotiations to a democratic settlement. He also thought that an end to the tour would only be water on the mill of his stubborn National Party counterparts in the negotiations. After firm undertakings from Craven and Patel, the ANC agreed that the test against Australia could take place the following Saturday. It did, and *Die Stem* wasn't played and a minute's silence was observed by the Newlands crowd – with a few exceptions. Australia beat South Africa 26–3.

It is difficult to explain why Luyt decided to do what he did. It wasn't a decision made on the spur of the moment – he admitted later that he had planned to play *Die Stem* all along. But this was the man who had broken ranks and talked to the ANC against the will of the government and his own rugby colleagues. This was the same person who helped form the Democratic Party with the express intent to wrest power from the National Party government and so end all forms of apartheid and establish a democracy. And now he was playing up to a right-wing constituency, in the process alienating the black majority and their leaders and jeopardising the smooth transition to normality in sport.

'That is typical of Louis,' an old friend of his told me when I asked him about this. 'Don't even try to get an explanation. He is erratic and utterly unpredictable. He has no ideology, no allegiance to anybody. He loves to show a big middle finger to anybody who has more power than him.'

It is hard to come to any conclusion other than that Luyt was either extremely opportunistic, or that he also, like those at the stadium, resented the loss of white Afrikaner power. Or perhaps both. Opportunistic in the sense that he knew that a large chunk of fanatical rugby supporters – and rugby administrators – were conservative, even right wing, and that his behaviour would make him a hero in their eyes. They had resented him when he went to meet with the ANC four years earlier, but his playing of *Die Stem* restored his image as a '*goeie Afrikanerleier*'. He was going to need the support of rugby clubs and unions when he made his bid for leadership of SARFU in eighteen months' time. He was saying to them: I brought international rugby back to South Africa, but now that we have it, I will fight all foreign elements who want to get their hands on our game. If that was his strategy, it seemed to have worked.

But it is also likely that Luyt, like so many white Afrikaner politicians, never really had a change of heart. Like them, he thought that apartheid had to end because it was making life unpleasant for whites, but he believed whites could share power without giving up power. Luyt could never establish a proper working relationship with any black rugby administrator, and set out to destroy the two black administrators who dared challenge him: Ebrahim Patel and Brian van Rooyen. When a black minister of sport criticised him, he crudely and publicly insulted the minister. It was this stubborn clinging to the old ways that in the end would cost him his whole public career.

The early 1990s also signalled the end of another era, the era of 'Doc' Danie Craven. In 1990, Craven was already eighty years old, but showed no desire to retire. Luyt was getting impatient with the old man who had been president of the South African Rugby Board since 1956, and started a campaign to get rid of him.

Craven was more than an institution in rugby and South African public life. He was a legend among rugby lovers worldwide.

Craven's grandfather, John Craven, was a Yorkshireman from the town of Steeton. He visited South Africa in 1860, but never left again. He met Thomas Bailey, father of the famous Sir Abe Bailey, on the journey from England and they started trading in the eastern Free State near the town of Lindley. He later married Catherina Roos, a local farmer's daughter, and settled on a Lindley farm, which they called Steeton. Their sixth child, James, married Maria Hartman. Their son Daniel ('Daantjie' and later 'Danie') Hartman Craven was born on 11 October 1910, the third of seven children. Despite being the son of a Yorkshireman, Danie's father fought with the Free State Commando against the British in the Anglo-Boer War. Like my grandfather, he was a prisoner of war in Ceylon (now Sri Lanka), and like my grandmother, Danie's mother spent most of the war in the Kroonstad concentration camp.

The Craven household had by now become completely Afrikaans-speaking, with English a third language after Sesotho. During the Rebellion of 1914, James Craven was an ardent supporter of Louis Botha and Jan Smuts. Danie grew up as a 'Smuts man' and called himself that until he died. Craven's biographer, Paul Dobson, says that although Craven's home language had always been Afrikaans, 'he claimed not to be an Afrikaner'. Craven's old friend and journalist, George Gerber, says in a book on Craven he wrote for the Stellenbosch Rugby Club: 'Dok never saw himself as an Afrikaner. When I once asked him whether he was an Afrikaner, he said: "What kind of a thing is that? I'm a South African."'

Craven went to Stellenbosch University after school and stayed in the famous Wilgenhof student residence, of which he later became warden. He was captain of the rugby team and the swimming team and played cricket for the university. He started off as a theology student, but ended up with three doctorates: in ethnology, psychology and physical training. In 1931 Craven was selected for the Springbok rugby side. He became a selector and coach of the Springbok team in 1949, and between 1956 and 1993 he was the president of the South African Rugby Board.

A more fundamentally different man to Louis Luyt one can hardly imagine. Luyt never liked him – he was everything Luyt wanted to be: he came from a rich family background, he was highly educated, sophisticated and revered nationally and internationally. The only thing Luyt and Craven had in common was a strong authoritarian streak. When he was a newspaper publisher, Luyt wanted to be like Piet Cillié; as an industrialist he admired Anton Rupert; as a rugby administrator he envied Danie Craven – all three of them prominent members of the somewhat exclusive Cape Afrikaner elite.

Craven was clearly overstaying his welcome as head of South African rugby – by 1990 he began nodding off during meetings, became forgetful and didn't have enough physical energy. But he was determined to oversee the unification of South African rugby and its re-entry into international competition, and he stayed on. It did not help Craven's cause when the Springboks appeared completely out of their depth with their first matches after re-admission: in 1992 they lost to Australia and New Zealand at home, and to France and England on tour.

Most people in the higher rugby echelons wanted Craven to go, but Luyt was the only one ruthless enough, and he orchestrated the campaign. His campaign was supported by an ambitious and clever sports writer at the *Sunday Times*, Edward Griffiths. Luyt later employed Griffiths as SARFU's media man and then as chief executive officer.

Public humiliation was not beyond Luyt. At a rugby ceremony in 1992, he said that special small steps had been built to the podium 'for people who walk with difficulty'. Craven feebly hit back that the steps were for Luyt, because he was overweight. Luyt countered: 'But I can go on a diet.'

Luyt criticised Craven because SARFU had not sent a representative to observe the 1992 currie Cup final at Ellis Park, knowing well that Craven had informed him that SARFU had asked the presidents of Transvaal and Natal to act as representatives of the union. Craven did not travel much any more, and his co-president, Ebrahim Patel, had another engagement that day. Luyt, clearly wanting to make the point that Craven was too old to fulfil his duties, said their absence was a slap in the face of Transvaal rugby and the sponsors. Craven was angry at Luyt's cheap shot. 'It is artificial to kick up a fuss because we were not there,' he said. 'Dr Luyt is now like a child who lost and then runs to his mother.'

At SARFU's special general meeting on 27 November 1992, Luyt proposed that the constitution be changed. He wanted the position of president to be changed into an honorary position, and a chairman appointed to run SARFU. Craven himself chaired part of the meeting, but not very well. Ebrahim Patel had to cover for him. Luyt's proposal was defeated only because Patel told them he would not allow Craven to be kicked out or humiliated. Such a step could threaten the fragile unity in rugby. 'That is the least we can do after all the man has done for rugby,' he said. Patel, whose relationship with Luyt was an acrimonious one, probably did it as much to spite Luyt as he did it out of loyalty to Craven.

Craven's biographer, Paul Dobson, says Craven knew what was coming. Three weeks before the SARFU meeting he told Dobson: 'I have acquiesced. I am finished.' Dobson recalls: 'At that stage he sounded depressed, barely coherent and no longer happy to chat.' During this time Craven fell down the stairs of his Velddrif cottage and was taken to hospital in an unconscious state. He was soon out of hospital, but it was a heavy blow to the old man. He was still president of SARFU, but he stopped making decisions or attending meetings. On 4 January 1993 Craven died, two months before his time as executive president was to run out, and thirty-six years after he became president. Fritz Eloff was the caretaker until March, when Patel's term was to start.

Craven had not groomed anyone to take over his position. He had said more than once that Jannie Engelbrecht, once a brilliant Springbok wing who became a successful wine farmer, would have been able to fill his shoes. Craven's friends say he once wondered out loud whether Morné du Plessis, former Springbok captain, would be his successor. It so happened that Engelbrecht became the Springbok team manager in 1993, and after he fell out with Luyt he was replaced by Du Plessis.

The power struggle in SARFU started months before the election of a new executive in March 1994. Luyt and Patel, the two early front-runners, were at each other's throats most of the time, with Fritz Eloff also a contender. Luyt had already outmaneouvred Patel by preventing his re-election to the Transvaal union executive. In late 1993 there was speculation in the newspapers that an outsider, a 'Mr X', could be the winner because the unions did not believe Patel was dynamic enough to lead SARFU, but they disliked Luyt too much to vote for him.

Luyt believed his time had come. The crown of South African rugby now had an additional attraction: the Rugby World Cup was going to be hosted in South Africa in 1995. He spent a lot of time and energy – and, some say, money – lobbying the various union representatives. He had Transvaal behind him, soon secured the support of Eastern Province, and then concentrated his powers of persuasion on the smaller and rural unions. His message, one of the officials in a rural union told me, was: 'You may not like me, but I am the strong man of South African rugby. With the World Cup coming and professionalism in rugby a virtual certainty after that, I'm the only man who can run rugby successfully. I transformed Transvaal from a bankrupt union and a weak team into the richest union and the strongest team in the country in six years. I have proved myself as a businessman. I will make South African rugby the richest and most powerful in the world.'

It was a very convincing argument, especially the financial one. By January 1994 Luyt also had Northern Free State, Vaal Triangle, Far North and Lowveld behind him, and Griquas followed. The Luyt camp then pulled a clever trick to counter Patel: they proposed Mluleki George, chairman of the National Sports Congress and senior ANC figure in the Eastern Cape, as senior vice-president, and three other black administrators as executive members: Arthob Petersen of Boland, Tobie Titus of Western Province and Mntwey Nkwinti of Eastern Province. Griqualand West chairman André Markgraaff was proposed as junior vice-chairman.

SARFU's first election at the Woodstock Holiday Inn in Cape Town on 11 March 1994 – just eight weeks before South Africa's first democratic election – turned out to be an anti-climax. Eloff had withdrawn earlier, and now Patel pulled out, saying his school, the Lenasia Muslim Primary School, needed all his energies. Luyt was the only nominee for president, and George the only nominee for senior vice-president. They were elected unopposed. Louis Luyt was now in charge of South African rugby.

It was agreed that four executive members should be from the old SARU structures: Mluleki George and Silas Nkanunu of Eastern Province, Tobie Titus of Western Province and Arthob Petersen of Boland. The other members of the executive were Ronnie Masson of Western Province, Hentie Serfontein of Northern Transvaal, Keith Parkinson of Natal, André Markgraaff of Griqualand West and Hennie Erasmus of South Eastern Transvaal.

Luyt's old enemy, Fritz Eloff, chaired the meeting in the place of Patel, who did not attend the meeting at all. But Eloff was graceful. Luyt was a controversial man, he said, but he did listen to advice. 'We need a strong leader to lead us on the road to the World Cup. Dr Luyt is such a man,' he said.

It must have been Eloff's conciliatory gesture that made Luyt refrain from one of his regular offensive speeches. He first told of how he had met with Reverend Arnold Stofile, a member of the interim executive and later Premier of the Eastern Cape, and said to him: 'I hope you are praying for me.' Stofile responded: 'Now more than ever.' Luyt smiled at the men just elected to be his executive and said: 'Now that I see the executive that you have given me, I don't think even that is enough.' There was general laughter – one of the last times the SARFU executive laughed at Luyt's jokes.

Luyt also undertook to work for South African rugby 'twenty-four hours a day'. He added: 'In the process I will tackle the problems of rugby fearlessly, because we are a rugby nation. We were the best. We have to become the best again.'

He kept his promise.

5

MAKING ENEMIES

*One has to start at the top. I looked at myself and found no
fault. So then I had to go downwards.*

— Louis Luyt, August 1994

Louis Luyt's election as the highest authority in South African rugby
at the age of sixty-one gave him immense satisfaction. He had not
only achieved one of his childhood determinations – to be a national figure who commanded respect – but he had done it in the face
of adversity. He had not got the job because he was a Broeder or a
member of a political party, he had got it because of his achievements and his cunning.

But Luyt, like most men with huge egos and despotic tendencies,
could not sit back, enjoy his achievements and rule South African
rugby with the benevolence of a Danie Craven. He also failed completely to read the fundamental shift in South African society around
the advent of democracy in 1994: there was a new openness, a new
preparedness to challenge authoritarianism, a new insistence on
democracy and transparency on all levels of society. This new culture also extended to the rugby establishment and the broad mass
of rugby fans.

Luyt was oblivious of this. Ten days after his election in March 1994, he started a programme of complicated legal (and some highly unorthodox) manoeuvres which would give him even more unchallenged powers at Transvaal rugby and Ellis Park stadium and built it into a family empire, employing his son Louis junior, his son-in-law Rian Oberholzer and even his daughter Corlia on occasion. And he treated Springbok rugby as he had Transvaal rugby for so long: constantly interfering with selectors, team management and players. In the international rugby community he quickly became as well known as Danie Craven. But while Craven was respected as an elder statesman of the game, Luyt was resented as a crude, boorish, xenophobic and power-hungry man.

It was well known in rugby circles in the early 1990s that Luyt had been bolder than any other rugby administrator in the world when it came to paying players and generally breaking the International Rugby Board's rules on amateurism. Transvaal captain François Pienaar wrote of Luyt in the early 1990s: 'He, at least, had long ago given up on the charade of amateurism.' The British media crucified Luyt when he then accused the England captain, Will Carling, of having become a 'pound millionaire' through rugby just as the England team arrived for a tour in South Africa. He later denied that that was what he meant.

Luyt got his first taste of what the South African rugby public were thinking of him at the second test against the English team at Newlands in June 1994. When Luyt was welcomed at the stadium over the public address system, a large number of the spectators booed loudly. Luyt remarked that he was clearly 'as popular at Newlands as in the British press'. The chairman of the Western Province Rugby Union, Ronnie Masson, later apologised to Luyt. 'I am very sorry about the grumbling among the spectators when Dr Luyt arrived,' he said. 'He is after all the president of SARFU and should be supported.'

At the reception after the test, Luyt made the kind of undiplomatic speech for which he became famous during his career as a top sports administrator. He addressed the English team manager, Jack Rowell, and said: 'Jack, you are a gentleman. I am not, so I will say what I want. The score today flattered you guys and I don't mind saying it. We will no longer need the country's tailors to mend our pants, because we are in the process of getting up from our knees, getting back on our feet. South Africa is back. We don't have to fear anybody.'

That wasn't exactly true. The old stalwarts of Springbok rugby like Naas Botha, Danie Gerber, Uli Schmidt and Wahl Bartmann were at the end of their playing careers. The Springboks were rusty and were playing isolation-style rugby, whereas countries such as Australia and England had developed completely new approaches. South Africa was lagging behind seriously, and Luyt and his associates did not seem to have the patience or the intimate knowledge of the new game to tolerate coaches slowly bringing the Boks back into the modern game. But South Africa certainly had enough talented players and more than enough determination to make a comeback.

John Williams was the first coach to be dumped in the deep end. He was a competent coach of provincial teams, but he did not seem to grasp the dynamics of the new game. He coached the Springboks like he did Northern Transvaal. It didn't work. At the end of 1992, his days were numbered: five tests played, only one, against France, won. The arrogant and rugby-hungry South African fans, as well as the SARFU hierarchy, were impatient. South Africa isn't a rugby-playing country, it's a rugby-winning country.

The most successful coach in South Africa at that time was Ian McIntosh of Natal. But he was not a rugby fraternity insider, or a former Springbok, and he was an English-speaking ex-Zimbabwean on top of it. Gerrie Sonnekus of Free State was appointed to take Williams's place, but before he could do so, his involvement in a financial controversy was revealed and he pulled out.

At the beginning of 1993, a few weeks after Craven's death, McIntosh was asked to coach the Springboks. He had a contract up to the World Cup in 1995. McIntosh was without the brilliant Naas Botha, but he had the services of another blond rugby genius: François Pienaar. Pienaar was captain of Transvaal and Luyt's blue-eyed boy. Pienaar called Luyt 'a benevolent and supportive' figure at the time: 'We respected him and liked him, and he played an integral part within what had become an extremely happy squad.' Before a home match, Pienaar said, they always had a team braai at Luyt's house, and after the match Luyt took them to a steakhouse. But the 'extreme happiness' with Luyt was not to last through 1994.

McIntosh appointed Pienaar captain of the Springbok squad. Jannie Engelbrecht, legendary Springbok wing of the 1960s, was appointed as team manager. In 1993, McIntosh, Engelbrecht and Pienaar took the Springboks on a crucial tour of Australia. Ebrahim Patel was still the executive president of SARFU and accompanied the Boks during the first part of the tour. McIntosh later said of the Australian tour: 'Both François and Jannie later reckoned the tour was the most enjoyable they had been on, and I was relaxed and happy in their company.'

Engelbrecht told me that he believed the tour was very success-ful, but very, very difficult. 'We'd just got back into the international arena and there were so many perceptions. The new generation Australians ... had never even seen the Springboks, just about never heard of them. The impact we as management and players had to make was not only about rugby. We had to go and sell South Africa. We had to prove that the new dispensation was working. We had to show the world who and what the Springboks were. We had to show the outside world who and what South Africans were; we had to show we were decent, civilised people with norms and standards.

'In that sense it was a very difficult tour. At the level of being an ambassador you had to go out of your way. I was literally working eighteen hours a day to fulfil both functions of ambassador and manager.'

McIntosh remembers that the South African ambassador to Australia told Engelbrecht in his presence: 'Jannie, you should have been a diplomat. You and your Springbok team have done more for the South African team on your brief trip than we have achieved in one year.' It helped that the Australians remembered Engelbrecht as one of the most prolific try-scorers in rugby history: forty-four in all. McIntosh says Engelbrecht was 'a wonderful character' with a 'phenomenal work rate' and a strong personality – so strong, he says, that players complained to him that Engelbrecht was dictatorial.

The tour to New Zealand the next year was in stark contrast to this success and happiness. Because, by this time, Louis Luyt had become the president of SARFU. In the words of rugby writer John Bishop: 'The 1994 season was to prove one of the most traumatic and acrimonious in Springbok rugby history, a year when play on the field was overshadowed by controversy and an undignified, public scrap between top South African administrators.'

McIntosh later remarked that he never, at any stage, felt that 'Luyt quite trusted me or had any faith in the game I was advocating'. The coach's first problem was that SARFU appointed a new selection panel of six, headed by former Springbok Hannes Marais. Many rugby journalists later concluded that Marais' job as convenor was to shackle McIntosh as much as possible. The coach did not have a happy relationship with Marais and the SARFU representative on the selection panel, Johan Claassen. Mac was quoted as saying of Marais: 'We disagreed often. Hannes may have been a great Springbok prop and captain, but there was no way I would accept that he knew more than me about my job, not with his limited coaching experience and background.'

Engelbrecht invited Luyt over to New Zealand for the first few matches, as he had done with Patel the previous year. McIntosh later blamed him for this. 'We were still in the process of establishing ourselves in the international arena,' Engelbrecht explains, 'and New Zealand is a very important rugby country. Our last tour over there was in 1981, and that was an unhappy, controversial tour that divided the people of New Zealand. We had to sell Springbok rugby and South Africa to them. That was my perspective. Louis was our president, our highest authority in rugby. I have to be proud of my president, and use him as a way of marketing our team and our country. Mac only thought about rugby, but I had a much wider perspective.

'That is why I asked Louis to come for a match or two. And Louis came, but unfortunately he decided to stay on. That is where the problems started.

'Louis wanted to be president and he wanted to be team manager. I did not think he had the capacity to fulfil that function. He had no experience, and I don't think he has the ability to communicate with people and be a real ambassador for his country. That was such a big problem in New Zealand.

'Louis just arrived. I told them that he was coming, but Louis never bothered to even make contact with his counterpart in New Zealand. That's the way it was always done. So he arrived uninvited by New Zealand. And when they did not supply him with tickets to a match, the hell was loose. When he did not have a hotel room, he shouted and screamed at the New Zealanders. From the beginning there was conflict between him and the New Zealand Rugby Union. It destroyed my vision of being an ambassador.

'But it wasn't only that. Louis caused conflict everywhere he went. He constantly interfered with the selection of players, which was the prerogative of the coach, the manager and the captain. We operated exactly like we did when I played international rugby from 1959 – when there is an injury and a replacement had to be sent, then you contact the convenor of the selection committee and say: we need a man, send someone. Not Louis Luyt.

'Kobus Wiese was injured and we had to send him home. So I phoned the chairman of the selection committee and said, send me a lock forward. They have a priority list of five locks, I have four, so they have to send me number five. The logistics of how he would get to us was SARFU's responsibility. But Louis wanted to do it. Louis wanted to decide who should be the replacement. He was incredibly angry that we didn't want to listen to him.

'At one stage I told him: Louis, please, I am the manager. I am autonomous in my decisions as manager. You are the president of the South African Rugby Football Union. But I am in charge of this team and you are unfortunately not. You better start realising that. And if you don't, we are going to have conflict [*koppe stamp*]. And that's what happened.'

McIntosh's biographer, John Bishop, says that even before the first test Luyt 'appeared moody'. The conflict between Luyt and Engelbrecht reached boiling point in the town of Timaru. Luyt was extremely upset because he had been given a tiny room in the hotel where the Springboks stayed. According to McIntosh and Engelbrecht, he accosted Engelbrecht in the corridor of the hotel and a screaming match ensued. He did not only feel humiliated because of his small room, he also voiced his anger at not being briefed about the decision to replace Wiese with Adri Geldenhuys. McIntosh was concerned that the screaming match would create a scandal and influence the players, and he took the two into Engelbrecht's room.

Engelbrecht confirms that Luyt indeed had a tiny room in Timaru. 'There were no rooms left. He was not on our list, because we never knew what he was going to do next. He just arrived at places. Louis was being extremely difficult. He wanted to continue the fight in the room, but I told him that I had a function to attend. Six hundred people were expecting me to make a speech, and I could not insult them by not showing up or coming late. I told Louis we could talk after the function. Louis was extremely upset about this. He felt that I was treating him as someone who wasn't that important. This incident was a turning point. After that the tour became a complete nightmare.' McIntosh said he thought that the row, which was to simmer between the two for the rest of the tour before coming to a head in August, 'had its seeds in Timaru'.

Fritz Joubert of the newspaper *Die Burger* reported at the time that one of the reasons for the bad blood during Luyt's stay in New Zealand was that he was not an official member of the Springbok tour group: 'Despite the fact that the New Zealand Rugby Union offered its help, he has made his own travel arrangements.'

After the first test Luyt publicly criticised McIntosh for not including a specialist goal-kicker, and blamed the defeat on bad discipline. In fact, he publicly blamed Engelbrecht and McIntosh several times for the 'indiscipline' of the players on the tour, although senior players and journalists on tour denied this. Luyt returned to South Africa shortly after the first test.

During the second test, prop Johan le Roux bit All Black captain Sean Fitzpatrick on the ear. That evening McIntosh, Engelbrecht and captain François Pienaar watched the video footage of the incident. It was clear for all to see that Le Roux bent down and applied his teeth to Fitzpatrick's ear. McIntosh said later that they agreed, 'and it was unanimous', that Le Roux should be sent home. Pienaar remembered it this way: 'After some discussion, we all decided that Johan would be sent home. I did not agree with the decision, and to my eternal regret, I did not disagree with the decision either.' Yet afterwards Luyt criticised Engelbrecht for the decision. It seemed Luyt wanted to take credit for handing down the punishment. He told journalist Dan Retief that Le Roux's banishment should have been seen as strong action by SARFU and not by the tour management.

Luyt also said that, if he had his way, Le Roux would never play rugby again – a statement that angered senior players. Engelbrecht and McIntosh criticised Luyt for saying this. They believed Le Roux's suspension until March 1996 was sufficient, even too severe. Luyt was livid when he read these criticisms in South African newspapers. He told journalists that Engelbrecht and McIntosh had been appointed by SARFU to manage and coach the Springbok rugby team, and not to criticise SARFU. 'These two don't realise that SARFU was under great international pressure since the Le Roux incident to eradicate dirty play,' he said. 'I have received phone calls from London and Australia about the ear-biting, and it is SARFU's job to restore South Africa's honourable rugby name. If we feel Le Roux should never play again, the tour management is not entitled to criticise us.'

Pienaar said after the second test that the defeat in that test, combined with the controversy over Le Roux's ear-biting, had 'knocked the stuffing out of the tour', and most players just wanted to return home. 'Everything that had seemed so fun and positive now seemed so negative.'

Luyt made serious derogatory remarks about Engelbrecht to players and other officials. Among other things, he said that Engelbrecht, an accomplished wine farmer and wine maker, had spent too much time marketing his own wines in Australia and New Zealand and not enough with the rugby tour.

McIntosh's reaction to this gossip was: 'Jannie's work rate on tour was phenomenal and it made me laugh, during the New Zealand tour, to hear the totally unfounded stories of how he was spending his time marketing his wines instead of attending practices. If ever anyone gets to know someone, it is a coach and a manager on a tour. I spent more hours and days with Jannie than anyone else, and he had no time for himself.' He said there was one, and only one, occasion when Jannie took a few hours off to take the wine maker at his estate, *Rust-en-Vrede*, to a distillery near Christchurch.

Engelbrecht bristled when I asked him about the rumours. We were sitting at a desk in the cellar of *Rust-en-Vrede* outside Stellenbosch. 'Louis started that gossip because it suited him,' he said. 'He always manipulated to drive a wedge between Ian and

85

myself. That's what he does: divide and rule. Because I didn't expect it, I never did anything about it. Somewhere in his book Mac says that I had been against him continuing as Springbok coach. That is not true, but Louis tried to drive a wedge between us. I still have my report.

'We had to entertain our guys on tour sometimes, and in New Zealand we had a choice: we could take the players to the Barossa Valley and show them the wine cellars, or find something else to do. Balie Swart was a qualified wine maker and many of the other guys were interested in wine, so they voted for going to the wine cellars. I had been there many times. I did not need to go again. That was the one trip. And then I had one afternoon off when Mac said there was not going to be a rugby practice and I had no other obligations. In Argentina I had absolutely nothing to do with wine. In England the Rugby Union organised a reception for us and to surprise me, they bought some of my wine in London and put it on the table. I had nothing to do with it; I had no idea they were going to do that. Now you have the total wine story. I don't market my wines, I have an entire marketing team dedicated to that. Louis just used it to sow a little seed of suspicion that I wasn't doing my job.'

Luyt went back to New Zealand before the third and last test. Engelbrecht says Luyt's last and biggest insult to his New Zealand hosts was not to turn up at the farewell dinner at the end of the tour. The New Zealanders had sent an official, written invitation to him as president of SARFU.

'I sat next to the New Zealand president at the dinner,' says Engelbrecht, 'and after a while he asked me where my president was. I said he was with me in the hotel shortly before the dinner, I don't know why he's not here yet. Louis simply didn't arrive. He didn't tell them he wasn't coming, and he didn't even apologise the next day. How can you operate like that? When I asked him he gave a silly answer that if he didn't want to go, he didn't have to. You can't operate like that.'

Luyt only explained his absence when he was asked about it by reporters back in South Africa. He said he was left on his own after the last test and got lost when he was looking for the changing rooms. When he found them, the last players told him that the bus was about to leave. Then he got lost again. He got a lift back to the hotel and started talking to representatives of the media. He then decided it was too late to go to the dinner. He said he still planned to apologise to the New Zealand Rugby Union president.

Engelbrecht rejected his explanation: 'The bus was right in front of the changing rooms. There is no way that he could get lost. He did not come to the dinner because he spoke to selected media people in his room about his plans for the tour management.'

On 30 July, in Canterbury, Luyt invited *Sunday Times* journalist Dan Retief up to his room. He told Retief that McIntosh had failed as a coach and had to go. Retief says he knew Luyt was feeding him the story for public consumption and wanted him to write it. But only a few hours after that conversation, Luyt told a press conference that there was too much pressure on the coach and he had to be supported. Retief was completely baffled.

The *Sunday Tribune* of 31 July carried a piece by New Zealand writer Mike McGrath which quoted Luyt as saying that he was mindful of the fact that, were McIntosh to be foolishly discarded, his successor would just have nine months to acquaint himself with the realities of modern test rugby before the following year's World Cup.

'We cannot go against the coach now,' Luyt told McGrath. He said it wasn't the time to talk about a new coach and 'you can't put pressure on McIntosh at this stage the way some are doing right now. It's terrible, terrible. He's aged a lot since I last saw him. We're not being human to the man. We put him under pressure and that pressure goes to the players. I am the one who has supported him right through so don't put pressure on me in the situation where I've got to say we've got to decide on this now. Let's support the man and see what he comes up with. There's is no way I can replace McIntosh. It's the full executive that can do that, not me alone. And when we appointed him, we appointed him until after the World Cup.' Luyt added that the job of coach was 'not on the agenda' for the next executive meeting of SARFU on 19 August.

But just days after this interview, Luyt told the Sunday paper *Rapport* that McIntosh and Engelbrecht had not performed up to standard and were going to be replaced. Pienaar wrote about this: 'When Louis Luyt suggested in a newspaper interview that both the team manager and the coach were "history", all spirit and morale appeared to evaporate. Everyone became more concerned with their own survival in the wreckage of the tour than what happened with the team.'

The South African Press Agency reported at the time that the senior members of the Springbok team supported McIntosh and Engelbrecht. Balie Swart was quoted as saying that many of the problems were due to provincialism. 'We as players in the national team have overcome that problem,' he said, 'but clearly a lot of the armchair critics are still struggling with it. McIntosh has not been given enough time in the international arena. He deserves another chance before he is thrown into the darkness.'

After the final test, a reporter went up to McIntosh and asked him whether anybody had spoken to him. McIntosh said no, and asked what he was referring to. The reporter said he had just talked to Luyt, and 'I think you have been chopped.' McIntosh addressed the players and told them that he had heard he was getting the boot. McIntosh recalls that some of the players seemed 'bewildered and surprised' at the news, but others appeared 'obviously aware' of the news. He says he 'always had the feeling certain Transvaal players were reporting to Luyt behind my back'. Dan Retief says it also appeared to him that the Transvaal faction in the Bok team never supported McIntosh: 'Even then, on tour, Pienaar, who was at that stage quite close to Luyt, was probably angling to have Kitch Christie appointed as coach.'

On the bus to the Auckland airport on the way home, Engelbrecht sat down next to McIntosh and told him that his wife had just called from South Africa. 'It has been on the news back home. You, me and Gysie [Pienaar, the assistant coach] have all been sacked.' Luyt was on the same flight, a very long haul first to Sydney and then all the way to Johannesburg. Luyt was sitting in first class, the coach, manager and team in the economy section. Luyt did not say a single word to them on the flight or on arrival at Johannesburg International Airport. McIntosh says he had been expecting the news, and was resigned. 'We had been expecting the worst, but it was the way the whole sordid affair was handled which aggravated an already painful situation.'

On 8 August, a week after his statements in the *Sunday Tribune*, Luyt told a press conference at Ellis Park that he wasn't prepared to work with McIntosh or Engelbrecht any longer. His main reason for wanting them removed was poor discipline. 'Look at what happened during the last three tours [to Argentina, Australia and New Zealand]. We suffered losses and we had people sent off on tour. Discipline was non-existent. I leave it to your imagination who was responsible.' Luyt also complained that McIntosh had not consulted him on the composition of the Springbok squad for the third test, and that Engelbrecht had never deferred to him as SARFU president. 'For that I can't blame Jannie Engelbrecht. I must blame the SARFU administration. Engelbrecht did not have his terms of reference and this was the cause of a number of things going wrong.' But Luyt also called Engelbrecht a 'has-been' and said South African rugby did not need him any more.

Luyt said that the original undertaking that McIntosh would stay on until after the World Cup was not binding, as it was not a written contract. 'It was an oral agreement. Also, it was subject to performance on the playing field. He could not achieve anything with three tours. The team came back from New Zealand as losers. It was also clear to me in New Zealand that some of the players had turned against him, although a few still support him.'

The *Sunday Tribune* of 14 August 1994 reported that Luyt said at a Cape Town lunch the previous week about his dismissal of McIntosh and Engelbrecht: 'One has to start at the top. I looked at myself and found no fault. So then I had to go downwards.'

Edward Griffiths, at the time still a sports writer at the *Sunday Times* but later the CEO of SARFU, writes in his book *One Team, One Country* that Luyt's style was to act on his personal instinct, 'swiftly and, if necessary, brutally', knowing that his executive committee would later back him up. Like Craven before him, Griffiths says, Luyt demanded total control, although Craven did it more subtly. 'The roots of this system lay in an essentially Afrikaans ethos which applied to pre-1990 politics as well as to rugby: that – while strict discipline, clear rules and stuffy procedures applied to everyone on the ladder – the leader could do exactly what he liked, how he liked and when he liked. No rules.'

Luyt's cruel dumping of the Springbok management raised a storm of protest that raged in South Africa for weeks and even reached Australia and New Zealand.

The protest was mostly about Luyt's outrageous style and about Engelbrecht, and only because Engelbrecht fought back hard. McIntosh went quietly, almost without saying a word. And few people spoke up for him – certainly not his captain or his players. His successor as coach, Kitch Christie, said much later: 'Many people in and around South Africa reflect on the brutal dismissal of McIntosh as unfair, but very few people said so at the time. This is the pattern within a game historically ruled by fear. Everyone speaks up some years later; no one speaks up at the time.' This was particularly true of the Luyt era.

Senior players, including François Pienaar, all later denied the allegations of bad behaviour and indiscipline, and some of them publicly criticised the sacking of their coach. But it took them years. The man known as 'The Rolls Royce of fullbacks', André Joubert, later said McIntosh was a 'brilliant coach' and that to fire him after the tour 'was so unfair, and just when everything was coming right'.

Pienaar, widely seen as one of those who undermined McIntosh on the tour and one of the players Luyt was referring to who had 'turned against' the coach, waited a few years before he had his say about McIntosh: 'Ian McIntosh did not deserve to be dismissed after the 1994 tour of New Zealand,' he wrote in his autobiography, *Rainbow Warrior*, first published in 1999. 'A decent and knowledgeable man, he had taken a young, emerging Springbok squad to Australia and New Zealand in consecutive seasons, and had narrowly lost both series when they might have been won.'

Natal Rugby Union president Keith Parkinson, a senior member of SARFU's executive, was virtually the only one who immediately called for McIntosh's reinstatement. 'I believe he has already achieved enough progress with the Springbok team to take them to the World Cup and win it,' he said at the time. Rugby writer Dan Retief, who had been critical of McIntosh during the New Zealand tour, later changed his mind about the coach: 'I now genuinely believe that we would not have won the World Cup the next year if it had not been for Mac,' he said.

Kitch Christie says of McIntosh in his autobiography written with Edward Griffiths, *Kitch – Triumph of a Decent Man*: 'If he had been able to choose the team he wanted, I am sure he would have had better results and would have stayed to coach the Boks at the World Cup, and I honestly believe he would have done extremely well. He's a fine coach. I did not think Ian McIntosh should have been sacked as Springbok coach in August 1994, and I still don't think so now.'

Edward Griffiths wrote later: 'He [McIntosh] returned from New Zealand and accepted his execution by decree with admirable calm and dignity. However, the downright cruel and despicable face of

South African rugby, the opposite to its honour and glory, revealed itself in the fact that McIntosh was not officially thanked for his services, no letter was written, no one faced him. Yet another decent man was ruthlessly discarded, and people standing by simply looked the other way.' As it turned out, Griffiths would get the same kind of treatment from Luyt two years later.

The SARFU executive was meeting in Cape Town on the Wednesday after the team's return, where Luyt's decisions had to be ratified. McIntosh thought he should have the right to defend himself, and phoned Johan Claassen about it. Claassen promised to do whatever he could, and said he would phone McIntosh back. He never bothered to phone back. McIntosh never had the opportunity to tell his side of the story before he was fired.

McIntosh told his biographer, John Bishop: 'The hurt I felt was not caused by the sacking but rather the way it was done – through the media. I had expected Louis Luyt to call me to his office to tell me the reasons for terminating my contract, face to face. I would have accepted that and, anyway, it would be my problem if I didn't. That would have been a gentleman's way of doing it. But decisions taken on my future were passed on through the newspapers and on television. It hurt my family and me.'

McIntosh says one of the first people to phone him after he was fired officially was Springbok captain François Pienaar. He was really sorry, Pienaar told him. McIntosh told him that he did not believe him. He says he told Pienaar: 'François, don't try and kid me. I really believe that I did not get your full support on the tour and, let's be honest, you've got what you want now and that is Kitch. And I understand that, but I don't believe you're being sincere now.'

Luyt did not speak to McIntosh for eighteen months. They briefly exchanged greetings at Eden Park in Auckland, New Zealand, when McIntosh's Natal team played against Auckland in the Super 12 competition. Luyt was booed by the Auckland spectators when he walked up to the podium. McIntosh says: 'The first time we spoke about my actual sacking was at the end of 1996 when Natal beat Transvaal in the Currie Cup final at Ellis Park. Louis came up to me at the function afterwards and told me that he had not been behind my sacking. And that was that.'

But while McIntosh accepted his unceremonious sacking, Engelbrecht fought back – and many with him, especially in his home province. The president of the Western Province Rugby Union, Ronnie Masson, protested: 'What happened wasn't good for South African rugby. When Dr Luyt went over to New Zealand, I thought they would make peace, but clearly it did not happen. It is a pity the differences were played out through the media.' Former Springbok and former Rugby Board member Butch Lochner said Luyt acted unprofessionally: 'A better manager than Jannie Engelbrecht you won't find in South Africa. Nobody is his equal when it comes to human relationships.' Former Springbok prop Hempies du Toit said: 'Dok Craven always said that when someone starts thinking he is bigger than the game, things go wrong. Mr Engelbrecht still puts rugby first. His heart is in the game. The management of SARFU is a bad example to the country's players.'

Even the previous selector and former Springbok captain Hannes Marais, a fierce critic of McIntosh's, attacked Luyt. The sackings were 'a continuation of Dr Luyt's management style,' he said, and what had happened was bad for South African rugby.

The Springbok captain of the difficult and controversial 1981 tour, Wynand Claassen, said that even during that tour Danie Craven never interfered. He remarked that it should not be forgotten that François Pienaar, as captain, was also part of the management and should also be held responsible. Another popular former captain, Morné du Plessis, said Luyt's actions made South African rugby appear ridiculous.

The newspaper *Die Burger* wrote in a main editorial: 'The bombs the president of the SA Rugby Union, Dr Louis Luyt, dropped yesterday are an undeserved blow to South African rugby. It can do the game more damage than good. In the eyes of the outside world it must be seen as a low point after the respect that South Africa enjoyed under the leadership of Dr Danie Craven. Luyt has neither the style, nor the respect, nor the authority of a Craven. He has messed up to such an extent after a short period in power that South Africa runs the risk of becoming the ridicule of world rugby.'

New Zealand's Minister of Sport, John Banks, expressed his deep disappointment at what Luyt had done, and said he was sending a fax message to President Nelson Mandela. Eddie Tonks, chairman of the New Zealand Rugby Union, said his union could not praise Engelbrecht and McIntosh enough. 'They were among the best tour managements we had here in years,' he said. 'The team and management were popular over here. Engelbrecht is a real asset.' He said the relationship between his union and Engelbrecht was always cordial and correct, and the behaviour of the players off the field was a compliment to South Africa. His union expressed their disappointment to SARFU in an official letter.

Public sympathy clearly lay with Engelbrecht, and media responses to Luyt's actions were sometimes nasty. In a piece titled 'wine notes', the *Sunday Tribune* quipped: 'Jannie Engelbrecht's Stellenbosch wine farm, *Rust-en-Vrede*, in the shadow of the Helderberg, has a history that dates back to 1694. This year's Luyt Harvest should be an amusing little wine.'

Engelbrecht didn't mince his words either. He called Luyt a 'tyrant' who was in rugby 'only to serve his own ego'. Engelbrecht promised to fight Luyt's 'authoritarianism' on behalf of South African rugby. He said South African rugby could not be managed 'with lies and half-truths'. The rugby officials and the rugby public to whom they are responsible should know everything, he said. In an interview on national radio Engelbrecht said that only SARFU, and not Luyt, could fire him. 'He always wanted to be the second manager. I will not allow anybody, and that includes Dr Luyt, to interfere with my work. I refused to obey his orders. There was only one manager, and that was me. I have received many calls from other unions supporting me and saying things cannot go on like this.'

Engelbrecht was correct in saying that only SARFU could fire him. The meeting where this was to happen was scheduled for a Cape Town hotel on 10 August. Engelbrecht insisted on attending the meeting and stating his case. Western Province rugby fans demonstrated against Luyt in front of the hotel, and the meeting had to be moved to another venue.

Engelbrecht picks up the story: 'I told them the meeting was supposed to start at seven, and now it was much later and I had an appointment to be on a television programme at nine. I said you can either fire me now, or you can wait until I'm back from the studio. Louis was livid. They moved to the TV room to see what I was going to say. I knew they were listening, and I said on TV that Louis tried to hijack the tour, that he tried to be manager and that it had negative consequences.

'They waited for me and I was back there just after ten. Mluleki George was the chairman. I was on my own. I defended myself, because I had nothing to hide. By half past eleven everything was on the table – all the allegations. There were no more questions.

'And then Louis got up and mentioned two incidents – incidents that had to prove that there had been no discipline on the tour. The one was about one of the players who broke one of the hotel room partitions with his elbow – they were wrestling or something. I told the players I didn't have a problem with it, I would tell the hotel management about it, ask them to fix it and give me the bill so I could get the money back from the player. That was it, nothing really.

'The other incident Louis mentioned was a taxi driver who came to see me and said one of the Boks slammed his car door so hard the lock broke, and then he kicked the door. I showed the driver the pictures of the players, and he identified the men involved. I called them and said: guys, what is your version of what happened? They

95

explained that they went to a nightclub and met a South African visitor there who wasn't exactly sober. When they arrived back at the hotel, the man slammed the door and kicked it. Well, I could not conduct a court case, because I didn't know where to get hold of this man. So I said to them I held them responsible. I told the taxi driver to have his car fixed, and bring me the bill. He brought it the next day, and I took the money off the players' payment.

'That was it. There were no more arguments why I should be fired. I even gave them the very favourable reports from New Zealand. But Louis doubted me. I said wait, I'll have my office fax through the receipts, I still have it. I have the receipts and the names of the hotel manager and the taxi driver. And with that the rug was pulled from under Luyt. There was no reason left why I should be fired.

'Luyt was dirty. Why had he not mentioned this to me before, in New Zealand or afterwards? It is a dangerous thing to say, and I have no direct proof, but I suspected Luyt had spies among the players who gave him feedback of every incident so he could use it against me. It is totally unacceptable to give a man the responsibility, a man with a long rugby history, with knowledge and management capabilities, a man who is running his own business successfully, who isn't dependent on SARFU for a salary; to appoint a man like that and then try to catch him through espionage and to confront him with it later. What kind of a person would do that?

'But I had answered all SARFU's questions, and there was no reason why they could fire me. So they appointed me manager for the tour to England. But Luyt was bitter. I wasn't in England for a week when he started talking to Carel du Plessis to become manager. Luyt's actions really are totally absurd.'

Luyt was outraged that Engelbrecht had outsmarted him, but his colleagues on the SARFU executive were concerned that the image of rugby had been tarnished by the public slagging match and could not ignore the strong public protest and support for Engelbrecht.

Mluleki George was apparently the one who insisted on a reconciliatory statement by SARFU in which Luyt and Engelbrecht pledged support and loyalty to each other. They emerged from the meeting with Luyt and Engelbrecht shaking hands for the press and television cameras, flashing rather plastic smiles.

Griffiths says Engelbrecht's continued presence in Springbok management was untenable. He says everybody noticed the negative electricity when he and Luyt stood together. Engelbrecht also snubbed Luyt in his presence when he said at a post-test dinner in Edinburgh that no one could ever follow in Danie Craven's shoes. Griffiths says it was clear that there could never be harmony with both of them in South African rugby management, but Luyt was the duly elected president and Engelbrecht only the appointed manager.

The day after the re-appointment of Engelbrecht, Luyt told the *Sunday Times*'s Dan Retief in a long interview that the pressure and the criticism were affecting him and his family, and that he was going to resign from SARFU. A while later he asked Retief to wait before he presented the story to his newspaper. On Saturday morning he summoned Retief to his home and confirmed that he had decided to resign. Retief says he remembers that Luyt's son, Louis junior, was also present and told his father: 'These people don't deserve you, dad.'

On Sunday 14 August the *Sunday Times* announced with a banner headline on its front page: 'Luyt Quits'. Retief wrote: 'Louis Luyt yesterday announced his resignation as president of the South African Rugby Football Union. In a move which is likely to send reverberations throughout the rugby world, Dr Luyt said he was severing all ties with SARFU and would also be standing down as chief organiser of next year's Rugby World Cup.'

Retief quoted 'a sombre Dr Luyt' as saying: 'I have to do the honourable thing and resign. I said that unless the Springbok team's management was changed, I would stand down, and that is what I'm doing.' Retief wrote that Luyt was 'adamant' about quitting: 'The emotions have gone so far against me now. My family and I are suffering greatly. We've been confronted with ugly letters in the press and I've received very nasty unsigned and dirty faxes. I'm surprised that people can go so low, to use words they do in faxes. I said I would do it, and I feel it is the proper thing to do (to resign). I can't take the hurt and insults any more and I'm not going to put my family in the firing line. That's not fair – to expose them to this filth. People don't seem to care about feelings. People say I've been through many fights and that I'm tough, but every time you do it leaves a scar.'

Luyt told Retief he was staying on as Transvaal president. 'I feel I have brought some professionalism to rugby administration. I wanted to put it right because it's a mess. It was my intention eventually to relinquish the Transvaal presidency to work only for South Africa; I thought I could do for SARFU what I did for Transvaal.

'But it's over now – I know I'm not the most liked person among the press simply because I tend to speak my mind. People don't like straight talk. They call beating about the bush diplomacy. But it takes an awful long time to get to the point and I don't have the time – I'm not a young man any more.'

Most rugby supporters and many administrators smiled over their Sunday breakfast. The last two weeks had been unpleasant, almost sordid. Nothing like this had ever happened in South African rugby. Now the source of all the embarrassment was getting out of the game, and rugby could get its dignity back.

They couldn't have been more wrong.

Retief's colleague on the *Sunday Times* who was appointed to the World Cup management team soon afterwards, Edward Griffiths, wrote in the same paper that South African rugby could not afford to lose Luyt. 'Yes, the man lacks airs and graces but he is the best man to lead SARFU forward to the World Cup. The big man must stay.'

That same Sunday afternoon, members of SARFU's executive were on their way to Cape Town for an emergency meeting the next morning. The president of the Griqualand West Rugby Union, André Markgraaff, told newspapers that Sunday: 'We cannot afford to lose Dr Luyt. Apart from his financial and organisational abilities, he is the only man we have who can be president.' SARFU's vice-president, Mluleki George, said: 'We cannot afford to lose a man who works 18 hours a day for rugby. People who cheer his resignation are short-sighted.'

After a four-hour meeting, Luyt announced that he had withdrawn his resignation. With the exception of Natal's Keith Parkinson and Western Province's Ronnie Masson, the SARFU executive had asked him to stay. He had called the bluff of those members of SARFU who were critical of him, and they had buckled. They had no answer to the question: who would run South Africa's staging of the Rugby World Cup, then just ten months away, if Luyt was out of the picture? The Minister of Sport, Steve Tshwete, had the same concern and he personally asked Luyt to stay on and manage the World Cup.

The Springbok captain, François Pienaar, broke his silence and said he was 'overjoyed' that Luyt had decided to withdraw his resignation. 'Rugby in South Africa needs someone such as Dr Luyt,' he said. 'Apart from his contribution to the World Cup, he means a lot to South African rugby in general. It is a good thing that he is staying on in his position.'

Luyt had gambled and won. His ego was bruised by the public outpouring of support for Engelbrecht and the demonstrations against him, and he wanted to show that he was irreplaceable. It was pretty obvious that he was calling his critics' bluff and playing martyr for a day, but it worked. Not only did his own executive and the Minister of Sport beg him to stay, he also forced a concession from SARFU to clip the wings of the Springbok team manager. From then on, the manager would have no say over team selections.

Engelbrecht's job became even more difficult. Apart from having less power, he soon faced a new foe: the newly appointed SARFU spokesman Edward Griffiths, who criticised Engelbrecht at every opportunity and insisted on writing Engelbrecht's speeches for him. Griffiths says in his book *One Team One Country* that Engelbrecht, in all his official speeches, talked about his own experiences as a Springbok player in the 1960s and did not appreciate the changes that had taken place in South Africa and in rugby. 'Engelbrecht's nostalgic approach may well have appealed to dyed-in-the-wool conservative rugby men in South Africa and around the world, but it jarred with the wider audience.' Engelbrecht was eventually sacked by Luyt and the SARFU executive in January 1995.

Jon Swift wrote in the *Weekly Mail* in late August 1994: 'The time for bloodletting and name-calling is over. There are simply not enough days left before the World Cup is scheduled to kick off to carry on with a domestic battle which has worldwide connotations. We have to get our ducks in a row now. That means stopping the humiliating business of sackings and resignations; ceasing votes on the merits or demerits of individuals and start thinking as a united body ... We cannot do otherwise if South Africa is to have any chance whatsoever in the meeting of rugby's top nations next year. Nor can we deviate if we do not want the rest of the rugby world to regard us as a clamorous rat pack of barefoot yokels squabbling in the dust of a distant country.'

Swift said what most sober South African rugby fans and administrators were thinking: it was time to consolidate and prepare for the 1995 Rugby World Cup.

6

THE RUGBY WORLD CUP

*[W]e did not have the support of sixty-three thousand South
Africans today. We had the support of forty-two million South
Africans.*

– François Pienaar, 24 June 1995

For many decades one of the favourite topics on winter evenings in
pubs in South Africa, New Zealand and even Australia, France and
Britain was: who were the real rugby world champions? When the
International Rugby Board eventually instituted a Rugby World Cup
in 1987 to make the answer to this question official, the question
could still not be answered with certainty, because South Africa was
barred from playing on account of its government's apartheid policies.

The first World Cup took place in Australia and New Zealand in
1987. Sixteen national teams took part. The New Zealand All Blacks
took the cup by beating France 29–9 in the final in Auckland. Wales
beat the Australian Wallabies 22–21 in the play-off for the third and
fourth place.

The 1991 World Cup was held in Britain and France, with the final
at Twickenham. The Wallabies beat England 12–6 in the final, and
the All Blacks beat Scotland 13–6 in the third-place play-off.

So these were the teams to beat: Australia, New Zealand, France, England, Scotland and Wales. Further down the line were Ireland, Argentina and Western Samoa, with Canada and Italy still stronger than Romania, Japan, the United States, Tonga, Russia, Zimbabwe, Kenya and the Ivory Coast. But, the only real question, at least in the southern hemisphere, was who was the strongest among Australia, New Zealand and South Africa.

In 1992, in the middle of intense negotiations with the National Party government to establish a democracy in South Africa, the ANC gave their blessing to the lifting of the ban on contact between Springbok rugby and the rest of the world. That same year the International Rugby Board appointed South Africa the host country for the 1995 Rugby World Cup. It was going to be the biggest international event ever hosted by South Africa.

By the time the World Cup took place, the New South Africa would be exactly one year old – the democratic election took place on 27 April 1994. South Africans, and the international community, were slightly nervous: could South Africa organise this huge event successfully? The task rested mainly on the shoulders of Louis Luyt, who declared right from the start: this was going to be the most successful and profitable Rugby World Cup ever. And from the politicians down to the rugby administrators, players and fans there was one shared dream: South Africa and South African rugby should win that cup.

At the time Ian McIntosh was fired as Springbok coach in August 1994, the South African team had started showing early signs of improvement, giving indications that they were adapting to the new international environment. But they certainly did not look like world champions – they had lost to every major rugby-playing nation by then.

Kitch Christie, then coach of a very successful Transvaal team, took over the coaching job. He had the advantage of two home tests against Argentina (which the Boks won easily) and a tour of thirteen matches to Wales, Scotland and Ireland to prepare his squad. The

Springboks won the tests against Scotland and Wales, but lost to an Irish Barbarians team in Dublin. There were also off-the-field incidents. The maverick Springbok wing James Small was involved in a nightclub brawl after the second test against Argentina, and Christie dropped him from the squad touring to Britain.

By early 1995 the new Springbok management team was in place – probably the most dynamic team ever assembled to guide South Africa's national team: Kitch Christie coach, Morné du Plessis manager, François Pienaar captain, and Edward Griffiths CEO of SARFU. Du Plessis had been the Springbok captain between 1975 and 1980, as had his father, Felix, in the 1940s. Already very popular, he was to become one of the most respected figures in South African rugby. For once, Luyt had not surrounded himself with weak yes-men.

Next came the announcement of the twenty-six-man World Cup squad. The biggest shock was the omission of one of the most famous loose forwards in a green and gold jersey in recent times: Tiaan Strauss. He went on to play excellent Super 12 rugby in Australia for five years afterwards and even made the Australian national side. Another somewhat surprising omission was Gary Teichmann, considered one of the best loose forwards in the country. Du Plessis and Griffiths organised a live announcement of the squad on national television – the twenty-six men walked on stage one after the other to stand behind a huge sign which read: One team, one country. The magic was beginning to happen.

The first match of the tournament was on 25 May, at Newlands in Cape Town. It wasn't just a match. It was the champions of the 1991 World Cup, Australia, against the home team, South Africa. Australia hadn't lost a test match in twelve months. But a defeat here could give the Springbok spirit a bad enough knock to cripple their tournament. After a glittering opening ceremony and a rousing welcome for President Nelson Mandela, the Australian captain, Michael Lynagh, kicked off.

The emotions among the spectators – and millions of South Africans watching on television – were see-sawing. At the first scrum, Joost van der Westhuizen was off-side. Lynagh's penalty kick was over. Three minutes later Joel Stransky kicked a penalty goal. Scores level. Then Lynagh's boot again: 6–3. Then André Joubert started an exciting move from deep in Springbok territory. The Boks suddenly looked dangerous when they were running with the ball. Another Stransky penalty: 6–6. And another: 9–6.

But the Springboks couldn't win their own ball in the line-outs. It wasn't looking too good. And then suddenly a skilful Wallaby movement, the ball going from hand to hand. Lynagh went over for a brilliant try, and converted: 9–13. South Africa was getting nervous. Just before half-time, James Small got the ball and ran like the wind. Passed to James Dalton, on to Mark Andrews. The ball emerged from the ruck and quickly went down the backline. Small ran with the ball again, and passed to Pieter Hendriks, who beat the famous David Campese on the outside and scored in the corner. South Africa exploded. It could still happen. Half-time score: 14–13.

Not long into the second half, a perfectly executed pre-planned move sent a storming Stransky over the line with the ball. It was Stransky's day – a try, a conversion, four penalty goals and a drop goal. A late Phil Kearns try did not even matter. Final score: South Africa 27, Australia 18. Wild parties broke out all over South Africa.

A first glimpse of what the World Cup could do for nation building in South Africa at a crucial time in its history came the next day. The black newspaper *Sowetan*, which rarely reported on rugby, ran a banner headline: 'AmaBokoboko!' An editorial in the business newspaper *Business Day* stated: 'The apartheid legacy is still with us. In its player composition and following, rugby is and will for many years be a predominantly white sport. But it is fair to say that it is no longer a specifically Afrikaner nationalist project, and that it is beginning to play a role in forging a new national identity.'

The English journalist, rugby coach and Labour Party politician

Derek Wyatt wrote about his experience of that day: 'Three hours after the event, and still sober, it seemed to me that on this great day for rugby, God had leased himself to the new rainbow nation of South Africa.'

After the first game, the road to the quarter-finals was relatively easy: South Africa 21, Romania 8; South Africa 20, Canada 0. In the quarter-finals South Africa demolished Western Samoa 42–4; France beat Ireland 36–12; England defeated Australia 25–22; and the All Blacks beat Scotland 48–30.

But the semi-final on 17 June against France in Durban was different, dangerously different. Heavy rain delayed the match for an hour. Televisions throughout the world showed women sweeping water off the field with brooms. When the match finally started, the French played their hearts out. They had played in the finals at the 1987 World Cup, but were defeated by England in the quarter-finals in 1991. They desperately wanted to play in the final of 1995, and the Springboks were in their way. Ruben Kruger scored a try in the first half, but the South Africans made many mistakes and French goal-kicker Thierry Lacroix's boot did not.

South Africa was leading 19–15 with only a minute of playing time left when France was awarded a scrum close to the Springboks' goal line. Flyhalf Christophe Deylaud kicked; Abdelatif Benazzi got hold of the ball and brought it down. Time was up. If it was a try, the French would go through to the final and the Springboks' campaign would be over. But referee Derek Bevan decided Benazzi had fallen just short of the line, literally a few inches short, it appeared. In the five-yard scrum that followed, the Springboks won the ball and Stransky kicked into touch. The final whistle blew. South Africa was through to the final of the 1995 World Cup.

The next day the All Blacks overpowered England 45–29. They had scored six tries – four by that awesome phenomenon of the 1995 World Cup, Jonah Lomu. Lomu even had a new Tongan volcanic island named after him by the end of the World Cup. Even before the England match, when the All Blacks trounced Japan 145–17 in an astonishing display, New Zealand became the firm favourites to walk away with the 1995 crown.

So far the World Cup organisation had run like clockwork. The airport facilities at Johannesburg, Durban and Cape Town were taxed to the limit, but there were no serious delays. South African Airways was outperforming itself in ferrying players and spectators from one centre to another. The hotels in the major centres coped well. Apart from the odd power cut, the stadiums in Johannesburg, Pretoria, Port Elizabeth, Cape Town, Stellenbosch, Rustenburg, Durban, East London and Bloemfontein were more than sufficient. The many hundreds of journalists and TV crews from all over the world had mostly favourable things to say about the World Cup management team, especially about media facilities and communication. There were no serious incidents of crime, and visitors were very complimentary about South African hospitality. With only the final left to play, Louis Luyt and his team were exhausted, but happy.

But the last week brought some controversy. The final was to be played at Ellis Park, and the New Zealand team was staying at the Crowne Plaza hotel in Sandton. Sean Fitzpatrick, the All Black captain, writes in his autobiography *Turning Point* that South African hospitality was superb, until the last week. Then, he says, everything changed. 'The first night a car alarm went off all night, every two hours. We asked why it wasn't stopped and the reply was that they were having trouble with the tow-trucks and that moving the car was a security risk because of the fear of bombs. And phone calls were suddenly coming through. People were ringing saying "Fitzpatrick, you are going to lose on Saturday." When you asked how that could suddenly happen, the excuse was, "Sorry, we had a new guy on last night who didn't know the procedure."' The All Black captain was subtly suggesting that there was a campaign to unsettle his team before the final, but he wasn't saying who was responsible.

The New Zealand coach, Laurie Mains, ordered the All Blacks to eat in a separate dining room to get the players out of the glare of the other hotel guests. Rory Steyn, the South African policeman assigned to protect the All Black team and former bodyguard to Nelson Mandela, said this was a mistake. The team normally ate in a cordoned-off part of the main dining room, and he felt that was safer. 'Anyone wanting to poison the team would therefore have had to poison every other guest as well and the hotel was packed to capacity,' he says in his book written with Debora Patta, *One Step Behind Mandela.*

And that is exactly what happened. About thirty-six hours before the final on Saturday more than half of the All Black squad came down with some form of food poisoning.

Steyn says on the Thursday evening before the final, he took some of the players to the movie theatres in Sandton City. By the time the movies were over, most of his charges were vomiting. 'When I got upstairs to the doctor's room it looked like a battle zone; like a scene from a movie – players were lying all over the place and the doctor and physio were walking around injecting them. Now, I was a police officer, I worked with facts. What my eyes told me that night was that the team had deliberately been poisoned.'

The circumstances certainly appeared very suspicious. After talking to all eighteen men affected, it was ascertained that the poisoning definitely happened in the hotel, because they did not have any food or drink from outside the hotel that day. And not a single other hotel guest, who ate from exactly the same kitchen, was affected.

The All Black management did not publicly blame anybody, but the New Zealand media were immediately suspicious, and asked out loud whether this could have been the work of South Africans who wanted their team to have an advantage. Thursday night was the perfect timing for this, some argued, because it meant that the men would have recovered sufficiently to play the final, but it also meant that they would probably be weaker than normal. And it would more than likely have an affect on their mental preparation for the big match, they said.

By late Friday afternoon most of the players were feeling better, apart from Jeff Wilson and Andrew Mehrtens. But several players said they were still feeling shaky by Saturday afternoon. Coach Laurie Mains said afterwards he would go to his grave wondering what would have happened in the final if the players had not been poisoned. Mains employed a private investigator, who apparently found that someone had paid a waitress named Suzie to put something in the All Blacks' drinking water.

The CEO of SARFU, Edward Griffiths, conceded that it was a blow to the team and that key players like Wilson were clearly suffering during the match. But he vehemently rejected any suggestion of mischief on the part of South African rugby: 'To hint that this illness was deliberately caused by South Africans, as some All Black officials did, was the sourest of sour grapes.'

Rory Steyn says: 'To my fellow South Africans I want to say this: stop all those cheap jokes about "Suzie", the "food poisoning" and "whingeing Kiwis". It happened. There is no doubt that the All Blacks were poisoned two days before the final.'

It appears to me extremely unlikely that the poisoning could have been an accident, a simple case of hotel food that went bad. The players did not eat anything that wasn't also available to other hotel guests. The Crowne Plaza Hotel has never had a case of food poisoning before or after this incident. The probability that eighteen New Zealand rugby players ate something that not a single one of the other hundreds of hotel guests ate, and that this should happen just two days before one of the most important international sporting contests in a long time, must be close to zero. It is also quite likely that the poisoning episode had some influence on the World Cup final two days later, although we will never know if it was a strong enough influence to have resulted in a different final score. My very strong suspicion is that someone indeed tampered with the All

Blacks' food or drink in order to weaken them before the big match and give South Africa an advantage. But we will probably never know whether the initiative for this unsporting and potentially dangerous act came from official rugby circles, from someone in the betting fraternity or even perhaps from an ordinary South African with a misguided sense of patriotism.

In contrast, things were really going well in the South African camp. On the day the All Blacks were poisoned, the Springboks held a huge international press conference, and they were joined by three national heroes from other sporting disciplines: world number two golfer Ernie Els, soccer star Marks Maponyane and popular cricketer Fanie de Villiers. The Springboks were always conscious that, for the first time in South Africa's history, the entire nation was fully and emotionally behind them. During their last training session, President Nelson Mandela personally phoned Pienaar on his cellphone to wish them luck.

The Springboks watched the video of the brilliant All Black performance against England in the semi-final over and over, especially the awesome performance of Jonah Lomu the Unstoppable. He was 6 foot 4 inches, but could cover the 100 metres in 10,8 seconds. The *Sydney Morning Herald* called him a rhino in ballet shoes. Was he going to be the Springboks' undoing? His opposite number on wing was a whole head shorter than him. But then, James Small probably had the biggest heart of all the players in the World Cup. He was one of the most passionate and determined players ever to wear the green and gold. The plan devised to tame the rhino was that Small would always stay on Lomu's outside, forcing him inside where the cover defence could help bring him down.

Pienaar wanted his men to be, in his words, 'the epitome of controlled aggression' on the field – to needle the All Blacks by shoving them, pushing them or holding them down, but never to be caught, and never to retaliate when the All Blacks lost their tempers. This was the tactic Sean Fitzpatrick had been using with his men for years.

Just before lunch on the day of the match, the Springboks got a taste of what that day was going to mean to South Africa. They went for a slow jog from their Sandton hotel, and the traffic stopped. Children and newspaper vendors of all races started running with them. Cars hooted. People cheered. Back in the team room, Du Plessis, Christie and Pienaar addressed the players. Pienaar said he had no doubt whatsoever that if the Boks 'played the game of their lives', they would win the World Cup. On the bus on the way to Ellis Park, Pienaar played a Roger Whittaker song over the public address system: 'No, I don't believe in "if" any more. "If" is for children. "If" is an illusion.'

In the changing room at the stadium, the players were stunned to see a tall black man walk in wearing a number six Springbok jersey: President Nelson Mandela. Pienaar's number was six. Mandela shook every player's hand and left.

This was not the only surprise. As part of the closing ceremony, a South African Airways Boeing 747 passenger jet flew extremely low over the stadium, with 'Good Luck Bokke' written on the undercarriage. It was a breathtaking moment. Ladysmith Black Mambazo sang the anthem stirringly, and the crowd exploded when Mandela appeared on the field with his number six jersey to greet the two teams. The All Blacks performed the *haka* with extra aggression. The 60 000-odd spectators sang *Shozaloza* with the help of radio DJ Dan Moyane. And then all that remained was to play a game of rugby.

The New Zealanders dominated the first few minutes, but the Springboks quickly recovered. About fifteen minutes into the first half, Lomu got the ball and ran down the field. He broke through two tackles, but Joost van der Westhuizen went in low and brought him down. Andrew Mehrtens kicked two penalties, Joel Stransky one. Then Mark Andrews broke away, passed to Joost, Joost offloaded to Ruben Kruger, who powered over the line. But referee Ed Morrison ruled that it wasn't a try. All the Springbok players near the ball afterwards swore high and low that Morrison had made a mistake. But the Springboks fought on. Stransky kicked another penalty and shortly afterwards succeeded with a drop goal. Half-time score: South Africa 9, New Zealand 6.

Early in the second half, Lomu got the ball at speed and ran around fullback André Joubert with the tryline in front of him. But across raced one of the most fearless of rugby players, Japie Mulder, and brought Lomu down with an absolutely beautiful tackle, probably the tackle that saved the game.

At full time, the scores were level at 9–9. Early in extra time, Mehrtens kicked a long penalty: score 9–12. Suddenly Chester Williams started running with the ball, passed to Joost van der Westhuizen, on to Joel Stransky. Stransky had nobody in front of him. He was going to score. But Morrison blew his whistle, to the utter chagrin of millions of South Africans. It was a forward pass, he said. This remained a debate for weeks and months afterwards: was the pass to Stransky really forward? At least the Springboks got a penalty shortly afterwards, and Stransky's kick was true. Second half of extra time, and the score was level at 12-all.

With just a few minutes left, the Springboks were awarded a scrum in the middle of the field. Stransky told Joost van der Westhuizen he wanted the ball fast and long and straight. He got it, and kicked a drop goal high between the posts – the most famous drop goal in South African rugby history. Seven minutes later the final whistle blew. The Springboks had won 15–12. They were the world champions. Sixty thousand spectators and many millions of South African television viewers went ballistic.

On the way to the podium, SABC television reporter David van der Sandt cornered Pienaar for a live interview. 'François, fantastic support from sixty-three thousand South Africans today ...' Pienaar's reply became famous: 'David, we did not have the support of sixty-three thousand South Africans today. We had the support of forty-two million South Africans.'

On the podium Nelson Mandela, wearing his green and gold number six jersey and a Springbok cap, handed Pienaar the Webb Ellis trophy, and the two created one the most magic moments in South Africa's history.

At the press conference after the match Pienaar said: 'Seeing Nelson Mandela wearing my shirt was the biggest thrill of my life. He came into the dressing room before the match and thanked us for what we had done for South Africa. We returned the compliment. I am the happiest man in the world.'

During all the excitement that day, Louis Luyt had to be content with standing in the background. Next to Mandela, next to Pienaar. Never the centre of attraction, yet this was his World Cup.

His chance came at the official Rugby World Cup 1995 dinner at Gallagher Estate in Midrand. As the president of the hosting rugby union, it was his privilege to make a speech. Traditionally, this is a time for graciousness and great sportsmanship – a time to thank and compliment each other and generally have a good time, because it is the only occasion where the players, coaches and administrators of the world's top rugby nations get together every four years.

This is what Luyt said: 'Ladies and gentlemen, of course for us South Africans this is a great day. This is what we have been waiting for for so many years. We boasted in '87 that the real World Cup was not won by New Zealand because we were not there. Then in '91 we boasted again. We were not there. Then, in 1995, we proved that if we had been there, we would have won.'

Luyt called his son-in-law, Rian Oberholzer, to the podium. 'I want to say one thing. So much has been said about the Rugby World Cup. If one man made this all possible, one man who worked round the clock, one who did everything for South Africa, it was Rian Oberholzer.

'I heard that my coach, Kitch Christie, today told his players he was not available henceforth. I want to tell you, you haven't spoken to me yet, pal. You will be available. So will you, Morné du Plessis. We build the perfect team around a perfect manager. The manager, Morné, the coach, Kitch, and the team …

'I thank you for your support and I thank you for coming here. I thank you for supporting this country. We went through very tremendous periods, tumultuous periods. There was a time when the Rugby World Cup could have been removed from South Africa. We fought for it, we kept it here, and we showed the world that we can host it, and host it in a way that will be very difficult, may I say to Wales, to emulate.'

The English team stood up and openly demonstrated their contempt for Luyt. Some of the All Blacks heckled loudly.

Luyt blundered on and gave a gold watch to referee Derek Bevan, instead of to Ed Morrison, who had handled the final. (Bevan was so embarrassed, he later auctioned the watch.) Luyt did not say a word about Morrison or the linesmen at the final. A group of World Cup referees sitting together at a table were visibly outraged by this weird behaviour.

It was deeply embarrassing to the South African players and officials. Pienaar said afterwards he was 'ashamed to see Springbok players feeling uncomfortable when they should have been enjoying the proudest evening of their career'. The English journalist and writer Derek Wyatt called it 'incredible, and in absurdly bad taste'. Luyt was like a cross between Marlon Brando's Godfather and Robert Maxwell, he said. 'The evening had been sullied; there was a nasty smell and for once it wasn't the Old Farts. Was this modern rugby?' The Irish representative on the International Rugby Board, Tom Kiernan, and All Black Mike Brewer apparently went up to Luyt and gave him a piece of their mind. All Black manager Colin Meads described Luyt's speech as a 'disgrace' and said it was an embarrassment for all the countries that had taken part in the previous World Cup tournaments.

Popular journalist and radio talk show host Jon Qwelane wrote in the *Saturday Star* of 1 July 1995: 'If anyone is still wondering why millions of blacks turned their backs against the game of rugby in the past they need only look at Louis Luyt's arrogant, piggish and utterly distasteful behaviour after the cup final … Luyt's behaviour at the post-match dinner explained most eloquently his spectacular rise to the top of the manure heap. He and his kind – there are hundreds of thousands of them, if not a couple of million – have never known or heard of humility and magnanimity. If that surprises you, believe me, in the ghettoes we know such behaviour to be the badge of honour of many whites. Luyt, as SARFU boss, and therefore the local rugby's chief ambassador, has sent out signals that the changes in the sport may very well be superficial. The apple may be tantalising in its outward appearance, but it is still rotten at the core.'

Even South Africa's Parliament criticised Luyt, albeit in a round-about way. The ruling ANC's chief whip, former rugby player Arnold Stofile, formulated a motion which was proposed in the House by a former athletics administrator and now ANC MP, Jannie Momberg. It read: 'The House

- Congratulates the national rugby team on winning the 1995 World Cup and expresses its appreciation towards the New Zealand team for its part in making Saturday, June 24 1995, a memorable occasion;
- Acknowledges the fact that New Zealand in 1987 and Australia in 1991 were worthy champions; and
- Confidently expresses the hope that South Africa will retain the World Cup in 1999.'

The CEO of SARFU at the time, Edward Griffiths, wrote later: 'The SARFU president left the podium to a silence punctuated by humiliating jeers. It was a desperately sad moment for a man who had worked tirelessly and effectively to organise the tournament, but it was a moment which he had brought entirely upon himself.'

7

'MONEY BRINGS EVIL'

The old administrators had played the card of 'loyalty' and
'pride in the jersey' to a point where they were no longer worth
anything. How could anyone be loyal to people who so callous-
ly exploited our position of weakness?

— Gary Teichmann, 2000

The 1995 Rugby World Cup did a lot more than put South Africa
firmly back on the world rugby map. It signalled the arrival of
professionalism in Rugby Union, exactly one hundred years after
the formation of Rugby League, as the professional rugby code – a
different game with different rules – is known. Professionalism in
Rugby Union had been inevitably growing for several years, but
was staunchly opposed by the International Rugby Board until after
the 1995 World Cup.

The decision to go professional changed the face of rugby fundamentally. And Louis Luyt was right in the middle of this revolution.
Of all the top rugby administrators in the world, he was the one best
qualified to lead rugby into the new era.

Luyt actually pre-empted the money revolution. He had been buying and paying players for a decade before it became legal. In the

early days it had to be done carefully: players would be attracted to a club or a union with a job offer or a business opportunity; players had to be remunerated by way of trust funds, free accommodation and sponsored cars. By the late 1980s players were paid large amounts of cash under the table to move to another club or union, and players in the bigger unions started getting match fees 'to compensate them for time away from work'. And, of course, some players became quite rich out of sponsorships. Luyt was bolder than most rugby administrators, and got the respect of players and many other administrators for his honesty.

Not only South African rugby players benefited. Luyt had also had a strong hand in the rebel New Zealand Cavaliers tour in 1986 and the South Pacific Barbarians tour in 1987. These players defied their own unions and the international sporting ban on South Africa, and they certainly did not do it for the love of the game or because they approved of apartheid. They were paid large amounts of money, although nobody could ever prove who paid them or exactly how much they were paid.

Money rugby started in 1895 in Britain. This was before the days of a five-day working week, and players in the rugby-crazy districts of Lancashire and Yorkshire could not afford to play rugby matches instead of doing a Saturday work shift. The Rugby Football Union put their demands for compensation to a vote, and decided to keep the strict amateur code. So some of the clubs formed Rugby League, paid players salaries and match fees, and changed the rules to make it more of a spectator sport.

Rugby League never took off in South Africa. But it did attract some very good players: in the 1920s two Springboks, Attie van Heerden and Tank van Rooyen, played for the League club Wigan in England. In the 1950s one of the most famous Springboks ever, Tom van Vollenhoven, as well as Springboks Wilf Rosenberg, Colin Greenwood and Alan Skene, switched codes to League. In 1962 League clubs such as Johannesburg Celtic were formed, but they never got off the ground. A South African League team travelled to Australia that year, but the team was completely out of its depth. In the early years, playing for League automatically meant a complete ban – and ostracisation – from all other rugby in South Africa. This was softened in the 1980s. When Springbok greats Rob Louw and Ray Mordt came back after a stint playing League rugby, they were eventually allowed back in the South African rugby fold – Mordt later coached Transvaal.

The man who did more than most to keep the amateur ethos intact was Danie Craven. He fought money in rugby tooth and nail almost until the day he died, although he did turn a blind eye when the rebel tour players were paid. He once told a journalist interviewing him that League players were 'like prostitutes. What they used to do for fun they now do for money.' In several interviews over a few years Craven said when asked about professional rugby: 'Over my dead body.' And so it was.

But not even a respected traditionalist like Craven could stem the tide of commercialism in South African rugby. As Luyt had demonstrated with Transvaal since 1984, there was big money in rugby. Television stations made lots of money out of broadcasting the popular sport; rugby unions became rich from sponsorships, advertising at stadiums, and gate money. At the heart of all of this were the players, but they were not allowed to get paid. Top players were highly marketable national heroes, but they had to decline a share in the money they generated. Top golfers, boxers, tennis players and even athletes were getting rich out of their sport, but not rugby players. More importantly, the demands of the new game were such that it was almost impossible for top players to hold down a proper job – playing rugby had been a full-time occupation long before the 1995 change of heart. Another factor was the institution of the Rugby World Cup in 1987. These were expensive tournaments, and huge sponsorships and television rights were essential to make it pay for itself.

In 1995, two very rich Australians, Rupert Murdoch and Kerry Packer, competed to dominate international rugby and commercialise it completely.

Packer employed a former member of the Australian Rugby Union and representative on the International Rugby Board, Ross Turnbull, to put his plan together. His man in South Africa was the young business genius and former Transvaal coach Harry Viljoen, who was to become the Springbok coach in 2000. The plan was for a completely new professional rugby championship outside the existing rugby structures. All major international teams had to be signed up, and rugby would be popularised in countries where it was lesser known, such as the United States, Canada, Japan, even Brazil. Packer wanted to make rugby a truly global sport, and make his millions off television rights. He called his project The World Rugby Championship (TWRC).

Three weeks before the 1995 Rugby World Cup final, Springbok captain François Pienaar was approached by his Transvaal teammate, Ian MacDonald, with an 'exciting but secret' idea. Pienaar was taken to Viljoen's mansion in Sandton where the Packer plan was explained to him. Viljoen asked Pienaar to sign up the entire Springbok World Cup squad for the Packer plan. He explained that there would be fewer matches played, but of much higher quality. For the purposes of remuneration, players would be divided into three categories. Top South African players would get salaries of between R500 000 and R1 million per year.

Pienaar was over the moon. Officially, the Springbok players were earning 'salaries' of about R70 000 per year at that stage. Pienaar had long been outspoken in favour of professionalism in rugby. A year earlier, in June 1994, he sent shockwaves through international rugby when he became the first top player to call himself a 'professional rugby player' in an interview with New Zealand television. 'We are professionals who play an amateur sport. I hope rugby will become a proper professional sport after the World Cup.' Pienaar promised Viljoen he would try to recruit the Springbok squad, but said he could do it only after the World Cup final.

A week later, Pienaar had a meeting with Turnbull himself in a Sandton hotel and gave a full commitment to the Packer plans. The Springbok captain secured an agreement that if the Packer project became a reality, he would receive an additional amount of US$300 000 for acting as the agent who signed up the Springboks. Especially in South African terms, that was a lot of money for a rugby player.

But, behind the scenes, Louis Luyt was making a different deal. On 23 June, the day before the Saturday World Cup final, SARFU CEO Edward Griffiths called an urgent press conference. When the journalists saw Luyt flanked by Leo Williams, the president of the Australian Rugby Union, Richard Guy, chairman of the New Zealand Rugby Union, and David Moffat of the New South Wales Rugby Football Union, they knew something big was up.

Moffat informed the conference that a new working body representing the rugby unions of South Africa, New Zealand and Australia had been formed and that he was going to act as its chief executive. This umbrella body was called SANZAR.

Next up was Luyt, chairman of SANZAR, who revealed that SANZAR had sold all their television rights for ten years to the News Corporation, the media company owned by tycoon Rupert Murdoch. Murdoch had earlier in 1994 announced plans for a Rugby Super League, not very different from Packer's new plans. SANZAR had talked him out of it, and instead offered to jack up their own rugby plans and sell the News Corporation their combined television rights. The amount agreed upon was staggering: US$550 million. Whether it was going to be the Packer show or the Murdoch show, clearly big money had arrived on the rugby scene. Nobody was going to stop it.

Murdoch's problems were bigger than Packer's. His $550 million deal with SANZAR would be absolutely worthless if most of the world's top rugby players had signed up with Packer. In fact, if

Packer's plans came off, SANZAR would be an empty shell, representing only those players not deemed good enough to be signed on by Packer. This was not going to be rugby exciting enough to broadcast globally. Murdoch, Luyt and his Australian and New Zealand counterparts were not going to accept this lying down.

Viljoen and Pienaar thought the Packer plans were a complete secret. But in the cut-throat world of big money, secrets don't last long. Edward Griffiths addressed the Springbok squad at the first team meeting after the final. He said the SANZAR deal with Murdoch's News Corporation would mean huge increases in players' salaries. And then he warned the players to wait for SARFU's official offer before they signed any contracts with an 'unofficial rugby circus'. Obviously, Luyt and his men knew about the Packer project and the offer made to Pienaar.

But the rest of the players had no idea what Griffiths was referring to. Pienaar hastily asked Griffiths and other non-players to leave the room so he could have a word with them. He then simply told them that there was a proposal outside SARFU that was so attractive they would be foolish not to consider it first. Pienaar promised to fully explain the proposal to the team before the end of the week.

The Springbok team were invited by the Sun International group and SARFU to spend the first weekend after the World Cup final at the Palace Hotel at the Lost City in Sun City. This was Pienaar's opportunity to sell Packer's TWRC plans to them. Harry Viljoen had earlier divided the World Cup squad into three categories – clearly some were worth more commercially than others – and Pienaar called these groups for talks in his hotel room one after the other.

Here, Pienaar explained the Packer project to the players and gave them an idea of how much money they could earn if it came off. The players were overwhelmed by the figures: it meant they would become millionaires within a short time. Pienaar's deal was that if they signed the contracts, he would lock them up in a safe and not disclose or give them to anyone until the whole team had

Rugby was young Louis' passport to acceptance by the *volk*

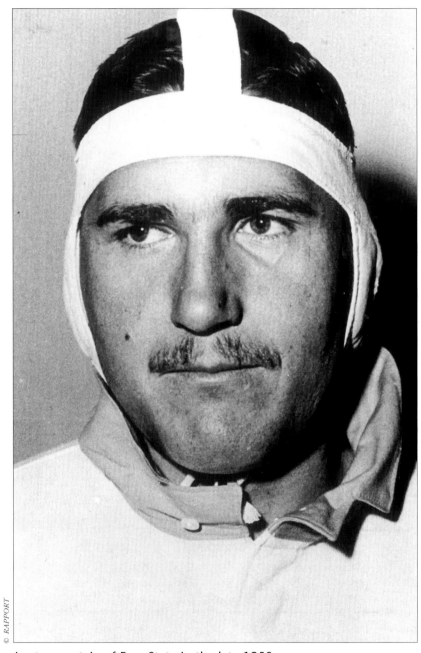

Luyt as captain of Free State in the late 1950s

Triomf Fertiliser – the business that made Luyt rich

Luyt receiving the Marketing Man of the Year Award in 1972. Behind him are Anton Rupert (far right) and Albert Wessels (right), the two top Afrikaner industrialists of the time

Luyt Lager. 'This is a good product,' Luyt said. 'It's got my name on it'

After becoming a millionaire by the age of thirty, Luyt bought himself an executive jet

Luyt at his Saxonwold mansion, Solitaire

King Louis

Luyt surveying his domain: Ellis Park

'One of the boys': Luyt at his home with Springbok rugby players (from left to right) Joost van der Westhuizen, James Dalton, Japie Mulder, Ruben Kruger and Chris Roussouw in 1995

Luyt shares a humorous moment with Springbok Kobus Wiese

Organising the World Cup: Luyt with his son-in-law Rian Oberholzer
(left) and Natal scrumhalf Craig Jameson

At the World Cup: Luyt is flanked by Sports Minister Steve Tshwete and President Nelson Mandela

Luyt looks on as Mandela shakes hands with victorious Springbok lock Mark Andrews

Nelson Mandela congratulates Springbok captain François Pienaar

Celebrating victory with the World Cup

The high point of his life: Luyt holding the Webb Ellis trophy

SARFU CEO Edward Griffiths and Luyt in 1995

Luyt and Mluleki George discussing the future of the Springbok emblem in 1996

Luyt campaigning in Alexandra: 'I have been here before, but many years ago when I sold beer illegally to shebeens'

A defaced Federal Alliance poster

Luyt is questioned by journalists in the week that he was finally ousted from SARFU in May 1998

Luyt at the Constitutional Court hearing in 1999

'No man is my master. I do not bend my knee for anybody other than my God'

weighed up all options and decided to go the TWRC way. He said that any player could pull out at any point and ask for his signed contract to be destroyed.

All of the players signed on the spot, although Chester Williams asked Pienaar a few days later to destroy his contract. Griffiths had a meeting with some of the senior players later that evening at the Palace Hotel and asked Pienaar directly whether they were considering options other than the SARFU proposals. Pienaar had to lie, because Ross Turnbull was in the process of signing up all the test players in Britain, Australia and New Zealand, and if news got to Luyt at this stage, it could jeopardise these efforts. Turnbull also started contracting senior provincial players in South Africa and the other countries.

Two weeks after the World Cup, the whole Natal team signed the Packer contracts, and other provinces followed. The Natal (later Springbok) captain, Gary Teichmann, says in his autobiography, *For the Record*, written with Edward Griffiths: 'Relations between administrators and players deteriorated to a point where the overwhelming majority of players would have no problem in deserting the official structure to join a rebel organisation that paid well. The old administrators had played the card of "loyalty" and "pride in the jersey" to a point where they were no longer worth anything. How could anyone be loyal to people who so callously exploited our position of weakness?'

According to Pienaar's version of events, some of the senior Transvaal players had an argument with the players' representative on the union committee, Uli Schmidt, the day after the Lost City weekend. Schmidt was conveying a message from Luyt that he was not prepared to concede to the demands they had made before the World Cup about retainers and match fees. The next day Luyt fired four of the players who voiced their opinions to Schmidt: Hennie le Roux and Johan Roux, who were ordered to hand back their sponsored cars immediately, and Charles Rossouw and Rudolf Straueli.

That afternoon the Transvaal players met at Pienaar's house, where it was decided he should approach Luyt. He saw Luyt the same afternoon, and arranged for a meeting the next morning at Ellis Park. At that meeting, says Pienaar, Luyt adopted 'a hostile and aggressive approach', and there was no progress. A team of second-choice players was selected to play for Transvaal against Eastern Province that weekend.

The Transvaal players read out a statement at a press conference, but refused to answer questions. According to Pienaar, they were 'so scared of saying something Luyt would be able to use against us, perhaps even in court. We should have answered questions, but we were generally terrified of the union president.' Eventually they proposed a compromise on their original proposals, which Luyt accepted after he forced the players to apologise to him in public. The morale in the Transvaal camp had plummeted from what Pienaar described in 1994 as 'extremely happy' to what he called, barely a year later, an atmosphere of 'bad feeling, mistrust, harassment and plain hostility'.

But this altercation between Luyt and his Transvaal team was a mere sideshow. The big question was still whether the world's best players would go with Packer's TWRC plan, or with their unions and therefore follow the Murdoch route. The head of News Corporation, Sam Chisholm, secretly made contact with Pienaar and asked him if the Springboks would be interested in an offer from News Corporation similar to the Packer proposal. Pienaar replied in the affirmative. Packer's son, Jamie, flew to South Africa to ask Pienaar to hand over the twenty-eight signed Springbok contracts, but Pienaar claims he told him this would have to be a decision made by the whole Springbok team. Packer clearly knew that Murdoch was going to make an equally attractive offer to the top players, and brought the message that they would pay the players 20 per cent more than any offer made.

Pienaar says in his autobiography, *Rainbow Warrior*, that he was favouring the Packer alternative. 'In my view, the players' choice was not between playing for South Africa and playing for Packer; it was between playing for Luyt or for Packer.' He says of Luyt during this time: 'His behaviour had been characteristically erratic: one moment, he was swiping at me, the next moment he was greeting me in the warmest possible terms ...'

Towards the end of July, Luyt had urgent talks with News Corporation on behalf of SANZAR. It was agreed that decisive action was needed to demolish Kerry Packer's TWRC plans, and that Luyt should do whatever it took to sign up the Springbok squad. Once they were on board, the Australian, English and New Zealand teams would follow.

On 30 July, Luyt invited a number of senior Springboks for brunch at his Saxonwold home. He walked up to Pienaar and declared: 'I will match Packer.' At a meeting at a Midrand hotel, the Springbok squad overwhelmingly voted for the SARFU option, mainly because their lives would not change at all: they would still be playing for their existing provincial unions and the Springboks.

Luyt's words 'I'll match Packer' were applied literally: the TWRC contracts, with a few minor changes, became the SARFU contracts. The players were impatient to sign. For most of them it meant a ten-fold increase in their income from rugby. As Griffiths remarked: 'If the 1995 Springboks had won the World Cup by a narrow margin, it would be accurate to suggest they romped to victory in the transition to professionalism.'

Luyt did exact some revenge, however. He changed the contracts to stipulate that the players would be paid in South African rands rather than American dollars. He knew the rand was inevitably going to weaken against the dollar – at the very least he was certain the rand wasn't going to get stronger. The players' contracts stipulated an exchange rate of R3,62 to a dollar. When the three-year contracts ended in 1998, a dollar cost R5,40. But SARFU was getting paid in US currency by News Corporation, which meant that for every R5,40 they received for the players, SARFU only had to pay out R3,62. The players were so eager to sign, they accepted Luyt's amendment almost without question. It saved SARFU millions – more than a third of the total cost.

After they had voted for the SARFU contract, the players were ushered into a room where Luyt's daughter Corlia, an attorney and the wife of senior SARFU official Rian Oberholzer, had them fill in their SARFU contracts and sign them. Luyt later taunted them, saying they had 'signed their lives away' to SARFU, and he certainly made them feel as if this was what they had done in the months ahead.

Some months later the newspaper *Beeld* reported that it had seen some of the SARFU contracts, and that senior players like Pienaar, Joost van der Westhuizen, Ruben Kruger, Joel Stransky and James Small would each earn at least R2,5 million during the contracted three years. Add to that their income from sponsorships, public speaking and advertising, and the total earnings of someone like Pienaar and a few others well exceeded R1 million per year.

Few, if any, of the Springbok players knew that Pienaar then pressured Luyt for the commission he was promised by Packer. He reminded Luyt that he undertook to 'match Packer', and that Packer had promised him US$300 000. Some months later Luyt sent Pienaar a Transvaal Rugby Union cheque of R1 million. After golfer Ernie Els and soccer player Lucas Radebe, Pienaar became the wealthiest sports personality in South Africa.

One of the wealthiest, perhaps, but not the most popular – not with Luyt, and not with the provincial rugby players. The senior players who had not been part of the World Cup squad felt betrayed by Pienaar and his teammates for killing off Packer's TWRC initiative. The TWRC proposal would have meant that they could get decent money for the first time – for instance, Gary Teichmann, captain of Natal, would have received in the region of R400 000 instead of R140 000 per year.

With the Packer deal dead, the provincial players had no bargaining power. The relationship between provincial players and members of the Springbok squad became very unpleasant, the players calling members of the World Cup squad 'selfish' and 'sell-outs', sometimes even to their faces. When SARFU eventually did pass on some of the News Corporation millions to provincial players, they only got one-year contracts to the Springboks' three years, and only a fraction of the money.

No one summed up the course of events better than Pienaar himself. In 1999 he said: 'Money brings evil. Money would bring greed, money would bring temptation, money would bring jealousy.'

South African rugby went through deeply unhappy times in the second half of 1995 and 1996, all because of money: who got how much money and who didn't. Luyt felt humiliated by Pienaar and his squad, and did everything to make their lives miserable. Nobody outmaneouvres Louis Luyt in business dealings, certainly not a mere rugby player. Kitch Christie's explanation was that every time Luyt had to sign a cheque for one of the Springboks, 'he saw Francois Pienaar's face on it'.

Pienaar later told the story of 'the man who used to call me "my son" in happier moments' standing next to him when the Transvaal team photograph was taken at the end of 1995 and saying: 'There is a thin line between love and hate, and I hate you.'

Relationships became so unbearable that Springbok manager Morné du Plessis organised a meeting between Luyt and a number of World Cup Springboks. He took Gary Teichmann along to speak for those players without three-year contracts. Teichmann remembers: 'I was taken aback when Luyt began the meeting by speaking aggressively and without pause for five minutes. The idea did strike me that, even if the World Cup Players were raking in millions, they were earning their money – working for an employer as hard as this.' When Luyt noticed Teichmann in the meeting, he shouted at him to get out of the room. Teichmann waited in the car park, and was later called in by Luyt to negotiate on behalf of players without contracts. According to Teichmann, Luyt said: 'We will offer the players without contracts a match fee of R30 000 per match. That is our final offer. You can take it or leave it. If you don't want it, let us know and we will find some other players.' Teichmann accepted the offer.

Strangely, the quality of rugby played by the Springbok squad did not seem to suffer during this early period of bad blood. During the first week of September 1995, the Boks beat Wales 40–11 in a one-off test at Ellis Park. Then came a short tour to Italy, where they beat the Italian national team 40–1. But the real test of strength came with a match against England, a team that had scored four tries against the All Blacks in the World Cup semi-finals. The Springboks played magnificently against an inspired England team, beating them 24–14. Their 1995 record was perfect: ten tests played, ten tests won. In 1996 they beat Tonga, pushing their record to eleven victories in a row.

In the midst of all the drama and back-stabbing, one man tried desperately to keep South African rugby on track and build on the glory of the World Cup victory: SARFU CEO Edward Griffiths. At a press conference immediately after the World Cup, he had outlined SARFU's challenge in the months and years ahead: 'It has given us the chance to become a truly national sport. The World Cup has aroused in the minds of millions of black South Africans a spark of interest in a game from which they have historically been excluded. It is now our challenge to fan that precious spark and set the game ablaze across the country.'

But this vision was clearly not shared by Luyt, other members of SARFU or the leadership of the provincial unions. Griffiths says Luyt's commitment to that mission was 'minimal' and that Luyt and the SARFU men around him, his son Louis junior and his son-in-law Rian Oberholzer, 'wallowed in their own sense of importance at the powerbase of South African rugby, but the concept of a national game seemed to draw a blank in their minds.'

Griffiths clashed with Luyt junior and Oberholzer on more than one occasion. Once, as he and Luyt senior were about to walk into an executive meeting, he asked Luyt to tell his son to stop behaving as if he was the one who took the decisions in SARFU. According to Griffiths, Luyt said: 'You're too sensitive. Louis doesn't want your job and neither does Rian.' Griffiths responded: 'That's lucky, because neither of them could do it in the first place.' Luyt: 'Yes, they could.' Griffiths: 'No, they couldn't. They don't know how to handle the players. They have no idea about the media and I don't think they have ever been to a township in their lives.' Luyt then stormed off. Really mature dialogue at the powerhouse of South African rugby.

On 12 February 1996 Griffiths received a six-line fax message from Luyt. It simply said he had been dismissed with immediate effect. He gave no reasons for this drastic step, and refused to take telephone calls from Griffiths for days. Griffiths asked to state his case before the executive committee of SARFU, but Luyt refused. Much later, says Griffiths, Luyt gave him the real reason: 'You have become too important for the position.'

Sports Minister Steve Tshwete lashed out at Luyt. 'For the umpteenth time, Dr Luyt has been given permission by his colleagues in the national executive committee to transmit a strong message to the country and the world that South African rugby remains trapped in the twilight of the autocratic, undemocratic and unaccountable past,' he said on 23 February at a sports awards dinner at the University of Fort Hare. He called Griffiths 'a young man who had worked hard to clean rugby of that repugnant past'.

The *Cape Times* asked in an editorial on 16 February: 'How much longer is rugby going to allow autocratic SARFU president Louis Luyt to dump the game back into the dark ages?' Dan Retief wrote in the *Sunday Times*: 'The resurrection of rugby's image as the preserve of the White Right is one of the consequences of Louis Luyt's dictatorial dismissal of Edward Griffiths.' He added: 'Mr Luyt's intractable style could influence those who remain unconvinced that rugby is ready to be a part of the new South Africa – who mistrust the euphoria which pulsed through the World Cup victory. It is precisely this constituency who have been most outraged at the treatment meted out to Mr Griffiths. Although Mr Luyt's latest act has sent shock waves through the rugby world it should not have come as a surprise; for the simple reason that behaving impulsively is so completely in character.'

Rian Oberholzer was appointed CEO of SARFU in Griffiths's place. The first member of the Dream Team – the World Cup management team of Griffiths, Kitch Christie, Morné du Plessis and François Pienaar – was gone. The others were soon to follow.

A week after Griffiths was fired, rugby writer Rodney Hartman wrote in the *Sunday Argus* that highly placed sources had told him that Luyt had approached the Department of Home Affairs with a view to having Griffiths deported back to Britain and so prevent him from fighting his dismissal in court. Luyt denied this and sued Argus Newspapers Ltd for R50 000 for defamation, but the matter was settled out of court.

A few months later Luyt mentioned a whole list of grievances against Griffiths in an interview with a sports magazine. He said Griffiths had clashed with Morné du Plessis during the World Cup, and had had altercations with Frikkie Erasmus – Chester Williams's lawyer – because Williams did not want to sign the SARFU contract. Luyt said Griffiths had threatened to go to the press with the story that Williams did not want to assist rugby development in black areas.

Luyt alleged that Griffiths had made decisions without consulting the SARFU executive. He made commitments to build a R5 million stadium in a black area in Gauteng and R9 million in an Eastern Cape township when SARFU did not have the funds, Luyt said. Griffiths's introduction of race quotas at schools rugby had embarrassed SARFU and 'took sponsors by surprise'.

Griffiths described Luyt's allegations as a 'collection of half truths, some of which are defamatory'. He said: 'If these were the reasons for my dismissal, I would have thought any reasonable person would have put them to me at the time of my dismissal so that I could have an opportunity to answer them.'

Two months after Griffiths was fired, coach Kitch Christie stepped down. He was battling a serious blood disorder, but this was nothing new: he had been doing so for years. He later wrote: 'I can't honestly say I resigned of my own free will. I was under the direct impression that Louis Luyt was in a hurry to appoint André Markgraaff as the Springbok coach.' The second member of the World Cup Dream Team was gone. Luyt immediately appointed Markgraaff as Springbok coach.

Markgraaff's claim to fame was that he had coached a small union, Griquas, and achieved quite a lot of success – partly by buying promising Free State players. But many players and journalists felt that he did not have the experience and credentials to coach the national side. His appointment may have had another explanation behind it: Markgraaff had been the staunchest Luyt supporter among all union chairmen for years. Players and journalists talked about a 'strategic alliance' between him and Luyt going back to 1994. According to this theory, which many believed to be fact, Luyt gave Markgraaff a lot of money to build up Griquas. The deal was that Markgraaff had to mobilise the support of all the smaller unions so that they would vote for Luyt when he stood for president of SARFU. At least that part was true: Markgraaff's lobbying did secure Luyt's unopposed nomination in 1994. The reciprocal part of the deal, so the theory went, was that Markgraaff would one day get the job of Springbok coach if Luyt was elected. So it was pay-back time.

Markgraaff was brimming with confidence, telling rugby journalists that his team was going to play rugby 'the world had never seen'. He was so confident that he ignored the Springboks' winning style of play and brought in new strategies. The first time his new style could be tested was at a Tri-Nations match against Australia. The Springboks appeared listless, ill-disciplined and without clear direction, and lost 21–16. A winning streak of eleven test matches had come to an end.

Building up to the Tri-Nations test against the All Blacks, the morale among the team was very low. But they knew the New Zealanders had been telling the world that they should have won the World Cup the previous year and that they were fired up for the battle. The Springboks played for their honour, and played their hearts out. But the team wasn't clicking as well as before, and with the help of some terrible refereeing decisions lost 15–11. Some of the senior players, led by Pienaar, were close to revolting against the new coach. Pienaar had several heated arguments with Markgraaff, at least two in the presence of other Springboks. This was unheard of.

The Springboks won the second match against Australia 25–19 with an improved performance. This was July 1996, just a year after the World Cup final with its extraordinary patriotic atmosphere, but the Free State stadium was full of the orange, white and blue flags of apartheid South Africa. Team manager Morné du Plessis issued a statement after the match expressing the national side's disappointment at this reactionary demonstration. The Springboks did not want support from people waving the old flag, he said.

Gary Teichmann called Du Plessis' response 'a perfectly reasonable statement, distancing us from all symbols that were widely interpreted as support for apartheid'. But Luyt and SARFU did not like it. They issued a statement coming close to all-out repudiation of the Springbok manager, saying he had made the statement in his personal capacity.

SARFU had sold out their own manager, and now the question was what the team was going to say. François Pienaar was their captain and spokesman. He was a personal friend of Nelson Mandela's – Mandela had attended his wedding not long before this incident.

He was widely seen as the transforming face of rugby. He also knew exactly what someone waving the old flag was trying to say. But Pienaar sided with SARFU and, in a devastating blow to the belea- guered manager, declared: 'We want to unite the entire country, whichever flag anyone is waving at the stadium.'

In his autobiography, Pienaar falls over his own feet several times to justify his statement. 'I understood what he [Du Plessis] wanted to say, but nobody had told me exactly what he had said,' he writes. 'Communications were breaking down and I suddenly found myself being asked to comment on the manager's remarks.' He says he tried to pacify those players who complained to him that their families were unhappy with Du Plessis' statement. And, he claims, 'I had tried to steer a tight middle line, but my comments were then received as implicit criticism of Morné and, amazingly, I found myself being cast in a public dispute with the most outstanding team manager in my experience.' How he could find this 'amazing', only Pienaar will know. Teichmann's comment on the incident was: 'We had all been let down by an absolute lack of leadership, conviction and support when it was sorely needed, and team spirit began to suffer.'

Morné du Plessis stepped down as team manager a few weeks later. He was arguably the best and most successful Springbok man- ager ever. In the book *Rugby DisUnion – The Making of Three World Cups*, Derek Wyatt wrote of the 1995 Rugby World Cup: 'The critical elements in South Africa's success were the management. Morné du Plessis was the key figure here. Despite his long absence from the game, his innate intelligence and catholicism was behind the team's thinking in terms of the larger society of which they had become a part in the 1990s. Ultimately, he was the real star of 1995.'

Of the World Cup Dream Team of a year ago, only François Pienaar was left. But not for long.

The last test of the 1996 Tri-Nations competition was played at Newlands. The Springboks lost 29–18 to the All Blacks. Pienaar was carried off the field with concussion in the second half. He was still lying on the treatment table in the medical room after the match when Thabo Mbeki, then deputy president of South Africa, Jim Bolger, then Prime Minister of New Zealand, and John Hart, the New Zealand coach, came to wish him well. But not his own coach and not his own union president.

Teichmann remembers: 'Our changing room was still afterwards, with André Markgraaff and Louis Luyt standing around. It did strike me at the time that neither of them had been to the medical room to enquire about François' health ... What was now clear was that neither the coach nor president was overly concerned about the captain.' When Pienaar walked back into the team room, Luyt was sitting with a beer in his hand and his arm around Teichmann. Luyt and Markgraaff ignored him completely. The captain was out in the cold. Markgraaff later told some of the players that Pienaar had faked his concussion, but denied this when an angry Pienaar confronted him in public.

Teichmann took over the Springbok captaincy for the period Pienaar was unable to play after his concussion. Pienaar played for Transvaal again after that, but when the squad for the coming tour to England and France was announced, his name was not among the thirty players selected. After three years as Springbok captain and only fifteen months after leading the Springboks to World Cup victory, he wasn't important enough for Markgraaff or Luyt to tell him the news personally or even phone him. That Sunday the newspapers all had Markgraaff's statement on their front pages: 'François Pienaar is not a part of my vision for the future.'

The last member of the World Cup Dream Team was gone. Ian McIntosh commented: 'It was an extraordinary decision. First Edward Griffiths, then Kitch Christie, Morné du Plessis and finally François Pienaar. With a huff and a puff, South Africa's fragile rugby

home had been blown over.' Kitch Christie said: 'It was all so unnec-
essary. We were winning. Why did Markgraaff have to break it all
down?'

The Springbok squad found a new name for Markgraaff: Saddam
Hussein. The public outcry over Pienaar's axing dominated the radio
talk shows and the pages of newspapers for weeks. More than fifteen thousand people phoned Radio 702 to demand Pienaar's
reinstatement. The newspaper *Beeld* received 349 faxes of protest
in one day. An organisation calling itself PAMAL – People Against
Markgraaff and Luyt – was formed and canvassed support on
Internet websites. A spokesman for the government of the Gauteng
province, Thabang Mamonyane, said: 'We are concerned about the
situation because, to many of our people, François Pienaar has
become synonymous with rugby.' *Die Burger* quoted from
Shakespeare's *Hamlet* in an editorial on Luyt, Markgraaff and
Pienaar: 'Something is rotten in the state of Denmark.'

Luyt's shadow fell darkly over the whole episode. His vendetta
against Pienaar from the day he had to tell him 'I'll match Packer'
had made it possible for a bungling, insecure Markgraaff to get rid
of him – that is, if Luyt did not actually engineer the axing himself.
Pienaar himself says there was 'no doubt in my mind that Louis Luyt
was not at all distressed by my demise'. Four years later Luyt said in
a television interview that Pienaar had to go because he was 'too
strong for Markgraaff'.

But at the time Luyt rejected any suggestion that he was involved
in the decision, saying he was 'completely amazed' by the allegations. 'François is one of the great Springboks and to suggest there
is some kind of vendetta against him is preposterous,' he told *The
Citizen* on 14 October. 'Like many in South Africa I am sad to see
François' name not among the list of 36 players, but the Springbok
coach and selectors are doing what they feel is best for South African
rugby.'

Jon Swift wrote in the *Mail & Guardian* of 18 October 1996: 'The public hanging of a national hero impacts not just on the game, but on the nation. What the good men like Pienaar, Kitch Christie and Morné du Plessis did for the game and the spirit they helped engender among the non-rugby playing public cannot be underestimated. There was then a feeling that this was truly a national game and not a pastime that was the sole preserve of the white Afrikaner. To have achieved this change in perceptions in such a short space of time was remarkable. To have gone as far down the road to the destruction of this perception as quickly as SARFU has managed to do, is a tragedy.'

Markgraaff started finding his feet as coach during the tour at the end of 1996 with Gary Teichmann as captain, Hugh Reece-Edwards and Nick Mallet as assistant coaches, and Carel du Plessis as technical adviser. The Springboks beat Argentina 46–15 and 44–21, France 22–12 and 13–12, and Wales 37–20.

But Markgraaff's reign as Springbok coach did not last long. In February 1997 a tape-recording of a conversation he had with a former Griqualand West captain, André Bester, was made public. Markgraaff could clearly be heard raging against the 'kaffirs' and against Pienaar. 'Naturally it is fucking politics,' Markgraaff ranted, 'with the whole fucking country behind him [Pienaar] … Now I hear that Mluleki George also wants to resign on Friday. It's kaffirs, man, it's the fucking NSC, the fucking kaffirs.' It was a huge blow to the already deteriorating image of South African rugby.

After defying anyone to call him a racist and declaring, 'I am considered quite liberal in my community,' a tearful Markgraaff had no option but to resign. Pienaar, who was now overseas, said knowingly: 'It now becomes clearer why I was dropped last year.'

However, most of the team stood by Markgraaff. Brendan Venter even said he felt 'sorry for the guy'. Breyton Paulse, however, thought that his comments were 'almost unacceptable, because how must people of colour feel if they play in his team?'

Carel du Plessis, one of the best wings in world rugby in the mid-1980s, was appointed Springbok coach with a contract going up to the 1999 World Cup. He replaced Reece-Edwards and Mallet with former Springbok loose forward Gert Smal. Under Du Plessis and Smal the Springboks accumulated an extraordinary string of defeats in 1997. The Springboks lost the first test against the British Lions 27–16, the second 18–15, and won the third 35–16. The Springboks lost the first Tri-Nations test against the All Blacks 35–32, the second against Australia 33–22, and the third against the All Blacks 55–35.

It was this last test that broke the camel's back. It was the first time in a full 107 years that the Springbok team had conceded more than 50 points in an international test match. The All Blacks scored eight tries. Teichmann writes in *For the Record*: 'A squad meeting was held later that night and it was James Small who showed the courage to say what every player was thinking. In the intimidating presence of Louis Luyt, the SARFU president, James stood up and said the players had been seriously let down by the management. That was a fact. We had. Luyt interrupted him. "You should be more careful when you talk about the people who are paying the mortgage on our house," the president said, sharp and threatening. The meeting instantly turned sour. I had to intervene. As captain, it was my duty. "Dr Luyt, you should know James is not expressing his personal view. I believe that is the opinion of the entire squad." The president mumbled on, and, amid the worst imaginable atmosphere, the meeting ended abruptly.'

It was the shock treatment that Springbok rugby needed. Two weeks later, the Springboks played Australia at Loftus Versfeld in the last match of the 1997 Tri-Nations series, already won by New Zealand. In an astonishing display of powerful, running rugby, the Springboks beat Australia 61–22. Like the last test against New Zealand, it was one for the record books: it was the first time the Australian Wallabies had conceded more than 50 points in an international test match.

But this one victory could not save Carel du Plessis' career as coach. On 30 August 1997 he addressed the SARFU executive at Ellis Park, and was dismissed. There was a groundswell of support in the rugby fraternity for a charismatic, intelligent upcoming coach who was described as a 'rugby visionary': Nick Mallet. He was chosen from thirty-nine applicants and appointed on 25 September 1997. He was the sixth Springbok coach since the return to international rugby five years before: John Williams, Gerrie Sonnekus, Ian McIntosh, Kitch Christie and Carel du Plessis had come before him.

Mallet presided over a remarkable run of seventeen successive test victories, but he was also axed as unceremoniously as his predecessors before his contract had run out. That's simply the way we do it in South African rugby.

8

TROUBLE IN PARADISE

*Even should a Commission of Inquiry determine that no irregu-
larities are found, there is an overwhelming public perception
… that the administration of rugby is defective, dictatorial and,
perhaps, even corrupt.*

— *Steve Tshwete, August 1997*

Louis Luyt would probably agree that his sweetest moment – perhaps even the high point of his life – was South Africa's victory in
the 1995 Rugby World Cup during his reign as president of South
African rugby. It was a triumphant event of which he was the master-
mind.

His graceless and embarrassing speech at the official dinner on
the last day of the tournament was the first big sign that not even
the recognition and satisfaction that came with the World Cup
success could exorcise the anger and bitterness at life that he had
harboured since childhood. His destructive war of attrition against
François Pienaar and his World Cup squad after he was forced to
sign huge contracts with them had done great harm to South African
rugby. Luyt had achieved so much, yet he remained a vengeful and
fundamentally insecure man, prone to bullying and pettiness. This

blinded him to the new realities of his own society and the significant changes in his environment.

By 1996 it was clear that Luyt was rushing headlong into self-destruction. Buying or bullying his critics and keeping everybody in the dark did not work as well in the post-1994 era as it had before. Accusations of financial mismanagement, nepotism, a dictatorial style of management, a lack of accountability and transparency, lack of representivity and even racism were flung at Luyt from all quarters, inside and outside the rugby world. Newspapers and talk radio stations were running polls on Luyt's popularity – a Radio 702 survey found that 862 people wanted Luyt to stay and 11 676 wanted him to quit rugby altogether. Luyt's reaction throughout was one of brazen defiance. It ended up with him challenging first the Minister of Sport, Steve Tshwete, and then the President of South Africa, Nelson Mandela.

The source of much of the unhappiness in the rugby fraternity was the way Luyt conducted the financial affairs of the Transvaal Rugby Football Union, which later changed its name to the Golden Lions Rugby Union (GLRU), and of Ellis Park stadium. Luyt had survived the criticism around his listing and delisting of Ellis Park and the controversial transactions that gave rise to allegations of insider trading. But on 21 March 1994 he took the unusual step of proposing at the TRFU's annual general meeting that *all* financial matters should henceforth vest in him as president. It has not been explained whether the union delegates were afraid of Luyt or whether they did not understand the implications of such a step, but they voted for the proposal, formally made by Luyt's deputy, Gert Augustyn.

This gave Luyt carte blanche to devise a new trust to take complete control of all the resources of the union as well as of the lucrative Ellis Park – control, as opposed to ownership, because the TRFU formally owned the stadium. The trust had five 'A' trustees, who could be anyone, and three 'B' trustees, who had to be members of the TRFU executive. Luyt appointed all eight trustees – all close associates and friends. He himself was an 'A' trustee, as was his son-in-law Rian Oberholzer. The other three were Willie Kruger, Avril Malan and Henry Vorster. Kruger had been a Luyt employee and board member of Luyt companies for more than twenty years. Malan, brother of the former Defence Minister, Magnus, was also a former Luyt employee. Vorster was a partner in the law firm Vorster Perreira, who drew up the trust deed. Vorster's partner, Perreira, had been a director of and attorney to Triomf Fertiliser. The 'B' trustees were old Luyt loyalists Jomo King, Hugh Bladen and Gert Augustyn.

The trust deed of the 'Transvaal Rugby Sports Trust' (later the Golden Lions Rugby Sports Trust) was made public for the first time in September 2000 when Luyt took the other trustees to court, alleging a conspiracy against him. It is an extraordinary document.

The document records that the Transvaal Rugby Union (TRU) and Ellis Park Rugby Stadium (Pty) Ltd (EPS) agreed to form the trust because 'the respective resources of the TRU and EPS can more efficiently be deployed in the furtherance of the common objectives of the TRU and EPS if those resources were to be consolidated and placed under one administration with the appropriate financial skills and experience.'

Clause 6.6 states: 'The financial statements of the trust are confidential and shall be published only in accordance with the decisions of the trustees from time to time provided that the beneficiary (TRU) shall be furnished with such financial information as may reasonably be required for the purposes of its own accounts and financial statements.'

Clause 7.2 declares: 'The trustees shall have full discretion in applying the resources of the trust in the furtherance of the objects of the trust and shall not be subject to the directions or instructions of any beneficiary or other third party.' That 'beneficiary' was the Transvaal Rugby Union, later the Golden Lions Rugby Union.

And if it wasn't clear enough that the TRU had signed away all its authority, clause 13.1 states: 'The TRU hereby makes over and places under the control of the trustees – 13.1.1 all voting rights; and 13.1.2 the right to receive dividends and/or interest, in respect of all shares and debentures from time to time held by the TRU and issued by EPS.'

Clause 13.2 makes it even clearer: 'In so far as may be necessary, the TRU hereby appoints the trustees as its agents with authority to exercise the voting rights specified in 13.1, which rights shall be exercised by any one of the trustees from time to time nominated by resolutions of the trustees.'

The trust deed also contained a comprehensive insurance policy for trustees: Clause 16.4. This clause states: 'The trustees shall be indemnified out of the trust fund against all claims and demands of whatsoever nature that may be made upon them arising out of the exercise or purported exercise of any of the rights of powers hereby conferred upon them or in the performance of any duties imposed upon them.'

The deed was signed on 5 October 1994 by: 'For Ellis Park Stadium (Proprietary) Limited: L. Luyt (duly authorised)' and 'For the Transvaal Rugby Union: L. Luyt (duly authorised)'. Luyt signed again as trustee, and then came the signatures of the other seven trustees.

This was a stroke of genius, although also perhaps highly irregular and unprecedented. In practice it meant that Luyt gathered seven of his cronies and took all power over the union and Ellis Park's assets and nobody could ever ask any questions about what they were doing. Ellis Park made millions every year – the last time its annual profits were made public was in 1992, when the profit was R9,3 million. That figure must have increased two- or threefold in 1995, the World Cup year. By 1998, the Golden Lions Rugby Trust must have received at least R50 million from Ellis Park, but it had only made one payment of R7,7 million to the Golden Lions Rugby Union, in 1996. But no one in the GLRU executive and no delegates to the union's general meetings could ask the trust where the rest of the money was. It was a recipe for controversy, if not for mischief.

In October 1996 the first dissent bubbled to the top. Luyt's vice-president at Transvaal, thirty-six-year-old accountant Brian van Rooyen, announced that he, like Chris van Coller six years earlier, was going to challenge Luyt for the presidency.

Van Rooyen, who still played for the club Eldoronians, told the *Saturday Star* on 19 October: 'There are many unhappy members on his [Luyt's] executive, but they are all scared of him. I'm not afraid. I once told him: "Dr Luyt, you owe me nothing and I owe you nothing, so don't try and bullshit me." My fight is for transparent administration, for collective decision-making and for a slice of the cake. Right now there's none of that.'

Van Rooyen was complaining about exactly the situation created by Luyt's Rugby Trust. 'There are fifty-five players contracted by Transvaal. I have not been privy to a single contract. Take the multi-million rand sponsorships Transvaal were involved with. I don't know how they are broken down or where that money goes to. The executive should be informed. I'm often told the union's doors are open. Yes, I agree, they are open. But they're open to go out, not to come in.'

Van Rooyen's other big fight was for rugby development. He represented a coloured club and believed the union under Luyt was not doing enough for black rugby or giving talented black players a chance to prove themselves. 'I have two sons who I want to see become Springboks,' Van Rooyen said. 'If I'm not going to pave the way for them, who is?'

But when Van Rooyen's challenge to Luyt came to a vote at the union's extraordinary meeting at the end of October, he received only three of the fifty-five votes. After his victory, Luyt turned on Van Rooyen with what *The Citizen* described as 'a tirade of abuse' and called him 'a fool' who was 'too stupid' to ask intelligent questions about the union's financial affairs. (Van Rooyen is an accountant.) Luyt said to Van Rooyen at the meeting: 'You're gone now, thank God you're gone. You may be in politics but you're out of rugby and we can do without you.'

But, like the election where Chris van Coller opposed Luyt in 1990, it wasn't an ordinary election. The rules again changed just before the voting started. One of Luyt's oldest lieutenants, Mickey Gerber, asked that the vote be done by a showing of hands, rather than by secret ballot as had been the custom for fifteen years. Van Rooyen commented: 'Although I only received three votes, I counted at least twenty-five abstentions. Had the ballot been secret, the twenty-five or so who refused to go with Luyt might well have put their cross next to my name. He knew a secret ballot could lose the presidency for him, or at best make him look bad.'

That weekend Colin Bryden wrote in the *Sunday Times*: 'With Luyt's powers of vengeance well proven, once it was decided voting would be by a show of hands, it was not surprising the unfortunate Van Rooyen received only three votes in his bid to replace Luyt as Transvaal rugby president. Van Rooyen is not alone in wondering about the financial workings of rugby, in particular the relationship between the Transvaal Union and Ellis Park Stadium.'

The *Mail & Guardian* said in an editorial: 'Van Rooyen, in his failed bid, mirrored many of the things this newly hatched democracy is still striving for: transparency, accountability and a system of open and collective decision-making.'

Luyt may have said 'goodbye' to Van Rooyen, but Van Rooyen wasn't going anywhere. He started compiling a dossier of complaints and allegations against Luyt, and requested Sports Minister Steve Tshwete to investigate Luyt and the TRFU. When Tshwete hinted at a possible investigation, Luyt came out with all guns blazing. He dared Tshwete to nominate independent auditors 'to establish whether any irregularities or payments had occurred *vis-à-vis* in particular Dr Luyt, members of his family, his family trusts and any other person.' Luyt also threatened to sue Van Rooyen 'and his cohorts, the newspapers, publishers and distributors who repeated the defamatory comments'.

On 14 February 1997 Tshwete announced that he was appointing a three-man task force to probe South African rugby. The three men were former judge Mervyn King, corporate lawyer Michael Katz and respected advocate Gilbert Marcus. Tshwete identified concerns about the administration of rugby, the development programme, the status of professionalism, the ownership of stadiums and television rights. Luyt hit back and demanded a copy of the 'Van Rooyen dossier', otherwise he would not co-operate with the task team. Tshwete responded: 'I will not be instructed by Louis Luyt or his lawyers. He will get the report when the time is right.'

But things were going horribly wrong for Luyt. Shortly after Tshwete announced the rugby probe, SABC television played the tape-recording of Springbok coach André Markgraaff's racist tirade over the air. When it became known that Luyt had known about the tape since 30 November 1996 and had done nothing about it, the ANC's Parliamentary Study Group on Sport asked the minister to put pressure on Luyt to quit.

The Markgraaff affair was not yet over when the *Sunday Times* published a damning front page report about the Luyt family's involvement in rugby. 'Fresh evidence of how Louis Luyt has turned rugby into a family business has emerged in leaked minutes of a South African Rugby Football Union meeting last year,' the newspaper reported. 'The minutes show that Luyt's son, Louis jr, stands to earn a ten percent commission on any sponsorship deal he arranges on behalf of SARFU. They also show he has been given a mandate to negotiate a proposed deal, which could be worth as much as R45 million, between South African rugby and Disneyworld in the US.'

The *Sunday Times* then listed who in the Luyt dynasty had what connections to rugby: Luyt himself was president of SARFU and the TRFU and a trustee of the Transvaal Rugby Sports Trust, which controlled Ellis Park, a stadium worth about R120 million; Louis Luyt junior was general manager of the stadium; Luyt senior's wife, Adri, was chairperson of SA Sports Management, long rumoured to be one of Ellis Park's main suppliers of refreshments; Luyt's daughter Corlia, who is married to SARFU CEO Rian Oberholzer, did legal work for SARFU as an attorney; Oberholzer was general manager of Ellis Park, tournament director of the 1995 Rugby World Cup, and then became chief executive of SANZAR before becoming CEO of SARFU. He was also a trustee of the powerful Transvaal Rugby Sports Trust.

Oberholzer reacted on Luyt's behalf the next day, calling the report 'mischievous, devious and libellous'. The next day Luyt himself announced that he had ordered his lawyers to 'sue the *Sunday Times* for millions'.

But the following week the *Sunday Times* went further in their reporting on the Luyt family connection. 'Luyt's son-in-law, Rian Oberholzer, is a director of a company that sells rugby kit to club, school and the Transvaal provincial teams. Luyt's son, Louis Luyt jr, heads Ellis Park Stadium (Pty) Ltd, from which Ellis Park suite-holders have to buy liquor and food. As marketing manager of Ellis Park stadium, Luyt jr wrote to suite-holders in 1995 reminding them of a condition in their contracts which stipulated that they had to buy their refreshments from the company.'

On 21 February 1997, Luyt, Mluleki George, Rian Oberholzer and other TRFU officials had a meeting with Steve Tshwete and his director-general, Mthobi Tyamzashe, about the proposed rugby task force. Tshwete talked about his own days as a rugby player – 'rugby is a sport that stole my passion' – and reminded Luyt that he (Tshwete) had helped to get SARFU to host the World Cup, had calmed people down when Luyt played *Die Stem* at Ellis Park in 1992 and had made sure the Australian test went ahead the following week, and had fought to retain the Springbok as the emblem of South African rugby. He said SARFU should know that his department was going to intervene in rugby, because 'rugby is not operating from Mars. It is operating from a specific framework in South Africa.'

According to a transcript of the meeting, Luyt raged: 'That document [the Van Rooyen dossier] is worth nothing and I want to put on record right now and this is the last time we are going to do it, that we want that document under Section 23 of the Constitution ... The Constitution provides for me to defend myself and I will defend myself.'

Later on in the meeting he said: 'Now you can go back to Parliament and make a law that you can fire me. Simply do that. We can all say that Mr Tshwete has fired me, Luyt, as a person. Yes sir you can do that, but I will not go down lightly.'

About Van Rooyen he said: 'Van Rooyen was running around, and where he gets the money, I do not know, but I will find out, I promise you that, I will find out where he got it, but he is running around to sow the sanctions against the sport. Now all of a sudden there is a crisis. The crisis emanated from a stupid report by Van Rooyen and now it has built up to a crescendo where it is a crisis – a crisis created by whom?

'... [This] started when Van Rooyen lost the election. Then he came to you with the dossier which I think he was helped with by *Finansies en Tegniek* [a financial magazine]. He was helped with a lot of private money. I know some of them. I will get to all of them and every single one of them will answer whether they like it or not. I shall pursue that until I bloody well die and it is a fact, but I will not die running away from gunshots. I will die fighting for that, because my name is at stake.'

Luyt was adamant that he wanted the Van Rooyen dossier, and the conversation became animated.

LUYT: 'You are not going to make a whatsitsname of the task force, I am telling you right now. I will walk out of here and I will say that ... I have come here, you have got the document, you have got to answer me and I am challenging you now to answer, tell me what the allegations are. That is why I came. I am here (inaudible) give it to me and let me answer it straight away.'

DIRECTOR-GENERAL: 'The allegations?'

TSHWETE: 'No you are not going to answer them here.'

LUYT: 'Yes, with evidence.'

TSHWETE: 'No you are not going to answer them here, the allegations.'

LUYT: 'Well ...'

TSHWETE: 'The allegations, you are going to answer them. There will be expert people who understand what is going on, what is contained ...'

LUYT: 'Well you should have had them here today because I came here. I am also with expert people. You mustn't take me for a bloody (inaudible) and then come here and you cannot give me the allegations. I will walk out of here.'

The two groups ended up agreeing to a joint press statement which said that SARFU would be given the opportunity to answer Van Rooyen's allegations; that the minister would appoint a task team under the leadership of the director-general; and that SARFU would apply to court for access to the Van Rooyen dossier.

On 24 February 1997 Luyt asked the Pretoria High Court to order Tshwete and his director-general, Mthobi Tyamzashe, to hand over the Van Rooyen dossier. Judge JP Roux found that Luyt's rights were indeed threatened, and ordered the handing over of the documents.

One of the interesting documents in the Van Rooyen dossier was a letter to Van Rooyen from the then Minister of Water Affairs and Forestry, Professor Kader Asmal. He wrote on the ministry's official letterhead:

Dear Mr Van Rooyen

I have watched the Louis Luyt spectacle with a sense of growing alarm, and I wish you to know of my warm support for what you have been trying to do. The juggernaut response by Luyt to your challenge and the juvenile way he attacked you suggest that – despite his apparent power – he is losing his grip.

Luyt is rooted in an era in which it was expected of people like him to do execrable things for the established order – such as fronting for the Government's *Citizen* newspaper – and of which he should be thoroughly ashamed. Yet he struts around the national rugby stage as if it is his private domain. He is having a grievously divisive effect on our public life, and your stunningly bold attempt to check him earns my warmest admiration and respect.

My hope is that the new moves to call him to account will be successful; and, meanwhile, may I warmly commend you for your courage and commitment to the new order that we are trying, despite the Luyts of our world, to establish in South Africa.

Warm regards

Yours sincerely

Prof Kader Asmal MP

Luyt was clearly very nervous about what could have been in the Van Rooyen dossier. But he need not have been so paranoid. It contained mostly newspaper clippings, court papers, Van Rooyen's view of Luyt, an analysis of the lack of transformation in rugby and questions that should be asked about Luyt's administration. The only concrete new material was details of SARFU's relationship with a marketing company called Megapro – according to the *Mail & Guardian* 'allegedly linked to Luyt' – in which Megapro's commission could amount to up to 25 per cent of SARFU's revenue.

Luyt's lawyers had in the meantime written to the Director-General of Sport that the task team was an 'illegally appointed body' and indicated that SARFU was not prepared to co-operate with it. But on 26 March 1997 the director-general, Mthobi Tyamzashe, warned Luyt in a letter: 'If you unreservedly agree to co-operate with the work of the task team we can immediately proceed. If not, the Minister will be compelled to request the Honourable State President to appoint a judicial commission of inquiry into the matter.' At a meeting between the task team, now joined by advocate Gcina Malindi, and a SARFU delegation on 3 April, Luyt assured the task team of SARFU's co-operation and support. On 4 May 1997 the task team published a notice inviting public representations on a wide range of matters relating to the administration of rugby in South Africa.

The SARFU administration and the various rugby unions indeed then co-operated with the task team. But Luyt ominously said at a SARFU executive meeting on 5 August 1997 that he was happy that the unions had co-operated with the task team 'because then I will hammer Mandela out of sight if he comes with a commission of inquiry when 80 percent already co-operated.'

SARFU's co-operation only lasted while they had easy answers to the task force's questions. When the forensics arm of the accounting firm Deloitte and Touche, acting for task team member Michael Katz, asked SARFU for information on some of the more contentious accusations of financial mismanagement, co-operation ceased. Deloitte and Touche asked for Ellis Park Stadium (Pty) Ltd's financial statements, details of the process of board appointments, details of directors' remuneration, a schedule of all subsidiaries and associates of the company, and 'the name and beneficial ownership of the entity which holds the liquor licence at Ellis Park'. It also asked for the trust deed and details of all investments and remuneration of the Transvaal Rugby Sports Trust, a copy of all sponsorship agreements, a copy of the $550 million Murdoch agreement and copies of the agreements between SARFU and rugby players.

Deloitte and Touche had clearly done their homework. Luyt couldn't possibly hand over all these documents without exposing all his financial wheelings and dealings. Deloitte and Touche's Mark Pinington also asked specific questions, such as how Louis Luyt junior had got his job at Ellis Park and what role Luyt's daughter, Corlia Oberholzer, had performed for the Transvaal Rugby Union. Pinington wanted to know whether any senior officials of the TRU operated businesses from any of the premises owned by the TRU or Ellis Park, and what commissions had been paid to whom in respect of sponsorship deals. And in an obvious reference to Luyt, Pinington asked whether the Sports Trust or Ellis Park had 'at any time considered or effected any resolution to purchase any moveable or immoveable property from any board member or other individual closely connected to a board member'.

Luyt, the TRU and the Transvaal Rugby Sports Trust never answered these questions.

SARFU's lawyers wrote to Director-General Tyamzashe, refusing all co-operation until they had been given particulars of all the accusations against them. On 30 July 1997 SARFU sent a fax to all the rugby unions stating: 'Unions are hereby advised that all co-operation with the Task Force appointed by the Minister of Sport and Recreation to investigate Rugby in South Africa must, with immediate effect, be suspended.'

Minister Steve Tshwete met with President Nelson Mandela on 5 August 1997 and told him of his intention to apply for the appointment of a judicial commission of inquiry. Mandela told him to prepare a written motivation. Tyamzashe issued a press statement the next day which was to play an important part in a subsequent court case brought by Luyt.

Tyamzashe's statement reported that, in response to the minister's intimation to the President that he intended to apply for the appointment of a commission of inquiry, the President 'happily responded' that 'a commission is yours if, in your best judgement, it is opportune'. The legal position is that a minister cannot appoint a commission, and the President can only do it if he has applied his mind to the matter properly. Mandela and Tshwete later declared that this statement had never been made, and Tyamzashe admitted that it was a fabrication aimed at persuading SARFU to resume co-operation.

On 15 August the task team reported that they could not proceed with their investigation and recommended to the minister that he apply to the President for the appointment of a commission of inquiry. They handed in their preliminary reports to the director-general.

Task team member Michael Katz reported: 'I felt that there was a reluctance of people to appear officially as witnesses for fear of adverse consequences.' Others, he said, would only speak to him 'on a personal basis off the record'.

Katz got to the heart of a long-standing problem in South African rugby when he said it had emerged from his discussions that the smaller provincial unions were financially dependent on the SARFU executive and didn't want to annoy them. 'Alienating SARFU's executive by the giving of evidence by a representative of a provincial union could result in the loss to that union of a test venue during a future tour. This would be very disadvantageous to that union.'

Task team member Gcina Malindi reported on her investigations into the development of rugby among black communities and charges of racial prejudice. She had very little positive to say about SARFU on this score, despite their stated noble intentions.

Malindi reported widespread unhappiness among black players and administrators about the pace of transformation since the agreement to rugby unity in 1992. The Springbok and provincial teams seldom featured a black face, and SARFU's administrative structures had not changed either: 'Blacks are mainly confined to development departments in the provincial unions.' Dissatisfaction was also expressed about the absence of a special effort to give talented black players a chance to show their stuff and perhaps qualify for Springbok selection. Malindi also reported that many witnesses had told her of widespread racism in provincial unions and clubs.

Task team member Gilbert Marcus reported on his investigation into rugby and television rights. He said his departure point was 'the desirability of ensuring that as many people as possible have afford-able access to television coverage' of rugby matches. 'The success of the national rugby team in the 1995 World Cup served as a catalyst for unprecedented interest in rugby, particularly in black communi-ties. The success of the national team was a vivid example of how sport was able to bridge historical divisions and in which there was a rare shared pride in the success of the national team.'

SARFU had the only and final say over television rights regarding rugby. It had sold the rights to provincial matches, the Super 12 series and test matches to Rupert Murdoch's News Corporation in 1995, although the details of this contract were never revealed. The subscription channel M-Net bought the South African rights from Murdoch, which meant that only a very limited number of South Africans could watch the sport – and because of class structures, this meant that most black South Africans were excluded. M-Net did agree to televise all tests played in South Africa in open time, when all television viewers could watch. The starting time of matches was changed to 5 pm, to coincide with M-Net's open time.

By late 1997 the hostility towards Luyt and his running of rugby had spread to official rugby structures inside SARFU. In August 1997 the Natal Rugby Union took SARFU to court over the restructuring of the teams to play in the new Super 12 competition. The union's CEO, Brian van Zyl, said neither Luyt nor Oberholzer had attempted to discuss the implications of the move with the major unions.

Natal was going for the Luyt jugular, accusing him of nepotism and improper conduct. Van Zyl stated in his court application: 'It is now a matter of public record that the South African Breweries who were the sponsors of the South African national side were unsuc-cessful in their attempt to renew their sponsorship. An agreement has apparently been reached in terms of which the international company Nike will now be the sponsor of the South African national side. This agreement was concluded by the President of the first respondent (SARFU) without reference to or consultation with the Executive Committee or the Finance Committee of the first respondent.

'Moreover, it is again a matter of public record that the son of the first respondent's President [Luyt's son Louis junior] whose occupation and present position is that of General Manager of the Ellis Park Stadium, is to receive a commission of R2 million for brokering the agreement between Nike and the first respondent (SARFU). I find it strange that a man who is a stadium manager should be entrusted with brokering a multi-million rand international contract.

'I make mention of these facts because it has become obvious that the President (Luyt) and/or his son and/or his son-in-law are negotiating with international companies to sponsor the new Super 12 structure and are on the point of concluding an agreement. The President's son having secured an extremely healthy commission in the last sponsorship deal, it may be inferred that the same monetary considerations are in play in ensuring that the proposed system is enforced. I say that these considerations are impermissable and extraneous to the powers and functions of the first respondent, as reflected in its constitution.'

Van Zyl added: 'It is not open to the first respondent (SARFU), its President or Executive Committee to contemplate contractual dealings calculated to ensure a personal benefit (directly or indirectly) which otherwise could accrue to the first respondent itself.'

In a replying affidavit, Rian Oberholzer said the allegations about himself, Luyt and Luyt junior were 'scandalous, without foundation and untrue'.

Public opinion was not far behind Natal and Van Zyl. *The Star* said in an editorial on 12 August: 'Louis Luyt should do rugby the courtesy of stepping down as South African Rugby Football Union president. On and off the field, rugby is being ridiculed, while the bull-headed Luyt is seen as a divisive element in South African rugby.'

Referring to SARFU's reluctance to co-operate with the ministerial task team, the newspaper said: 'If Luyt has nothing to hide, why does he protest so much? Luyt has led us to believe that he is self-lessly serving the interests of rugby – and not his own. Perhaps the task team would put any doubts to rest that he is a law unto him-self.' *The Star* concluded: 'With Luyt at the helm, South African rugby will remain at war with itself and the spirit of the rainbow nation.'

In the meantime, Sports Minister Steve Tshwete started preparing the proposal to President Nelson Mandela for the appointment of a judi-cial commission of inquiry. He employed attorney Edward Nathan to assist him. The proposal included seven hundred pages of support-ing documents when it was handed to the president on 12 August 1997.

In his application to Mandela, Tshwete gave a broad overview of rugby in the social and political context of South Africa. 'It has been maintained that rugby in South Africa is, to a great extent, the Afrikaner's game. This may be an established perception in South Africa and abroad. In the former "white" circles of rugby, neverthe-less, fierce rivalry has always existed between Afrikaners and English speaking schools and clubs and even those provincial structures that were predominated by the one language group or the other. Black and coloured South Africans, furthermore, have a long and remark-able rugby history which, too, commenced in the early stages of British colonialism, and developed prior to and during the apartheid era. A proliferation of administration boards, reflective primarily of the racial divides, illustrated the political and social segregation.'

Tshwete outlined the efforts in the early 1990s to unite the vari-ous sporting bodies and the amalgamation of the black South African Rugby Union and the white South African Rugby Board to form the South African Rugby Football Union. This new body declared in its constitution that it 'shall, at national and at all other levels – right down to club and school level – pursue policies and programmes aimed at redressing imbalances and at creating a genuine non-racial, non-political and democratic union; such policies and programmes to be aimed at achieving, expeditiously, the non-racial, non-political and democratic structuring of the Union and all its constituent elements.'

Tshwete then remarked: 'The establishment of a documented sense of unity, for boardroom talks, was one thing. Ensuring that the policy was accepted and implemented down to the lower ranks remains entirely another. Racial and political sensitivities, irrespective of the constant application of pressures and the introduction of development programmes, continue at least in perception. Rugby, at national and international level, remains predominantly white in representation. Widespread speculation and accusation exists as to the reasons for a lack of full racial integration and representation.'

Tshwete put Louis Luyt in the centre of all these issues, quoting a description of him as 'an archetypal worst of old-style white South Africans – brash and arrogant, proud of his lack of concern for the fellow citizens'.

The minister concluded: 'The matters of public concern, which find continued expression in publications and other fora, remain. These are not matters which are restricted to private enterprise, but affect the national sport of rugby and the nation's concern therein ...

'Even should a Commission of Inquiry determine that no irregularities are found, there is an overwhelming public perception that has become abundantly clear to the Ministerial Task Team members collectively and through their individual exposure to members of the public, that the administration of rugby is defective, dictatorial and, perhaps, even corrupt.

'No organisation or institute can effectively operate under such a cloud, more particularly, one that is responsible for national activity. The position requires to be investigated to determine whether or not that perception is justified.'

On 22 September President Mandela announced the commission of inquiry and the appointment of acting judge Jules Browde as its chairman. But Browde never held his inquiry. Before he could start, Luyt took Mandela to court to stop it.

Luyt described the commission of inquiry as 'the worst thing in the world' on the weekly television rugby programme *Boots and All.* 'I'm fighting for the principle and for the rights of SARFU, the Gauteng Lions and everybody else involved. I don't believe that Steve Tshwete should have the right to tell me to hop, jump or sit.' He warned that when he eventually left South African rugby, it would 'fall apart'.

But there were many senior rugby figures who did not think that Luyt was fighting for them. In October 1997, SARFU's senior vice-president, Mluleki George, declared to newspaper reporters: 'Louis Luyt must be ousted as president of the South African Rugby Football Union', and stated his intention to oppose Luyt for the position of president at SARFU's meeting on 4 November.

It was significant that it was George, president of the Border Rugby Union and an ANC member of Parliament, who was opposing Luyt. It would be the first time a black rugby official stood for election to SARFU's top post. George had been a Luyt supporter for years, and had even defended Luyt during the negotiations with Steve Tshwete and his department around the task team that was to probe rugby. George was a veteran of the old non-racial sports movement and the black South African Rugby Union.

Shortly after George's announcement, the Natal Rugby Union president, Keith Parkinson, announced that he also intended challenging Luyt. George was unmoved. 'The important thing is that Louis Luyt must be removed as president of SARFU,' he told the Independent Newspapers group's rugby writer Liam del Carme. 'He is not good for the game and we need to change the image of the sport now. We must democratise rugby and that cannot happen if Luyt remains in charge. It is in the interest of rugby if Luyt goes. We must remove this cloud of suspicion over the game.'

George denied that his old friendship with Luyt was over. 'Louis and I are still friends. He was very courteous when we were at a meeting last week. There is no animosity between us. I admire him for what he has done for rugby in the past. I cannot deny he did the game a lot of good before the World Cup. I think he should have stepped down while he was on that high though. Rugby does not have the moral high ground it had after the World Cup.'

Steve Morris wrote about Luyt and George in the *Mail & Guardian*: 'Both men are as tough as they come. Both are inveterate survivors: Luyt a castaway, increasingly marooned on a lonely island of power forged by his own ego; George a patient stalker of the halls of power that were so long denied him in the days of apartheid.'

The opposition to Luyt slowly became more and more political, with racial undercurrents. In late October, Achmat Esau, a Western Province rugby administrator who coached rugby in the Bo-Kaap, a 'coloured' suburb of Cape Town, said in a newspaper interview: 'I am involved with rugby at a grass roots level and I know that basically nothing is being done for poor players. It is all very well for the national team to include players like Breyton Paulse, Dale Sandton and McNeil Hendricks, but still no real money is being spent on developing the game. People like Edward Griffiths wanted development to take shape, but Luyt is always against this. I think I should be the first person to say to Luyt's face that he is a racist and is damaging the image of rugby beyond repair.'

A few days before the election, Parkinson made it clear that he wasn't holding his breath: 'Luyt shrewdly won the loyalty of the smaller unions in South African rugby and therefore I don't think I stand a realistic chance,' he told reporters. But he added: 'Maybe I will not win this time, but we will get rid of Luyt eventually.'

And then the fourth of November arrived. Parkinson was of course right about the smaller unions – Luyt has always had them in his pocket, literally. But more than just these unions backed him.

Parkinson and George had hopelessly overestimated the willingness of the country's rugby administrators to go against Luyt. Many of those who had promised George their votes backed Luyt once again. Luyt got thirty-three of the forty-seven votes.

Looking back, it is difficult to comprehend why so many of the SARFU delegates decided to give Luyt a huge motion of confidence at that critical stage. He was one of the most unpopular public personalities in South Africa; he was in public conflict with the most popular public personality in South Africa, Nelson Mandela; a commission of inquiry into South African rugby was about to be launched, which they must have known would hurt Luyt badly; and there was serious disunity in South African rugby over Luyt's role.

But that is the way it had been with Transvaal rugby since 1984 and with SARFU since 1994: the executive committees of the unions and of SARFU refused to take any responsibility. They basked in the glory of Luyt's successes and rolled around in the money he made for rugby, and when things went wrong, Luyt took all the flak. Luyt became one of the most maligned public figures in South Africa in the second half of the 1990s, but seldom were the union bosses and the rest of the SARFU executive held responsible for the disasters. He could not have done any of the controversial things he was criticised for if it hadn't been for their backing.

Luyt was again triumphant after the humiliating defeat of George and Parkinson. 'I will go when I'm ready to go,' he said after his victory.

This time he was wrong. When his lapdogs finally realised which way the wind was blowing, they turned on him.

9

CHALLENGING MANDELA

*I will hammer Mandela out of sight if he comes with a
commission of inquiry ...*

— Louis Luyt, August 1997

On 20 October 1997 Luyt launched a legal challenge against the government that would make legal history – and make him one of the
most resented men in South Africa. On the one hand he may have
relished the idea of taking on the greatest icon of the late twentieth
century – he had boasted in August that he would 'hammer' Mandela
out of court. But, on the other hand, he had little choice but to resist
a commission of inquiry with everything at his disposal, because he
knew that nothing could be worse than answering under oath the
questions already put to him.

The application to the Transvaal High Court to have President
Nelson Mandela's decision to appoint the commission of inquiry set
aside or declared null and void was brought by SARFU, the Gauteng
Lions Rugby Union, the Mpumalanga Rugby Union and Luyt himself.
The respondents were the President of South Africa, the Minister
of Sport and the Director-General of Sport and Recreation.

In his founding affidavit, Luyt listed the events and tournaments

organised by SARFU and commented: 'I can say without fear of contradiction that these events are successfully organised. I verily believe that
no other type of sport in South Africa can claim the efficiency in organisation which SARFU has demonstrated in its organisation.'

Luyt also boasted about SARFU's development programme to
stimulate black rugby: 'I can say with complete confidence that
SARFU's programme is the most successful and largest programme
of its kind in all types of sport in South Africa.' SARFU's staging of
the 1995 Rugby World Cup was 'internationally regarded as one of
the major successes ever in that it generated a profit of approximately 28 million pounds (approximately R210 million).'

Luyt explained that SARFU had initially opposed Tshwete's
appointment of a task team but later agreed to co-operate. 'In this
regard I emphasise that it was never agreed nor contemplated that
the Minister, Director-General or Task Team would have carte
blanche to subject SARFU or its unions to interrogatories or unlimit-
ed or unspecified open ended investigations or searches.' When
SARFU received a request from Deloitte and Touche for financial
statements, documents and minutes of SARFU, the TRU, Ellis Park
Stadium and the Transvaal Rugby Sports Trust, it became clear to
him that the agreement between SARFU and the Minister of Sport
was not being honoured. That agreement was a binding one that
could not be annulled by a commission of inquiry. He claimed that
Tshwete was engaged in a 'vendetta' against him.

Luyt's basic argument was that the legal prerequisites for the
appointment of a commission stipulated by the Commissions Act
had not been satisfied. The Act determined that the matters to be
inquired into had to be 'a matter of public interest'. This does not
apply to 'private autonomous associations such as SARFU and its
constituent unions, and in any event not to its internal management'.
He stressed that SARFU and its provincial unions were all non-
governmental, non-statutory organisations which were not funded
by the state or taxpayers' money. 'Although the public at large and

in particular the rugby viewing public, have an interest in rugby as a sport in the sense that it is something that interests them and which they enjoy, the public have no legal interest in, or interest in the sense of concern or legitimate interest in, the internal management, policies, administration or practices of SARFU or any of its constituent unions.'

When Mandela decided to appoint the commission, Luyt said, he had no substantiated information about any wrongdoing in SARFU apart from the 'scurrilous Van Rooyen dossier'. Mandela clearly had not given any consideration to the fact 'that SARFU and its unions are in terms of the Constitution entitled to freely conduct their own internal affairs; that SARFU and its unions are entitled to conduct their affairs without state interference; that the appointment of a commission would constitute a severe infringement of their entrenched rights to freedom, security, equality and privacy; that the appointment of a commission would constitute an act of drastic state intervention in the affairs of a private sporting body, reminiscent of the apartheid era's intervention in sport'.

Luyt's other argument was that President Mandela had not properly considered the matter before he made his decision. 'In all the circumstances the decision by the President to appoint a commission of inquiry is so unreasonable that it can only be explained on the basis of a failure on the part of the President to properly apply his mind to the matter. The public concern, if it is found to exist at all, as opposed to mere curiosity, is so limited, trivial and insignificant that it could never weigh up against or justify the potential and actual prejudice that will result to SARFU and its unions as a result of the commission and its intended activities.'

These were basically the arguments Luyt's legal counsel tried to prove to the court when the hearings started on 26 January 1998, after months of legal skirmishes between the two sets of legal representatives.

The application was heard by Judge William de Villiers. He was

very much an 'old order' judge and had surrounded himself with
controversy, years earlier, when he opposed the racial integration of
the Pretoria Bar. I had personally appeared before him seven years
earlier when the Commissioner of Police requested an urgent interdict to stop me from publishing facts about a handgrenade attack
on the home of the leader of the Labour Party, Reverend Allan
Hendrickse. The attack was launched by a security police officer
who was ordered to scare Hendrickse after he embarrassed the PW
Botha government by going to swim at a whites-only beach. The
police then blamed the ANC for the attack. Judge De Villiers granted the interdict after a short hearing behind closed doors, ordering
me never even to mention the incident to anyone. It was a terrible
decision, and the judge was wrong. The source of the story was a
very senior police officer who was part of the chain of command
when the order for the attack was made, but I had promised not
to divulge his name. Every word I wanted to write was true and
was verified after 1994 – my only mistake was to ask for the
Commissioner's comment before I published and so give him an
opportunity to stop me. My personal impression was that De Villiers
was never interested in the truth and had decided to grant the order
even before my lawyer opened his mouth. But it is, I suppose, also
possible that he simply could not believe that the revered men in
blue could be so devious and dishonest – a whole bench of the
Appellate Division made that mistake when they caused me to lose
a multi-million rand defamation suit brought by the head of the
SAP's forensics laboratory whom my newspaper had accused of
preparing poison to use on anti-apartheid activists …

Wim Trengove, SC, appeared for Mandela and Tshwete, and Mike
Maritz, SC, appeared for SARFU and Luyt. They are two of the
sharpest legal minds in South Africa, and it showed during the weeks
of acrimonious hearings.

The case started on a controversial note. Maritz asked the court to order that President Nelson Mandela, Minister Steve Tshwete and Director-General Mthobi Tyamzashe be called to give oral evidence and be cross-examined. Judge De Villiers granted the request.

This was highly unusual. Never before had a South African head of state been forced to appear in court to answer for his actions and to be cross-examined. It was unheard of, not only in South Africa, but in most democracies. It could set a dangerous precedent.

The judge's decision to force President Mandela to testify was sharply criticised by lawyers, commentators, the ruling ANC and members of the public. Apart from the legal considerations, it was seen as an extreme gesture of disrespect to allow a man closely associated with the country's apartheid past to challenge the leader of the democratic movement and President of the new South Africa in such a way.

Oral evidence in the case started on 26 February. The hearing was held in Pretoria's divorce court. The two friends who had become arch-enemies, Steve Tshwete and Louis Luyt, sat two chairs away from each other. Norman Chandler, reporter for *The Star*, described the scene: 'The burly Luyt sat with his lawyers for the first one-and-a-half hours of proceedings before Tshwete arrived at 11:30 am and took his seat. The SARFU chairman, with an impervious stare, dismissed the minister's presence. Tshwete did not even look at his rival who, from time to time, smiled to himself as evidence was led by Mike Maritz.' Luyt, Rian Oberholzer and SARFU's Johan Erasmus were the first to give evidence, followed by Tyamzashe, task team members Michael Katz, Gilbert Marcus and Gcina Malindi, and finally Tshwete.

Luyt testified mostly about the meetings he had had with Tshwete and Tyamzashe about the task team, and the correspondence between the two groups about it. He insisted that the assurances that SARFU would be given an opportunity to answer the allegations against them if they co-operated with the task team, and that it would not lead to a wide-ranging 'fishing expedition', constituted a binding contract between the minister, the director-general and SARFU. Tshwete and Tyamzashe denied this in their evidence.

Tyamzashe had a tough time, especially about the press statement he had issued in August the previous year. He had said in the statement that when Tshwete told Mandela he was going to apply for a commission of inquiry, the president 'happily responded' that 'a commission is yours if, in your best judgement, it is opportune'. Tyamzashe now explained that he had put words in the president's mouth and that the press statement was incorrect. He had lied in the statement because he was trying to influence SARFU to co-operate with the task team and thought the threat of a commission would sway them. He had lied, but it was 'an honest lie', Tyamzashe said.

> MARITZ: 'You always knew that you falsely attributed those words to the President, or rather that is your story?'
>
> TYAMZASHE: 'I acknowledge that I attributed words to the President.'
>
> MARITZ: 'Yes, now we don't accept that, because I'm going to argue that that is not true. I am going to argue to his lordship that you did not falsely attribute words to the President, you are lying under oath here to save the President. You have become the fall guy in this case, that is what I'm going to argue. You can comment on that.'
>
> TYAMZASHE: 'Certainly, I'm not lying.'
>
> MARITZ: 'Yes?'
>
> TYAMZASHE: 'And I do not know if I am the fall guy.'
>
> MARITZ: 'It is not even an honest lie, you say.'

But the whole country was waiting for Nelson Mandela's appearance in court. He was due on 9 March, but because of affairs of state he could not be there that day. Instead, Trengove applied for an order revoking the decision to force the President to give evidence and be cross-examined. Judge De Villiers dismissed the application with costs. Mandela had to go.

10

MANDELA IN COURT

I am telling you that the allegation, rightly or wrongly, is that Dr Luyt is a pitiless dictator, and no official, I understand, can stand up to him. You cannot talk about democracy in that sense.

— Nelson Mandela, March 1998

Just after ten on the morning of 19 March 1998 President Nelson Mandela raised his right hand in the Pretoria High Court, swearing that he would tell the truth, the whole truth and nothing but the truth. This was constitutional history. The courtroom was packed with journalists from all over the world, and dozens of international television teams were waiting outside the court. Before he went in, Mandela told them he had 'grave reservations' about being ordered to appear by Judge De Villiers. Since becoming President he had appointed twenty-six different commissions of inquiry. If he had to go to give evidence in court about every decision, Mandela said, it would completely undermine the functions of government.

David Beresford wrote in the *Mail & Guardian*: 'Looking the epitome of dignity in a charcoal suit, the president made a point of demonstrating his respect for the court by refusing to take a seat offered to him by Judge William de Villiers. However, he did not address him by the respectful "my lord", instead calling him "judge". In the witness box, the president put on a masterful performance, at times reducing spectators to laughter as he crossed swords with advocate Mike Maritz, one of the most highly regarded silks in the country. Telling Maritz to "speak up" and rebuking him for repeating the same question in different guises, Mandela showed himself to be completely in command of the issues before the court.'

In fact, the President almost lost his temper with Maritz several times during the two days and ended up insulting him. I have read the transcript of the entire case, and I found myself wondering many times how on earth Maritz could treat a man like Mandela, quite apart from his being the President of South Africa, almost like a naughty and rather stupid child. It was a complete insult to Mandela's intelligence, as well as his integrity. Of course Mandela is not above the law, but I thought Maritz demonstrated an extreme lack of respect for Mandela's public office, age, history and standing in the international community. It was like hammering Mother Theresa with trick questions about child abuse, or badgering the Pope about stealing money from the collection plate. I know advocates like to believe they live in a macho world where they have to serve their clients regardless of any consideration, but I have serious doubts about whether Maritz would have treated former president FW de Klerk with so much disrespect.

In the process, Maritz was not serving his client well – at least not in my judgement. He could have achieved exactly what he wanted without trying to humiliate the President of South Africa. By doing so, he stirred up deep resentment among ordinary South Africans towards Luyt, because in the public's view Luyt was the one who forced Mandela into court. This resentment permeated even the rugby community, and by the end of the case, win or lose, Luyt's public position was untenable.

Maritz adopted the typical advocate's schoolmasterly style and didn't budge from it one inch. Mandela had to remind him a few times that rugby wasn't his only responsibility in life; that he was actually the head of the government of South Africa with an incredibly busy schedule. In fact, Mandela indicated several times that his national and international schedule was so hectic that he wanted his time in court to be as short as possible.

Maritz virtually never accepted a reply given by Mandela; he always reworked it, rephrased it or just asked it again, to the point of being ridiculous. Mandela told him many times that he objected to the tactic of asking the same question over and over in the hope that the witness would 'trip up'. The judge never rebuked Maritz, and instead always ordered Mandela to answer the question. I hope I will never be cross-examined by Maritz, because I am very sure that I will also tell him, like Mandela did, to 'go throw himself in a pool'.

This is how it went:

TRENGOVE: 'May it please the court, I call the President.'

JUDGE DE VILLIERS: 'Mr President, you may sit down.'

MANDELA: 'Thank you, judge. If I get tired, then I will take advantage of your kind offer.'

TRENGOVE: 'Mr President, you have already made affidavits in this matter on the appointment of the Browde Commission of Inquiry. SARFU, however, disputes the truth of your affidavits. At its request this court has ordered you to appear in person today to be examined and cross-examined on the following questions that I wish to put to you. Firstly, who made the decision to appoint the commission?'

MANDELA: 'I did.'

TRENGOVE: 'Secondly, did you personally consider the matter before you made the decision?'

MANDELA: 'I did.'

TRENGOVE: 'Thirdly, did you merely rubber-stamp a decision

made by the minister to appoint the commission?'

MANDELA: 'I made the decision alone. If I made that decision alone, there is no portion of rubber-stamping at all.'

TRENGOVE: 'Fourthly, Mr President, did you say to the minister in your meeting with him on Tuesday, 5 August last year, and I quote: "A commission is yours if in your best judgement it is opportune"?'

MANDELA: 'I never did.'

TRENGOVE: 'Thank you, my lord.'

DE VILLIERS: 'Thank you, Mr Trengove. Mr Maritz?'

MARITZ: 'Mr President, unfortunately this matter has come to a situation where it is certainly my unpleasant task of putting questions to you, but the occasion will not obviously detract me from doing what I have to do and I'm sure as a lawyer you will appreciate that. The rugby saga in South Africa, Mr President, has, as the rest of South African society, a history of racial divide. Not so?'

MANDELA: 'That is a matter of common knowledge.'

MARITZ: 'Now I think it is important because it has a bearing on the question to what extent you actually considered the matter to have some regard to the role of players in bringing about unification in rugby.'

MANDELA: 'I have the highest regard for all those who contributed towards making this sport not just the question of apartheid on the sports field, but turning it into a national asset in which all population groups support it. I have in mind an organisation like SARU, which was one of the first to drop the racial tag of coloured … They dropped that tag and became the South African Rugby Union and they campaigned throughout this country, convincing rugby players, rugby supporters that the time has come in the history of our country where we should have one unified sport. Then there are people like Dr Danie Craven whom I saw immediately after my release from jail, accompanied by Minister Steve Tshwete. We had a discussion with him in his house in Stellenbosch and we put forward this idea to him. At first he was not so co-operative, but, my lord, because it is so easy to convince an intelligent man to change his views, it is only the most stupid that you can never persuade to change his views. We were able to agree with the late Dr Craven that he must now commit himself to non-racialism in sport. He did that very well. There are others like Morné du Plessis, like Edward Griffiths, and like François Pienaar, who led our team so brilliantly during the world rugby tournament in 1995. There is also Mr Steve Tshwete. As I have said, he did monumental work. Then there is Dr Luyt. Dr Luyt, we were collaborators, we were partners. It was in the course of our trying to normalise rugby as a national sport that I came to earn high regard for him. I still have that high regard for him. There are of course very serious allegations which have been made, but my approach to him is determined by my experience when I worked closely with him, and I will not give credence to the allegations that are being made. I hope that – subject to what the judge will decide in this case – I hope that commission will have the opportunity to sit down, to probe these allegations, and if that commission decides that there is no substance in these allegations, I will be one of the happiest men in this country because that will then free rugby from the paralysing atmosphere, environment, in which it has been plunged today. I will be very happy. But at the same time, judge, if that commission decides that there is substance to the allegations, then I cannot allow personal relationships, however strong they are, to override the national interest. Those who are found to be responsible for doing things which have put rugby in disrepute, if those allegations are substantiated, they must pay the price. But until then, all the officials with whom I have worked, I have the highest regard for them.'

MARITZ: 'Mr President, you mentioned a couple of people, but you have also mentioned Dr Luyt and I understand that he was instrumental, as were others, including Minister Steve Tshwete, in the unification process in South African rugby.'

MANDELA: 'That is true. I have already said that.'

MARITZ: 'And he together with Minister Steve Tshwete and others played a pivotal role in such unification process.'

MANDELA: 'That is correct.'

MARITZ: 'I understand that already as long ago as 1988 Dr Luyt met with ANC delegates both in London as well as Frankfurt and later in Harare in an endeavour to breach this racial divide and achieve unification. Are you aware of that?'

MANDELA: 'I would not be sure about the years, but I am aware that he did play that role – which at that time could be played only by people who are independent, fearless and committed to the principle of non-racialism.'

MARITZ: 'I am told that at that time these discussions took place completely contrary to the then government policy.'

MANDELA: 'That is correct.'

MARITZ: 'And much to the chagrin of the then government.'

MANDELA: 'That is true.'

MARITZ: 'Ultimately some common ground was achieved as a result of these efforts on both sides, which then led to a negotiating committee of which Dr Luyt was the chief negotiator on the part of the then South African Rugby Board – one of the two rugby bodies. Are you aware of that?'

MANDELA: 'I would not have put it as high as all that, because, as I have already said, the question of promoting non-racial rugby and of turning it into a national asset, which we now all support, is the result of a collective effort as I have pointed out, and in that context Dr Luyt has played a critical role.'

Maritz then talked about the rugby unification process and started reading out sections of the SARFU constitution, pausing after every sentence for Mandela to say 'that is correct.' But after a while Mandela became impatient and said: 'I can say, to shorten the cross-examination, as far as I am concerned, I have gone through that constitution and it cannot be faulted on the question of non-racialism. It is absolutely committed. It is one of the best constitutions we have.'

MARITZ: 'Thank you, Mr President. That, I think, does curtail it somewhat now. You would also have noticed from going through that constitution that it is capable of a self-regulating process in the sense that it makes provision for regular general elections.'

MANDELA: 'That is correct. But I hope that question does not suggest that the government may not under certain circumstances set up a machinery in order to probe problems that have arisen. With that qualification I accept that.'

MARITZ: 'In other words, Mr President, if it is capable of self-regulation, it would mean that if anybody interested in rugby, if any of the members of SARFU is not satisfied with what is taking place in the management or the administration, it could resort through the ordinary democratic process at annual or whatever general elections to ensure that the governing bodies are not re-elected.'

MANDELA: 'That is correct, but subject to the fact that when there are serious allegations that cannot be resolved internally, and where the leadership of the organisation, rightly or wrongly, has lost credibility, even legitimacy, you cannot use that as an answer when throughout the country there are serious allegations such as have arisen. But I want to make it clear that I am not saying so because I believe that allegations have been proven. I am merely saying that the rugby officials, especially those of SARFU, are not in a position to allay the concern, the public concern in the country, because they are directly involved. In fact one of the criticisms is that there is no transparency and there is authoritarian rule by one individual who is feared by all the other officials. Whether that is true or not will only become clear if and when these allegations are probed.'

MARITZ: 'The principle that I am putting to you, Mr President, is that ...'

MANDELA: 'Can you please raise your voice?'

MARITZ: 'I apologise. The principle that I am putting to you is that in terms of its constitution, there is a self-regulating capacity in SARFU.'

MANDELA: 'I have already conceded that, and I hope Mr Maritz will not repeat questions which I have already answered because that can waste a lot of time. I have already conceded that in the context of what I have told the court.'

MARITZ: 'The position further, Mr President, arising from this self-regulating capacity or capability is that people involved in the sport and who belong to SARFU or its constituent unions, they have the ability to change things internally if they are not satisfied with it.'

MANDELA: 'Judge, to declare certain clauses in a constitution, to discuss them in broad terms is one thing, but to be committed to those principles in actual fact is something totally different, and that is the perception that has arisen in this country: that there is a cleavage between theory as expressed in the constitution and the actual practice.'

MARITZ: 'What I have difficulty with, Mr President, is that people not directly involved in the sport, sitting outside the sport, raise a number of concerns, but the people in the know, involved in the sport, taking part in the process of SARFU, they don't seem to be bothered by that.'

MANDELA: 'I do not know if anybody can have the courage to

make that blunt statement in the light of the allegations and the perceptions that exist countrywide. You heard, I am sure, the court may have noticed, that Mluleki George, vice-president of SARFU and also a member of Parliament, said in regard to pay television and the granting of rights to Murdoch [indistinct] He said he did not know about this. He just saw it in the paper and the Natal Rugby Union went to court precisely on the basis they were dissatisfied [with that]. I think it is a blunt statement to say that the players and the unions are not complaining. Let us withhold that judgement until, if the court so decides, this commission goes to work and probes this allegation.'

MARITZ: 'Now the Natal Rugby Union in fact commenced court proceedings as you quite rightly pointed out and they did so successfully. Not so?'

MANDELA: 'I believe so.'

MARITZ: 'Does that not illustrate the very point that there is every capability of self-regulation?'

MANDELA: 'Well, you know my answer. I would appeal to Mr Maritz not to repeat questions I have answered. I say until those allegations, those perceptions, those rumours, those suspicions as to what is going on have been probed, and thoroughly, and a decision made, it is premature to put forward this statement.'

MARITZ: 'The question I put to you, Mr President, is does the Natal court application not illustrate that if there is an aggrieved party, he can resort to court, in other words, utilise the internal mechanisms of the court?'

MANDELA: 'The court was concerned with the issues placed before it. There are more serious allegations I believe before the court than in that hearing, and we cannot avoid the fact it is believed by the public that there is something drastically wrong with the administration, the management, the control, the financial affairs of SARFU. There are even allegations that members of one family are being favoured in regard to sponsorship, contracts, commissions and employment. I do not know whether that is true or not, judge, but it can be established only if there is an independent commission of inquiry.'

MARITZ: 'Mr President, if Mr George felt that the Murdoch contract that had been entered into unauthorised, he could have dealt with the matter internally through annual general meetings or extraordinary general meetings or he could have resorted to court, not so, to have it declared unauthorised?'

MANDELA: 'Judge, I have already answered that question. I have said the leadership of SARFU is under a cloud of suspicion. As far as the public is concerned, they are not competent, they have not got the credibility to probe this question and make a finding which will satisfy the public. There was a great deal of concern on my part when François Pienaar was dropped as captain of the Springboks; the young man who led our team so brilliantly and who made a statement at the end of that match that we are not playing for the spectators here, we are playing for each and every South African. I might add, judge, that one of the first steps I took when I became President of this country was to invite François Pienaar for tea in the Union Buildings. I did so because he was the cornerstone and ground-plan of the victory which put South Africa on the map and opened the doors for South Africa to the entire world. I invited him and I had tea with him. I have been in contact with him and when we went to England, I invited him and his wife to my official residence. I have been hurt by the fact that he was dropped. And I want to say then, judge, that I do not know what the purpose is of pursuing this line, because I admit that the internal structures are there, but the point is that the officials of SARFU are under a cloud of suspicion. They have no credibility in matters of that nature.'

MARITZ: 'Mr President, can I again ask you the question? Perhaps I did not express myself clearly. Do you accept that Mr George that you referred to earlier could have taken SARFU to court if he was not satisfied that the Murdoch contract had been properly authorised?'

MANDELA: 'Judge, I must repeat I have already answered that question. The repetition of one question in different forms must not be permitted ... I have said in regard to the Natal case, the court was concerned with issues that were before the court that day. Some of the rumours, these allegations, my lord ... There are charges of nepotism. They are concrete in that form. But at the same time they are vague, unclear. There is no proven evidence at this point in time, and I think it would be futile to take a matter of that nature to court and that is why we think an independent commission like the Browde Commission is the right body, because questions of policies are going to be involved here. You cannot go to court and say to a court of law I want you to make a decision as far as this policy is concerned.'

MARITZ: 'You mentioned François Pienaar and the fact that you were unhappy when he was dropped. Is it not a fact of life, Mr President, that there are always younger, more able, more talented people who take the place of those who went before them in the sporting fields and sport sides?'

MANDELA: 'Well, the performance that he showed in the tournament did not suggest that he was so old as not to be fit for leading the team. Now if perhaps I was asked now to be captain, then of course SARFU would have all reason to say no, we cannot have you. But this is a young man, judge, who did a wonderful job. I went to see the South African team in Silvermine when they were going to play the very first match against the then reigning champions, the Australians, and I said to François Pienaar and the rest that the team that wins this game will go right through to the end. I was there in almost every match which our team played during that tournament except the Natal match because I was engaged. I wanted them to know that I was there. And I was particularly impressed by the leadership of François Pienaar and I felt that this was not only a young man who had the skill to play rugby, but that in future this is going to be one of the kingmakers in our attempt to unite the nation and to promote reconciliation. That is the reason, judge, why I was shocked when he was dropped. And then the remarks that were made by Markgraaff when he commented, when he was asked as to why his decision was made, were most unfortunate. And that tape, which showed that, insofar as he was concerned, he was a racist, created a very unfortunate impression. That is why I say this was regrettable and it is not just a question of going to court. The fact that the officials of SARFU took that step, it knocked the confidence almost irreparably in SARFU, and I am very happy that [indistinct] has done very well in the matches that he played and I had to phone him and thereafter invited him to my official residence together with Nick Mallett, Arthob Petersen and they thought that I, as President of the country, could say to young people who had done so well: thank you very much on behalf of South Africa.'

MARITZ: 'I want to get clarity on one aspect, Mr President. Are you saying to his lordship that at the time when François Pienaar was dropped, he was still the best player on merit in that position?'

MANDELA: 'I am not saying so. But I say if you take it in context, that decision was unfortunate, especially if you link it with the new coach, Markgraaff. I think that after the release of that tape, when he was relaxed, when he was not bluffing the public, when he was expressing his point of view, a coach to make such a statement and to use language which we are beginning to forget, it created such a stink that even SARFU could not bear to keep him. They dropped him.'

MARITZ: 'What about Kepler Wessels, captain of the Springbok side, was he not also dropped?'

MANDELA: 'Well ...'

MARITZ: 'Cricket side.'

MANDELA: 'I did not consider that, but I thought Kepler Wessels also was a very capable captain, like Clive Rice. Clive Rice and cricket did remarkable work, and Hansie Cronje is also one of my heroes in cricket. He has led our cricket team very well and it has stressed me a great deal when he was criticised when he lost in Pakistan and in Australia because sport is such that you will win today, the following day you lose. That is not how you assess the performance of any team, but when you take a total picture, then there is no doubt that you will produce a wonderful team led by a young man who is skilled, who has got the technique and the capacity of leadership.'

MARITZ: 'While we are talking about people being dropped, was Neil Tovey not dropped as captain of the football side?'

MANDELA: 'Well, some cases, judge, may be quite justified. I do not know, but I knew François Pienaar and that is the reason why there was such a human outcry when he was dropped. I am saying if you put that in the context of what Markgraaff said, you will understand the reason for such shock on the part of the public. There is genuine public concern in regard to what is happening in rugby today. It is a national asset and it is our duty, whoever we are, to ensure that that national asset is protected because it plays a very important role in nation building in this country. I have used all sports for that purpose because sport speaks a language which reaches areas where a president and politicians cannot reach. Therefore anybody who has got the depth of thinking, who has got a vision, will immediately accept the importance of sport ... And I believe that it is not only me, it is not only Minister Tshwete, it is not only Dr Luyt, but right across the border, rugby is regarded as a national asset. And what has been happening is a matter of public concern.'

MARITZ: 'Is it not exactly for that reason that we have selectors ...'

MANDELA: 'A little louder please Mr Maritz.'

MARITZ: 'I apologise, Mr President. Is it not exactly for that reason why each sporting code has its own selectors to decide who the best players are at a particular point in time?'

MANDELA: 'My lord, with due respect, I have already answered that question. Under the present leadership, nothing which they do will have credibility, and those selectors are appointed by the officials of SARFU and I would not like to be repeating the same question when I say, rightly or wrongly, the leadership of SARFU is tainted and I do hope that the court may in due course pass judgment which will allow that commission to do its work and I am prepared to abide by its decision.'

MARITZ: 'Would you agree with me, Mr President, that the World Cup rugby event hosted in South Africa by SARFU was a masterpiece of management, organisation and efficiency?'

MANDELA: 'I have already answered that and I said that victory by the Springboks further opened the doors of the world to South Africa ... a country which was the polecat of the world for more than forty years ... was now welcomed openly by the entire world. That is because not only did we win at the game, but because of good organisation and people like Minister Tshwete, Dr Luyt, who were responsible for that.'

MARITZ: 'We know that there were elections in SARFU towards the end of last year, and, notwithstanding all these allegations and gossip and speculation in the newspapers, Dr Luyt was over-whelmingly re-elected as president.'

MANDELA: 'One of the perceptions, judge, rightly or wrongly, and I do not say so because I believe in these rumours – I want to make that point very clearly: Dr Luyt is somebody I hold in high regard – but a perception is that he is authoritarian, that every official fears him, they tremble. I have been briefed that there are many top officials in SARFU, in the provincial unions, who are thoroughly dissatisfied with Dr Luyt, but they fear that if they stand up, they will immediately be victimised, and they have pointed to people who have been dropped. They say they are not going to take the risk, as some of these unions cannot make money. They rely, I am told, on Dr Luyt, and it is one thing to discuss in boardrooms. As far as the implementation of that policy is concerned, it is a totally different matter. I believe that as far as SARFU is concerned there is a bit of representivity. I believe there are four blacks and four whites, but if you go to the 14 provincial unions, you find a totally different picture: only whites. A game which we have worked hard to transform to make it non-racial. After four years in government, I cannot say with any measure of authority that non-racialism is being applied in sport. There are those perceptions.'

MARITZ: 'One gets the government that the people elect whether it is in national government or whether it is in cricket or whether it is in rugby. That is the democratic process.'

MANDELA: 'No, I conceded. So what about it?'

MARITZ: 'If the people elect someone that has a strong personality, that is their choice.'

MANDELA: 'Why don't you deal with what I have said? I am telling you that the allegation, rightly or wrongly, is that Dr Luyt is a pitiless dictator, and no official, I understand, can stand up to him. You cannot talk about democracy in that sense. We have seen throughout the world, judge, where there are bills of rights. Mangope in Bophuthatswana had a bill of rights, but the suppression, the gross violation of human rights in that bantustan was beyond words. Elections are part of a democratic process, but there are other things that one has to consider. You cannot just pin yourself on elections. I do not think – it is my own personal opinion – I do not think Dr Luyt is a man who has underhand methods ... But it is quite possible. We know that some candidates will bribe voters and promise them money and positions and knowing that this is a man who can [indistinct] if I do not beg him. People who have no backbones and who are frightened of being victimised as others have been will vote. So you must take a broad view. I can say that the message that is conveyed by the founding affidavit of Dr Luyt, it is a message which he does not want us to know ... all that it means is that he has something to hide, because a man who is clean would welcome such a probe. He would say I have nothing to hide, I have nothing to fear, and say please, you are free to look, to probe thoroughly and without restraint. But I believe that the moment the task team wanted to investigate financial affairs, he saw red and said there is going to be no co-operation. That is what I am informed, and therefore just to concentrate on the question that he was elected is meaningless in the light of the experience that we have.'

MARITZ: 'Do you regard Dr Luyt as a good administrator?'

MANDELA: 'Yes.'

MARITZ: 'We have seen some articles in the newspaper that he took over the Transvaal Rugby Union when it had a debt or a loss of some R54 million which he turned around successfully into a huge profit and balance.'

MANDELA: 'Well, that is one of the reasons why I have respect for him: because he has done that. I believe also from the point of view of sponsorship, he raised that sponsorship from R30 million to R85 million and that the world tournament in 1995 was fantastic in the sense that in the Olympic Games they also came out with a loss, but I am informed that in that tournament we made a profit of 28 million pounds sterling. That is a remarkable achievement. That is why he has earned my respect. He is a good organiser. But it does not answer the question, the suspicion that there is no transparency in SARFU and that there are

a lot of irregularities, no development programme, no representivity, there is nepotism. Those are allegations that are there
and I would expect a man who is claimed to have said I have
nothing to hide not to say by word of mouth, because it is quite
possible to say things you do not mean. We must combine that
theory with practice and that is what Dr Luyt has refused to do.'

MARITZ: 'Do you regard this as a form of government interference
into sport or not?'

MANDELA: 'Oh no. It is not. I am the President of this country. I
was the President of the ANC. Judge, I do not want to beat my
own chest, but I took the initiative and put my future on the
line by going around the country, mobilising [indistinct], following the example of SARU, NOCSA, the National Sports
Council and saying to our people: your attitude was correct
when you opposed the sportsmen and women in this country
because they were part and parcel of the most brutal system of
racial oppression that has taken place in this country. You are
quite right. But we are changing now and we would like you
to change your attitude and support this organisation. Judge,
you do not know that in Natal in Durban I addressed a meeting. Some of the people say it was about 50 000 people when
I said ... to them, after making all these elaborating relations, I
said: do you agree with me? I think not more than ten said yes.
I asked again. I say, I appeal to you this is critical for the history of our country. We must win the section of our community which regards rugby as a matter of sport. Let us win them
because they are critical to the building of national unity. Will
you agree with me, will those that agree with me, stand. I do
not think that we had more than 1 000 who stood up. So it was
a very discouraging assignment, but I did so successfully, and
the leadership of François Pienaar helped to cement that work.
But even more, you will recall that the National Sports Council
had decided that the Springbok emblem should be dropped

and that we should only have the Protea. I knew what the community that is associated, rightly or wrongly, with rugby, would think. This would introduce a state of insecurity, because throughout the world when there is a transformation, the minorities have concern. I went to Eersterust. I did not consult even my own organisation – not even the Minister of Sport, because I know when he opposes something, it is like asking Table Mountain to be moved. So I did not consult him. I did not consult with the deputy president, Thabo Mbeki. I went to Eersterust and I said this is a matter which is under the jurisdiction of the National Sports Council. I hope in due course they will agree with what I am going to say, and I said I propose that we should restore the Springbok emblem. Almost every member of my organisation were up in arms. I had to call all leaders of the sporting bodies to tell them why I took this decision. I called almost all the major ones – rugby, soccer, cricket – and I explained to them. It is only then that they were able to agree with me. Again I put my whole future on the line. You cannot say now after we have done that work … It is not only SARFU officials, it is the unions, it is the players, it is the spectators that take interest in this game. You cannot boast that this is a private organisation, this is an autonomous private organisation where the government should not get involved. The decision by the Minister of Sport to set up a task group to discuss the matter informally was a correct one. And when he came to me on 5 August … and briefed me on what had happened, I was still not convinced, but I understood his problem and I asked him for a motivation. When I started that motivation and when I discussed the matter with my own advisors – the director-general, Prof. Jakes Gerwel, Prof. Fink Haysom, my legal advisor – we decided that the minister had made a case for the appointment of a commission and I, and I alone, supported that commission. You cannot plead that rugby is an autonomous private organisation when members of the government have taken interest in promoting that game.'

MARITZ: 'The then Prime Minister John Vorster said that the government had an interest in sport and we know that there was serious intervention by government in sport in those days. Not so, Mr President?'

MANDELA: 'That is true.'

MARITZ: 'Now what is the difference between this type of intervention when you are not happy with what happens in SARFU by appointing a commission and the intervention that we had in those days?'

MANDELA: 'Well, I would have hoped that Mr Maritz would know the difference. You had on the one hand a minority government representing the community of less than 14% with a most cruel and insensitive policy which permitted gross violation of human rights. You have another government which is committed to democratic values, which has had a record of over four years of trying to mobilise the entire country under the slogan "*laat ons die verlede vergeet*". Let us concern ourselves with the present and the future. That government believes in transparency. Whatever problems we have in certain sections of the government, this government is committed to honesty and transparency, and when we find a situation where a game which is a national asset is under a cloud of suspicion, the government will be neglecting its duty if it did not take steps to have those allegations thoroughly proved by an independent commission.'

Maritz then questioned Mandela on the press statement Director-General Mthobi Tymazashe issued on 7 August 1997 on Tshwete's approach to Mandela for a commission to be appointed.

MARITZ: 'Looking at paragraph 3 thereof, Mr President, it reads: "The President happily responded as follows: A commission is yours if in your best judgement it is opportune."'

MANDELA: 'That is incorrect. What you are dealing with here is hearsay. It is hearsay which is complicated. It is not just hearsay from one individual. This was a report by SAPA. It was published in a number of newspapers. Those newspapers said this is what Minister Steve Tshwete said of what he is told by the secretary-general was said by me, by the President. That is the type of hearsay that we are dealing with here. I attach no value at all to it except that I did not say this and the director-general who was giving evidence here has testified under oath as to the reason why he made the statement. Also Minister Tshwete has repudiated this statement … Why should they not believe a minister of state when he said that the President has never said so? What remains of this document?'

MARITZ: 'Mr President, that is the very function of this court: to determine what the truth is, and that is the function of me asking you these questions, and as you stated under oath, it is a matter of public concern that the truth be found. Not so?'

MANDELA: 'Judge, I do not blame Advocate Maritz for asking these questions to me. He is perfectly entitled to do this and he must do his duty to the best of his ability. But I'm saying this is such a useless document. Why must he attach value to it when a minister of state, a director-general has repudiated it? I also, in my affidavit, have repudiated the fact that I said anything of the sort and the whole context of our case is that we and we alone signed the instrument setting up the commission. This was done on 22 September, long after the meeting of 5 August.'

MARITZ: 'Are you saying, Mr President, that we should believe the director-general?'

MANDELA: 'It is not only the director-general now. It is Minister Tshwete, who is very much concerned about sports, who is a

184

friend of Dr Luyt. It is also the President of this country who has made a statement under oath. Let me say, judge, I never imagined that Dr Luyt would be so insensitive, so disrespectful, so ungrateful as to say of the President of this country that when I gave my affidavit and signed it under oath, I was telling lies. I was not being honest, that is what he says. I never imagined he would do a thing like that. There must be some reason why he is resisting an investigation to find out what is going on in SARFU. People who know say he was all right: he was prepared to work with the task team when they limited their investigation to SARFU. But once they decided to probe the financial affairs of the organisation, Dr Luyt saw red. It was like a red cloth in front of a bull, and I think Dr Luyt in his founding affidavit is giving a message that he doesn't want us to know. He is saying: I have something to hide. I might just add, just to round up this matter, that in December last year, he telephoned me to say he wanted to see me and because of my respect for him, notwithstanding the tight programme I have, I said he should come immediately. His request was that I should withdraw this commission. I spoke to him earnestly as my collaborator. I said: Louis, do not ask for that, because the message you will be sending, you will be saying I have something to fear; I do not want transparency about the affairs of SARFU. Don't do that. He has done that notwithstanding the advice I gave to him. The Dr Luyt projected in that founding affidavit is somebody totally different from the one I knew. I just wondered to myself: What has gone wrong with Dr Luyt? What has he done to the affairs of SARFU? Only if he has got something which is irregular, which puts him on a lower moral ladder, could he challenge, could he refuse that there should be a probe. Because if he knows that he has done nothing wrong, he would welcome a commission so that we can rescue rugby from this unhealthy environment.'

After a break in the court proceedings, Maritz continued his cross-examination on the press statement.

> MARITZ: 'Paragraph 3 of the press statement, do you agree with me that what is stated there, if true, would amount to the President having given the minister carte blanche?'
>
> MANDELA: 'Judge, Dr Luyt himself, if we are going to consider his action, he does not believe in this. If he believed that I have abdicated my authority to Minister Tshwete, he would not have come to me in December and asked me to withdraw the commission. He would go to Minister Tshwete, the man to whom I have abdicated my constitutional rights and the fact that he came to me is an illustration that he does not believe in what is written here.'
>
> MARITZ: 'I will repeat the question Mr President.'
>
> MANDELA: 'Just repeat that please.'
>
> MARITZ: 'The question that I put to you was that paragraph 3 of the press statement, if true, would amount thereto that you had given the minister carte blanche.'
>
> MANDELA: 'Well, I have answered that question. I say your client himself, by his action, does not believe in this. Why come to a person who has abdicated his responsibility, who merely rubber-stamped what the Minister of Sport and Recreation had asked me about? He would have gone to him. There is a conflict between what appears here – which he believes, pure hearsay, not said by Minister Tshwete himself – and his action coming to me, at his own request ... I have fully answered the question. I will not answer it again. I am not going to be answering these repetitive questions.'
>
> MARITZ: 'Mr President, with great respect, I do not think that you have answered the question and I am going to ask you again. Paragraph 3 of the press statement, if true ...'
>
> MANDELA: 'It is totally untrue.'

MARITZ: 'Yes. If it were true, would it amount thereto that you had given the minister carte blanche?'

MANDELA: 'I am not prepared to speculate. I have given my answer and I am not prepared to reply again to Mr Maritz on this question.'

MARITZ: 'Mr President, this document that we are looking at now is an official document, not so?'

MANDELA: 'I have answered that question. I am not prepared, judge, to be answering the same question. I say the document, this statement, is false. It has been repudiated by the director-general. It has been repudiated by Minister Tshwete. It has been repudiated by myself, and Dr Luyt's conduct has repudiated this document. I am not going to worry. I will not answer any further questions on that point.'

MARITZ: 'This document was intended for publication as a press statement by the Ministry. Is that correct?'

MANDELA: 'I am not answering that question at all.'

MARITZ: 'This document was in fact widely published in the media, both on the television as well as in all the national newspapers.'

MANDELA: 'Mr Maritz if you want to continue talking like a gramophone record, you can do so. I am not going to answer that question. I have answered it. Unless the court says I should answer, I will not do so. I do not want to say you are abusing your right to cross-examine. I say whatever has been done with this document, no matter by whom, it is untrue that statement.'

Maritz then reminded Mandela that he said in his affidavit that he was 'an avid newspaper reader, radio listener and television viewer'.

MARITZ: 'Now it is because of that statement that I am asking you whether you were aware of the newspaper reports on 8 August dealing with this press statement.'

MANDELA: 'I have answered your question, judge, but I want to point out that the misconception on the part of Mr Maritz as to think that the single duty that I have is about this case … judge, is perhaps one of the most popular in the history of this country. It is unbelievable the number of correspondence that we receive a day. I asked my director-general to check the information I had been given in the past but he has not given me that information. I asked him to check it because I did want to explain this point to the judge. I am not concerned only with the problems of SARFU, I am concerned with the problems of the country and with some problems of the world. And this is only a part of my duties. I go to the office, judge, with an empty briefcase. At the end of the day when I have to go back I can hardly close that briefcase because of the number of documentation given to me which I have to read and I have never noticed this article either in the print media or in television.'

MARITZ: 'Now if you had seen it Mr President, and if you had read that particular quote in terms of which you had given the minister carte blanche, would that have upset you?'

MANDELA: 'Oh yes, because for a director-general to make a statement of this nature, and have it published notwithstanding this explanation that he made, is totally unacceptable and I condemn it in the strongest terms.'

MARITZ: 'Is that something that has ever happened before in your presidency, that directors-general issue false press statements falsely quoting you?'

MANDELA: 'I do not know if this has ever happened. It may have happened but what concerns me is that this particular statement, to attribute a statement like this to me is totally unacceptable.'

MARITZ: 'The difficulty, Mr President, is that the ordinary people like SARFU, and the ordinary members of the public, they are dependent on what they read in the newspapers.'

MANDELA: 'Well it is their own fault because newspaper reports are frequently not true, and, with respect, I wanted to quote an example, judge. I saw in *Rapport* of last Sunday a disclaimer by Dr Luyt when he was accused, and I say this with respect, when he was accused of inviting the presiding judge in this case to a match in Ellis Park. He had to come out to say: no it was not the presiding judge, it was Izak de Villiers, the former editor of *Rapport.* Mr Maritz himself, I read in the paper – I do not know whether it was yesterday or the day before yesterday – he expressed his indignation about this false report. Why should this be something unique when the press makes, very frequently, false reports?'

MARITZ: 'But in this particular case, for a change maybe, the press got it right. They made no mistake. They reported accurately on the press statement.'

MANDELA: 'You are asking me for an opinion because a release by the director-general contained a false statement. I say however accurate they may have been, in the light of what the director-general himself said in his affidavit, in the light of what the minister said in his affidavit, in the light of what I have said as the President of the country, any other person would accept. To question the statement made by the President of the country made under oath is an experience that is new. I do not know, and I say this again with respect, I do not know if under the previous order a thing of this nature would have happened.'

The members of the public sitting in the courtroom agreed so boisterously with this comment, that Mandela as well as De Villiers asked them to behave.

On the second day, Mandela repeatedly objected to Maritz's attitude. 'I do not expect Mr Maritz not to put questions on behalf of his client, but his whole way of cross-examination is based on the fact that I am not telling the court the truth. It is his duty to do so but it is based on that understanding – a person who doubts that the statement by the President in an affidavit is true – that the President is telling lies ... Now that was one thing I was taught never to do.'

Mandela quoted a Dr Jensen, who lectured him at Fort Hare University sixty years before: 'There is common agreement right down history that readiness to dismiss people as liars is actually a reflection of the character of the man who makes the accusation.' Maritz could see it as his duty to call him a liar, Mandela said, 'but he must know that in my mind it is a reflection of his own character. That is the basis of this lengthy and boring cross-examination.'

A little while later, when Maritz had rephrased the same question for the umpteenth time, Mandela responded angrily: 'I do now want to keep on reminding the court that I have already answered this question. Mr Maritz's way of cross-examination is one of distrust and he tries to catch a witness by repeating the same question in different forms. I am not going to play ball. You play that game alone.' A few minutes later Maritz did it again, and Mandela lamented the 'tragic case of Advocate Maritz', suggesting that 'nothing short of him being sent to a refresher course' was needed. Judge De Villiers intervened: 'Mr Mandela, you must bear with the court and you must bear with the cross-examiner.' Not ten minutes later it happened again. Mandela reacted: 'I am saying he is not going to get my co-operation in asking the same question in different forms. It is a cheap trick to, what do you call it, to trip up a witness. When I was as young as himself I used that also as a lawyer, but now I am more mature. I am going to be eighty in a few months time.'

The court case ended on 6 April 1998 and the court reserved its judgment.

11

LOUIS GOES – ALMOST

Rugby paid me back precisely what I did not deserve. The divi-
dend is too negative for me to accept. I will not rest. No man is
my master. I do not bend my knee for anybody other than my
God.

– Louis Luyt, May 1998

Challenging Nelson Mandela and forcing him into the witness box
of a civil court was a huge mistake – probably the biggest mistake
Luyt ever made. This was one lion he shouldn't have tickled. Luyt
and his legal team should have accepted the affidavits Mandela
made before the case started.

The African National Congress – a movement supported by close
on two-thirds of the South African population – viewed the treatment of their leader by a white Afrikaner man from the 'old order'
as an insult to all black people and a sign of disrespect towards
the new democracy they had fought so hard to establish. It was
probably also the view of a large number of South Africans who
did not support the ANC. Mandela was not only the President of
South Africa; he was the man who had been jailed by apartheid
governments for twenty-seven years and had emerged without a

trace of bitterness towards whites; he was the symbol of reconc-iliation and hope; he was as close as one can get to an international saint.

Mandela had just finished his testimony in the Pretoria High Court when the ANC-dominated National Sports Council (NSC), the high-est sporting body in South Africa, issued their ultimatum: Luyt and the entire executive of the South African Rugby Football Union must resign, or face an international ban on Springbok rugby. The Council said they would lobby all international rugby unions to isolate SARFU, and ask the Department of Home Affairs to restrict the trav-el movements of rugby players and administrators. There would be no more rugby tests and no Super 12 competition. Ireland and Wales were scheduled to tour South Africa at the end of April, and England was due in the country in July.

The president of the NSC was none other than the former execu-tive vice-president of SARFU who had been stripped of his position five months earlier, on 4 November 1997 – Mluleki George.

Gideon Sam, who chaired the marathon Sports Council meeting where the ultimatum was decided on, said afterwards: 'We will tell our friends in those countries that we are in the process of sorting out one of our members, SARFU, who is not in good standing. We would request them to postpone their coming to South Africa.'

An equally serious threat came from M-Net, the television company that held all the broadcast rights in South Africa for the Super 12 matches and the Tri-Nations competition with Australia and New Zealand. The head of M-Net Supersport, Russel Macmillan, told Luyt in early April to resign with his executive, or face a complete tele-vision blackout of rugby matches in South Africa.

But the biggest surprise was the position of the black members of SARFU's executive: senior vice-president and lawyer Silas Nkanunu, Paarl schoolteacher Arthob Pietersen, Peninsula Technikon registrar Tobie Titus, and Boland Rugby Union president Jackie Abrahams. They had deplored the appearance of Nelson Mandela in court, but opposed the call for Luyt to resign. 'We run rugby as a collective body,' Nkanunu told newspapers on 9 April. 'Luyt is not the problem. If there are problems in rugby, then we must tackle them. Whether Luyt should go or not, rests with the people who voted him into office.'

There was shock and consternation when Judge William de Villiers announced on 17 April 1998 that he had decided to set aside President Nelson Mandela's decision to appoint a commission of inquiry into South African rugby. It was the first time since the fully democratic election in 1994 that a High Court judge had overruled the President of the country. De Villiers only gave the reasons for his decision four months later.

Luyt was triumphant, and reminded some of his associates that he had told them a year before that he was going to 'hammer Mandela out of sight'.

Most South Africans were extremely angry at what was perceived by many to be Luyt's 'victory' over Mandela. Judge De Villiers was maligned in ANC statements, by columnists and commentators, in letters to newspapers and by callers to talk radio stations as an 'apartheid judge'.

Luyt may have won the legal battle, but the whole case was a total public relations disaster for him and for SARFU, and not only among black South Africans. The storm of protest suddenly became a hurricane.

SARFU's crisis meeting eventually took place on 7 May 1998. By the end of it, the face of South African rugby had changed forever. SARFU not only told Luyt to resign, they decided to apologise to Mandela and to agree to a commission of inquiry. SARFU described the events in a statement to the media:

The South African Rugby Football Union extraordinary general meeting decided that SARFU reject the ultimatum of the National

Sports Council (NSC) that its entire executive committee resign and be replaced by an interim management committee appointed by the NSC.

There was agreement amongst council members that the executive committee was a democratically elected body and as such could only be removed from office by the members of SARFU.

There was a general sentiment that rugby matters be resolved by those involved in the sport and that the current administrators at all levels were more than capable of running the game.

It was therefore agreed that SARFU would continue with a process of consultation and negotiation with the NSC. SARFU decided that it is, in principle, in favour that the matters of SARFU be investigated by an independent commission, the composition and terms of reference of such a commission to be negotiated by SARFU, the NSC and the government.

The SARFU delegation will be headed by Mr Ronnie Masson and will include Mr Hennie Erasmus, Mr Keith Parkinson and Mr Rian Oberholzer.

The issue of President Mandela's court appearance was also discussed and the following decision was taken. Insofar as SARFU had any part in Judge De Villiers' ordering the State President to give evidence and be cross-examined, it wishes to express its regret and apologises therefore.

It must be noted however that the following distanced themselves from the decision: Dr Louis Luyt; North West; Northern Free State; and Golden Lions.

Dr Luyt was requested by the following provinces and Executive Members to tender his voluntary resignation as President of SARFU: Western Province; Eastern Province; Griquas; Natal; Border; Boland; South Western Districts; and Messrs Masson, Heunis, Titus, Nkanunu, Verster, Petersen, Abrahams and Smith.

Dr Luyt refused this request.

Further, the following executive committee members tendered their resignations: Mr Silas Nkanunu, Mr Tobie Titus, Mr Jackie Abrahams, and Mr Arthob Petersen.

It was a stab right into Louis Luyt's heart. Four of the smaller unions that had been his loyal servants for years and three bigger unions had abandoned him. The four men who quit in protest when he refused to resign were the black executive members who less than a month earlier had declared their unqualified support for Luyt.

But what must have hurt him most was that his protégé and son-in-law, the man he had called to come forward at the World Cup dinner, Rian Oberholzer, had also turned against him. Luyt promptly banned Oberholzer and his wife, Luyt's daughter Corlia, from the Luyt family home.

A few hours after the SARFU meeting ended, the National Sports Council issued a statement quoting its CEO, Mvuzo Mbebe, saying: 'We were most concerned to learn that Dr Luyt has refused to accept the outcome of the meeting. He had explicitly asked the NSC to extend their deadline for the implementation of the NSC resolutions in order to take guidance from his Council. Now that the Council has provided its decisions, he has chosen to ignore it. The NSC has called for its support groups to remain calm and not take action before it has provided them with a guideline for the action to take. We especially ask them not to disrupt the matches this weekend by the Western Stormers and the Coastal Sharks.

'We remain committed to the sanction measures we outlined at our recent council meeting, which include amongst others the isolation of the South African Rugby Football Union. We will continue to campaign for this to happen. An executive meeting of the NSC will be called tomorrow to decide how these resolutions will be implemented. We will not alter our call for the resignation of the full executive of SARFU. SARFU has allegedly proposed sending a delegation to negotiate with us. The NSC will not undertake any discussions with this body given that the only four black members of that executive have resigned.'

The Minister of Sport, Steve Tshwete, said in a statement issued by his office that the developments strengthened the government's resolve to have the affairs of South African rugby investigated by a judicial commission of inquiry. He said it was time for Luyt to go: 'Any self-respecting person would read the sentiments of eight out of fourteen of the affiliated provinces to mean that he has outlived his usefulness and should accordingly do the honourable thing.'

'Outlived his usefulness' was the correct term for Tshwete to use, for he was the one who exactly four years earlier had pleaded with Luyt not to quit his SARFU position.

South African rugby's main sponsor, Vodacom, welcomed the SARFU decisions. 'It is encouraging that through their democratic vote, South African rugby administrators have effectively sought to initiate the process of putting their house in order. In particular we welcome their apology to President Mandela, as well as their call for an Independent Commission of Inquiry into the affairs of SARFU,' Vodacom CEO Alan Knott-Craig said. 'The overwhelming call by rugby administrators for Dr Luyt to resign his position is a clear message that his reign in rugby has come to an end. We join both the administrators of rugby and the vast number of interested parties in calling upon Dr Luyt "to do the right thing" in order that the continuing damage to the name of rugby in South Africa ceases and that rugby sportsmen and rugby lovers might get on with the game of rugby.'

It was deeply ironic that it was the sponsors of rugby, among them Vodacom and M-Net Supersport, who played such an important role in Luyt's demise, seeing that it was Luyt who pioneered the sponsorship of rugby.

South Africa's largest trade union federation, the Congress of South African Trade Unions (Cosatu), threatened 'rolling mass action' to force SARFU to obey the NSC demands. Cosatu said that if the NSC decided to go ahead with its threat to isolate SARFU, it would picket international matches and urge its international allies to take similar action when South African teams played abroad. Cosatu's then general secretary, Sam Shilowa, called for the reinstatement of the Browde Commission of Inquiry and the resignation of Judge William de Villiers.

Not even the mighty Louis Luyt could withstand this pressure. He also knew that the rugby unions were organising a special SARFU meeting where he would be kicked out following SARFU's constitutional stipulations.

Three days after the SARFU crisis meeting, on 10 May 1998, Luyt capitulated and handed in his resignation as SARFU president.

But Luyt did not go with a whimper. 'Spineless white people. I can put it no other way,' he said in an angry interview with the Bloemfontein newspaper *Die Volksblad* on 13 May. 'There is no marrow left in their bones. The white person no longer believes that he can protect that which is precious to him.

'I am not a racist. Each nation has something it would like to preserve. What do we still want to protect? Nothing? That is when people turn against you when they should stand up. That is the worst of all.

'Rugby is not Louis Luyt's be all and end all. I was initially dragged into rugby against my will when Transvaal were in financial difficulties. It was a challenge to lead them out of it. Now I only think day to day and not long term.

'I do believe by far the majority of South African rugby players and supporters support me. I think they will be bitterly disappointed if I do not remain involved in a watchdog capacity. But nothing is over. I am a life member of the Golden Lions.

Luyt was particularly livid about the white rugby officials who had, after such a long time of supporting him, now turned against him. 'I am not bitter, but I really did think that there were more people with backbone. But their positions were too important for them.

There was pressure from the large sponsors. Therefore they were with me the one moment and against me the next.'

Luyt was clearly a bitter man, despite his denial. 'Rugby paid me back precisely what I did not deserve,' he said. 'The dividend is too negative for me to accept. I will not rest. No man is my master. I do not bend my knee for anybody other than my God.'

In a statement after Luyt's resignation, Steve Tshwete called it the end of one of the 'saddest chapters in the history of rugby': 'Louis Luyt's departure from the centre stage of South African rugby has ushered in a breath of fresh air for many rugby-loving people here at home and abroad. His autocratic behaviour and outright arrogance as he presided over the fortunes of one of the country's most treasured assets was a painful embarrassment for rugby in particular and sport in general.

'He shall be remembered more by the consistent manner in which he resisted all efforts to take rugby across the threshold into the new era and the way in which he alienated this sport from the majority of our people. Under his autocratic leadership rugby deteriorated to a point where it had become a divisive instrument in the hands of a man who "will not bow to any man".'

On 21 May a SARFU delegation met with President Mandela to apologise officially for dragging him into court. A week later, Silas Nkanunu became the first black president of the South African Rugby Football Union. Rian Oberholzer, no longer on speaking terms with his father-in-law, not only stayed on as SARFU's CEO, but was allocated extended powers. The head of one of rugby's biggest sponsors, Russel Macmillan of M-Net Supersport, explained the new regime: 'The role of the CEO will be expanded and the role of the president will become mainly an honorary title. It is vital to ensure the president can never again have the power to force unions to toe the line against the wishes of the majority. The CEO will be the decision-maker, answerable to a board of executives.'

Luyt was out of SARFU, but the drama around his court case against the Mandela government was far from over. The anger at De Villiers reached new heights with the release of his detailed judgment on 7 August 1998. It now became clear why De Villiers had waited four months to give his reasons: his full judgment was 1 159 pages long. In his explanation for the delay, De Villiers said the judgment was a 'Herculean task'. He clearly knew his decision would be taken on appeal, and made sure that he explained every decision and comment in the finest detail. He analysed every meeting, every document and every bit of oral evidence brought before him.

De Villiers not only called the Minister of Sport, Steve Tshwete, and his director-general, Mthobi Tyamzashe, 'liars', he cast serious aspersions on the integrity and credibility of President Nelson Mandela. The insulting language used in public forums against De Villiers became so vitriolic that Judge President Frikkie Eloff warned publicly that contempt of court charges could be brought.

De Villiers stated in his judgment that 'to my mind, the evidence of the President is not credible. That may be due to lack of veracity, or unreliability, or a combination of these factors.' He also said: 'The President's performance on the witness stand was less than satisfactory. His overall demeanour is, to my mind, subject to material criticism. The court is conscious of the fact that the President is no longer a young man, that he has suffered much and that it must have been a particularly traumatic and humiliating experience to have been compelled to testify under the circumstances where he perceived his veracity to be doubted.'

Nevertheless, the judge said, the President 'flatly refused to answer a number of questions', and 'to some extent the court was used as a podium for political rhetoric'. De Villiers also criticised Mandela for 'suggesting to the court whom of the witnesses should be believed', for 'querying the rulings of the court' and for being 'argumentative'. He called some of his testimony 'far-fetched' and accused him of unleashing 'unbridled insults at the cross-examiner'.

Of Tshwete the judge said that he had lied in court, demonstrating 'evasiveness, hedging, lack of candour and inconsistency'. He said Tshwete's evidence sometimes 'bordered on the ludicrous' and was 'farcical'.

In contrast, Judge De Villiers found Louis Luyt and Rian Oberholzer 'truthful and satisfactory witnesses in all material respects' who 'made a favourable impression', whose demeanour was 'that of truthful and honest witnesses' and whose evidence the court had 'no hesitation in accepting as being truthful and honest'.

The ANC said in a statement that the judge had overstepped 'morally acceptable limits of commentary expected from the bench'.

Judge De Villiers found that by not telling the President that the government had reneged on its agreement to supply them with all allegations, Tshwete had wrongly informed Mandela about why SARFU had refused to co-operate. This meant that Mandela based his decision to appoint a commission on inaccurate information. This amounted to an improper exercise of discretion.

The notorious press statement by Mthobi Tyamzashe also played an important role in the judge's decision – the one where Tyamzashe stated that Mandela had told Tshwete after he was asked to appoint a commission that 'a commission is yours if, in your best judgement, it is opportune'. According to the judge, who did not accept any of the three men's versions of how the statement came about, this meant that Mandela had abdicated his responsibility. Tyamzashe, the judge said, had not been truthful when he said he had lied in the statement, because he knew if he didn't the government's case would be blown. The judge found that the President merely dressed up the minister's decision to appoint a commission as his own.

The judge also found that Mandela had violated SARFU's right to procedural fairness under common law and the Constitution. He ought to have afforded SARFU a hearing before he appointed a commission.

But this was not the end of the story. The government appealed to the Constitutional Court. Wim Trengove not only contested all De Villiers's findings, he set out to prove that the judge was motivated by bias in his handling of the case and in his findings, which were consistently wrong and always in favour of Luyt.

But Luyt also launched an accusation of bias. Just as the appeal case started, his legal counsel applied for the recusal of five of the Constitutional Court judges. They were likely to be prejudiced against Luyt because of their links to the ANC, he said. The judges were the President of the Court, Arthur Chaskalson, and judges Albie Sachs, Zac Yacoob, Pius Langa and Johann Kriegler. The objection against Kriegler was later dropped.

When the judges refused to recuse themselves, Luyt walked out and withdrew from the case, saying he had 'lost all faith in the process and in the court'.

The Constitutional Court judgment of 10 September 1999 was as devastating to Luyt as it was to Judge De Villiers. The judges did not even call De Villiers, as is traditionally done by judges referring to each other, 'the learned judge'. They simply called him 'the judge'.

The Constitutional Court completely exonerated Mandela. The judges said the President may have been bad-tempered, angry and insulting at times, but there was no evidence to suggest that he was not telling the truth. De Villiers was wrong in finding that Mandela's version of events should not be believed.

The court said that while the President should not be regarded as above the law, he should only in highly exceptional circumstances be called to give evidence as a witness in a civil case. This was not the case with the SARFU application.

Louis Luyt had lost in court and had been kicked out of SARFU. But he wasn't out of rugby yet: he was still the president of the Golden Lions Rugby Union.

12

BACK INTO POLITICS

I'm not a little opposition guy. Power is what counts and it is the only language people, black and white, know and understand.

– Louis Luyt, October 1998

After his victory in the Pretoria High Court – popularly seen as a victory over the ANC government – Luyt was loathed by most South Africans, but some regarded him with admiration because he had dared to stand up to Nelson Mandela and his cabinet.

The former CEO of SARFU, Edward Griffiths, told the Australian radio programme *The Sports Factor* in April 1998: 'He [Luyt] has now in many people's eyes become a white man who's standing up to the ANC; who's not being told what to do by the blacks; who's standing up even to Mandela; who's not scared of anyone. I think white people who felt that their power was being given away, and that all their privilege which they had over the years has been lost, have now found somebody who they can perceive as a hero.'

The Conservative Party said in a statement issued on 1 April 1998 that the ANC's problem with Luyt was that he was an Afrikaner. 'It is good that SARFU does not allow itself to be threatened by the

ANC,' the party stated. 'But the problems will not stop here, the onslaught will only get fiercer. For the Afrikaner there is only one solution, and that is to obtain full control over his own sports affairs.'

Luyt was deeply wounded by his unceremonious ousting by SARFU: being the big chief at Ellis Park was simply not enough. He was a national figure, dammit, and if he couldn't be that through rugby, he was going to do it through politics. As Howard Barrell wrote in the *Mail & Guardian* on 12 October 1998: 'Now Luyt evidently needs a new battle, preferably a bigger one. For fighting seems to provide one of the ways he can satisfy his need for outrageously improbable fantasies of power. And how, other than through those fantasies, can he cope with his own and his kind's disempowerment? His guiding maxim appears to be: I fight, therefore I am.'

In August 1998 Luyt told the Johannesburg newspaper *Beeld* that there was a 'strong demand' from people all over the country for him to get actively involved in the political arena. 'I know I have many followers who respect me because I stand up for what I believe in. I think to some extent I am a strong man and a leader.' Luyt said he was 'colour-blind' when it came to politics, but believed South Africa was on the wrong path, especially with the high crime rate, the weak economy and the influx of illegal immigrants. It was time for resistance against the ANC government, he said.

But Luyt had a problem. The party he had helped create in the late 1980s, the Democratic Party, did not want to be associated with him at all. His authoritarian streak, his unpopularity in many sections of the sports community and the negative reaction to the court challenge to Mandela would make him more of a liability than an asset. I suspect the DP leader, Tony Leon, and his lieutenants would also have been slightly nervous about a leadership challenge from such a powerful man. He could not go back to the National Party, even if they had wanted him, which they did not. He wasn't a right-winger by nature either, so the Freedom Front was also not an option.

So what do you do when you are politically ambitious and no political party wants you? You start your own political party, of course. Especially if you have lots and lots of money. And that's what Luyt did: on 1 October 1998 he announced the formation of a new political movement, the Federal Alliance. Leader: Louis Luyt.

Journalist Ryan Cresswell wondered out loud in *The Star* what Luyt's party's logo would look like: 'Could it be crossed rugby boots against a background of green and gold, or will it depict some powerful, enraged animal?'

At first it wasn't meant to be a political party, it was supposed to be an alliance, as the name indicated – an alliance of those parties that opposed the ruling ANC. With the announcement of the new movement came an invitation to all opposition parties to become part of the Luyt alliance: the Democratic Party, the National Party, the Inkatha Freedom Party, the Freedom Front and the United Democratic Movement. But one after the other the parties not only scorned the invitation, but also warned that Luyt was about to fragment the opposition even further. So Luyt became a one-man alliance, and started campaigning for the 1999 general election.

In a wide-ranging interview with *Rapport* on 4 October 1998, Luyt said his court case with Nelson Mandela had played an important role in his decision to go to Parliament. He was inundated with calls from the public to do something about the political situation. 'Perhaps they gained respect for me because I did not allow myself to be overwhelmed by the power of the state and the charisma of Mandela. I have noticed that people need someone to lead from the front and take the pressure, but also to dish it out.'

Luyt said he wasn't getting involved in politics to be in opposition. If the voters wanted him, he would be available to become the President of South Africa. 'I'm not a little opposition guy,' he said. 'Power is what counts and it is the only language people, black and white, know and understand.'

Luyt said he wanted to tell people who said his Federal Alliance was an alliance without partners that 'we are already an alliance in the broad sense, the *gatvol* alliance'. The *'gatvol'* group, those who were just sick and tired of the present circumstances, was becoming the biggest group of voters in the country, and they were going to vote for him, he said.

But if anybody expected Luyt to campaign on a right-wing ticket or a fight for white rights, which he could have done so easily, they were in for yet another Luyt surprise. The Federal Alliance's rather skimpy political manifesto stated that it stood for a free, democratic and non-racial South Africa with a vibrant free-market economy that would benefit all South Africans. In his political speeches, Luyt concentrated on the high crime rate, deteriorating health care and inadequate education, and accused the ANC of not delivering on its promises.

But mostly, the Federal Alliance was built around the personality of Luyt. The party's website plugged him more than the party: 'South Africa got to know Louis Luyt as a successful entrepreneur who had created a business empire, challenging the big monopolies head-on.' And: 'Louis Luyt is a deeply principled man who challenges sacred cows, not for the sake of challenging but out of conviction. Louis Luyt deeply believes in South Africa and the people of South Africa. He also believes in good, solid government. Every South African, regardless of race, religion or gender deserves quality government providing in every need. Louis Luyt believes that good governance is a combination of solid business acumen, dynamic and forceful leadership, administrative skills and above all sound, principled convictions.'

In fact, Luyt went to canvass for political support in the black townships of Soweto and Alexandra. He asked a black journalist, Shalo Mbatha, to take him to one of Soweto's most famous taverns, Wandi's Place. According to Mbatha there was pandemonium when people recognised him and wanted to shake his hand: 'Not exactly the sort of reception one would expect of the man many black South

Africans are said to view as a racist relic of the past,' Mbatha wrote.

Luyt apparently bonded with the locals, telling them about his life. He said he had four hundred families working on his wine farm, and he cared for them better than all the farmers in the area. He paid for their health care and contributed towards their pension schemes, which was why not one worker had ever resigned. 'I often hear people call me a racist. How do you define racist? My driver is black and has been with me for thirty years. He was very concerned about me going to Soweto with a stranger. I treat him like a member of the family.

'Tomorrow I'm going to call a staff meeting and talk about my wonderful experience here. I will encourage them to get out of their fearful mentality and come here to Soweto,' Luyt said. He even asked if he could buy a house in Soweto.

Mbatha wrote: 'He also said it was a pity that white people left it too late to live in harmony with blacks. Strangely enough, it doesn't sound like campaign talk. If Louis Luyt fakes sincerity, he fakes it well.'

In Alexandra, Luyt had a robust exchange with an ANC supporter in a shebeen, to the enjoyment of many other patrons. His view that there should be much better control of immigrants coming into the country was popular among many. Luyt told journalists: 'I have been here before, but many years ago when I sold beer [Luyt Lager] illegally to shebeens.'

At a meeting with the Parliamentary Press Gallery in March, Luyt was asked why he opted for active politics. 'I have a right to be in politics, because I have more investments here than the rest of the politicians.'

Luyt's strongest draw card was his stubborn determination. As he told the press gallery: 'My reputation is that I'll do what I say. A lot of people make a lot of promises and don't stick to their word. Look at my record.'

The Federal Alliance did get at least one other party to become a partner – former ANC National Executive Committee member Rocky Malebane-Metsing and his People's Progressive Party. Malebane-Metsing was also the leader of the abortive 1987 coup in the Bophuthatswana homeland.

Luyt commented on Malebane-Metsing's joining: 'Our chances have become even better to form the next government. We are working for an alternative government, not an opposition, and this is the first step for us to become the government.'

Luyt seemed to think he was going to give the other opposition parties a run for their money in the election. He repeatedly said his party was going to draw the bulk of the more than 25 per cent undecided voters. His critics and opponents, on the other hand, thought he could never get more than a few thousand votes. In the end, the Federal Alliance received only 0,54 per cent of the vote, sufficient for two seats in the National Assembly and one in the Gauteng provincial legislature.

If the Federal Alliance's moderate political stance was a surprise to some, then Luyt's behaviour as a member of Parliament and his relationship with the ruling ANC in the house was even more unexpected.

In July 1999 the ANC appointed Luyt as a member of the Judicial Services Commission, which makes recommendations on the appointment of judges. This position was supposed to go to Douglas Gibson, a member of the official opposition, the Democratic Party. Luyt's appointment came shortly after he launched an attack on four judges of the highest court in the land, the Constitutional Court, questioning their impartiality and that of the court itself. 'This man is, according to the ANC, a fit and proper person to now judge the judges,' said Tony Leon, leader of the Democratic Party. 'How humiliating and profoundly disrespectful to our courts and the concept of judicial independence. If Dr Luyt wishes to be the useful idiot of the ANC, or their *werfbobbejaan* [tame baboon], then good luck to him even as he betrays his few voters.' Louis Luyt the ANC's *werfbobbe-jaan?*

The official spokesman for the Federal Alliance, Jan Bosman, said in a statement: 'The Federal Alliance is proud of the fact that the talents and capabilities of its leader were acknowledged with his appointment to this prestigious committee, and that he can serve South Africa in this regard.' He added that the party was 'now more determined than ever' to play a constructive role in South Africa and in Parliament, as opposed to the confrontational style of the Democratic Party.

There was clearly a strong element of trying to spite the Democratic Party in the ANC's appointment of Luyt to the Judicial Services Commission. But the ANC also facilitated his membership of four other Parliamentary Portfolio Committees: Finance, Justice and Constitutional Development, Public Accounts, and Sport and Recreation.

A very senior ANC parliamentarian told me that Luyt was 'always very charming' in Parliament, and that 'his contributions in the Finance and Public Accounts Committees were always very positive and helpful'. In fact, the source told me, 'I hated Luyt when he came to Parliament, but by the time he left, I was sorry to see him go. He clearly knew what he was talking about, and went out of his way to be constructive rather than to shoot us down. I was often surprised at the way he seemed to crave being liked by the black members of Parliament.'

People who expected fireworks from Luyt the Politician were disappointed. In stark contrast to his controversial and stormy career as an industrialist and rugby administrator, he rarely spoke in Parliament, and when he did it was mostly constructive and non-controversial, even when he criticised the ANC government. He got on well with most in Parliament – apart from Steve Tshwete, that is, whom he continued to resent fiercely.

A senior opposition politician told me that Luyt became bored with Parliament within the first few months. 'I don't think Louis really understood what parliamentary politics was about when he got there. He is a man of action, and he thought he could quickly help fix things that were going wrong in government. When he was confronted with the cumbersome way democracy is now practised in our Parliament – mostly through committees and tedious debates – he lost interest. Being just another tiny cog in a huge machine wasn't what he had envisaged being a politician and a member of Parliament. Louis is not a political animal at all. He saw government as a business; as something that just had to be done efficiently and nothing more. When he realised he wasn't going to be a main player, he left.'

A year after he was elected to Parliament, Luyt and his party joined the alliance of the Democratic Party and the New National Party, called the Democratic Alliance. In August 2000 he announced that he was retiring from Parliament and from politics, which he did after the last parliamentary session of the year.

13

THE FINAL RETREAT

I do believe by far the majority of South African rugby players and supporters support me. I think they will be bitterly disappointed if I do not remain involved in a watchdog capacity. But nothing is over. I am a life member of the Golden Lions.
— Louis Luyt, May 1998

The last chapter in Luyt's life as a public figure – that is, if he doesn't make an unexpected comeback – is the hardest to understand and one that must make even him sad. It was almost as if Luyt could not bear being out of the headlines for so long. A week after he announced his political retirement, he dropped a bombshell which would again end up in unsavoury mud-slinging and a court case.

On 24 August 2000 Luyt issued a statement from Ellis Park – he was still chairman of Ellis Park Stadium and of the Golden Lions Sports Trust – accusing his own CEO, the union's coach and a former Springbok of being involved in a 'devious conspiracy' against him. The accused were Johan Prinsloo, CEO of the GLRU and a long-time Luyt associate and confidante; Laurie Mains, Golden Lions and Cats coach and All Black coach between 1992 and 1995; and Hennie le Roux, former Springbok and Golden Lions flyhalf. The conspiracy, Luyt said, would have 'seriously undermined' the union and the trust.

Luyt said he had received information from two independent sources that 'sensitive issues' discussed at Ellis Park were being leaked to a third party. He added: 'A process of elimination followed, implicating only Mr Prinsloo. We approached a private security company to gather more information and their advice was to tap his phone. It is our considered opinion that this action was lawful.' Luyt's spokesman, Jan Bosman, admitted the next day that Luyt had also ordered Mains's phone to be tapped after Luyt became convinced that the coach was also involved in the conspiracy.

Mains said he found it hard to believe that the man who hired him as coach was now accusing him of conspiracy. 'I'm dumbfounded. It's unbelievable,' Mains told the *New Zealand Herald*. Mains admitted conflict with Luyt's son Louis junior and said he was aware of 'minor rumblings' about players' salaries, 'but to suggest a conspiracy is total fabrication'.

In an interview with *Punt Geselsradio* the day after Luyt's statement, Prinsloo gave the first indication of what lay at the heart of Luyt's paranoia: it was Luyt's clever brainchild, the Golden Lions Rugby Sports Trust, which had taken all control over the union and the stadium back in 1994, that had come back to haunt him. The sin committed by the 'conspirators' was that they wanted the control over the rugby players taken away from the stadium company (of which Louis Luyt was chairman) and given back to the union. Prinsloo told the radio station: 'Some of us in the Golden Lions thought that rugby did not belong with Ellis Park. Rugby belongs with rugby people and that is the Golden Lions Rugby Union.' Prinsloo stressed that he had done 'some work' around this issue, but that did not mean it was scandalous or a conspiracy. He admitted that there were 'problems' among the players and with the coach, and expressed his disappointment that the issues could not have been resolved internally, 'with Dr Luyt as part of the solution'.

The radio journalist, Andries Cornelissen, asked Prinsloo: 'Is it not also about clashing personalities, like Hennie le Roux and Dr Luyt?' Prinsloo responded: 'Well, clashing personalities – I wouldn't say they were like Bostik or Vasvat [brands of glue] all these years, but I'm sure each of them is entitled to his own opinion. Hennie as a player is surely entitled to his own opinion, as Doc Luyt is entitled to his own opinion. We all know Dr Luyt is entitled to his opinion ...'

Golden Lions Rugby Union president Jomo King and the Golden Lions players issued statements denying involvement in any conspiracy, although they confirmed that there were player-related grievances. The players stated that both Prinsloo and Mains had acted in the best interests of the union and the players. 'The players hereby give their unequivocal support to Laurie Mains and the Golden Lions Rugby Union,' the players' statement said.

Luyt seemed increasingly isolated – he had accused the union's CEO and director of Ellis Park, Johan Prinsloo, and the union's coach, Laurie Mains, of conspiring against him, and now the players and the union's president turned against him. Luyt's old friend, Gert Augustyn, quietly resigned as trustee of the Golden Lions Rugby Sports Trust when the storm broke.

But Luyt wasn't backing down. He hit back with a statement that same day demanding Prinsloo's immediate resignation as trustee of the Sports Trust and director of Ellis Park. 'I am astonished by the denial of the conspiracy by the Golden Lions Rugby Union President Jomo King,' Luyt said in the statement. 'When he was shown the transcripts of the telephone discussions of Mr Johan Prinsloo, Mr King was appalled at the contents and the nature of the conspiracy. He took it upon himself to resolve the matter, which included procuring the resignation of Mr Johan Prinsloo as a trustee from the Golden Lions Rugby Sports Trust and as a director of Ellis Park

Stadium (Pty) Ltd. We have correspondence to this effect. This he hasn't done thus far. It is therefore extremely strange for Mr King to now deny this.'

Luyt said King was also informed of a document signed by five senior players in which they aired their grievances and made certain demands. 'Mr Hennie le Roux attended a meeting at Sun City between Mr Laurie Mains and the Golden Lions players where this document was discussed,' he said. 'This past Monday Mr Le Roux addressed the Executive Committee of the Golden Lions Rugby Union at a players' practice where the executive was handed this document.

'In every conspiracy there is a whistle-blower and it was a player who brought this document to our attention. Mr Laurie Mains cannot therefore deny his involvement,' Luyt said. The 'whistle-blower' later turned out to be James Dalton, a former Springbok, Golden Lions and Cats hooker, who later also played for the Bulls. Dalton was, astonishingly, also one of the players' elected representatives to liaise with the union.

Luyt restated the legal position on which structure had what say: 'Since 1 January 2000 the professional teams from the GLRU have fallen under the financial management of Ellis Park (Pty) Ltd and the uncertainty of the CEO of the GLRU, Mr Johan Prinsloo, about the position of the professional teams leaves us amazed.'

Legal experts were surprised at the time that Luyt had so readily admitted to his old habit of tapping the phones of adversaries. The tapping of phones is not only in contravention of the Telecommunications Act, it is also in breach of the Bill of Rights entrenched in South Africa's Constitution, which protects citizens' privacy.

Luyt reacted to these legal opinions in his statement of 25 August: 'Before the security firm started with the tapping we obtained legal opinion on the legality of such a procedure. There are ample common law cases and a decision by the High Court of Appeal, which clearly distinguishes between lawful and unlawful tapping under certain circumstances. We are of the considered opinion that what was done was lawful and in the interest of the company and the Trust. The law cannot only protect conspirators, it is also there to protect those who are conspired against.'

The police did not think it was such a clear-cut case, and investigated possible criminal charges against Luyt and the security company. At the time of writing, the director of public prosecutions of the Witwatersrand, Advocate André de Vries, SC, was in possession of the police dossier and was considering at least three criminal charges against Luyt and 'other persons' involved in the tapping of the phones.

On 8 September 2000 Luyt applied for an urgent interdict at the Witwatersrand High Court in Johannesburg. He asked the court to remove Johan Prinsloo as a trustee of the Golden Lions Sports Trust. He also asked that, pending his removal, Prinsloo be prohibited from 'acting contrary to the interests of the Trust' by making public statements calculated to damage the trust in its work; by hindering or preventing the trust's exercise of financial control over the professional rugby division of the GLRU; and by criticising the trust, its policies or the conduct of its trustees to the public, members of the union or the players.

In his supporting affidavit, Luyt explained that since October 1998 the Golden Lions Rugby Union had entered into contracts with the union's top rugby players, by now professional sportsmen, and then ceded those contracts to Ellis Park Stadium (Pty) Ltd. When the Receiver of Revenue withdrew the tax exempt status of the union in July 1999, the professional arm of Golden Lions rugby was transferred to Ellis Park Stadium by agreement between the union, the Trust and the Ellis Park Stadium company. Since then, financial control of the professional rugby division vested in the company.

Luyt could not help but tell the court of his own achievements. 'I point out that when I became president of the Union in 1984, it was in dire financial straits. The lease of the stadium had been ceded to Volkskas Bank to whom the Union was indebted for an amount in excess of R26 million, which it was unable to pay. The Trust now has cash of approximately R80 million. Under my stewardship the Union operated profitably. Since I retired as president, the losses incurred by the Union which required to be funded by the Trust, have been substantial. There is accordingly a need to ensure that strict financial controls are exercised as to how the monies of the Trust are utilised for the benefit of the Union.'

Luyt then described how he uncovered the alleged conspiracy. He said he had meetings with representatives from other unions on proposals for the re-organisation of professional rugby, especially regarding the control of revenue from television and sponsorships. 'It was therefore a matter of great concern to me to receive reports from two independent sources that confidential discussions held at meetings at the stadium between me, other rugby officials and the first respondent (Prinsloo) were somehow being immediately report- ed to the management of SARFU and, in particular, one R Oberholzer (the CEO of SARFU). It was obvious that there was a leak within the Trust or the (Ellis Park) company. In particular, the information given to me indicated that confidential discussions held between me (rep- resenting the Golden Lions Rugby Union and the other entities men- tioned) and representatives of certain other unions had been divulged. These discussions had concerned the strategy to be adopt- ed to deal with the controversial proposals regarding the realign- ment of professional rugby.'

The 'one R Oberholzer' Luyt was referring to was, of course, his son-in-law, Rian. Oberholzer denied Luyt's allegations. 'I know absolutely nothing of any conspiracy in Gauteng Lions circles,' he told *Beeld* in an interview. 'Nobody in those circles has leaked infor- mation about confidential discussions or meetings to me. I have received no calls in relation to such meetings. My point of view is that neither I nor SARFU should get involved in this matter, because it is an internal issue that the Golden Lions must handle on their own. Why my name is now being dragged into it, I don't know.'

Luyt said he suspected Prinsloo was leaking the information, and decided to tap his phone to make sure. He said he was 'extremely reluctant to follow such advice because I questioned its legality and morality', but he had to protect the entities he represented.

He then presented the court with transcripts of Prinsloo's conversations with recently resigned trustee Gert Augustyn, union executive member Sampie Pienaar, two with Hennie le Roux and one with Laurie Mains. These transcripts, Luyt said, demonstrated that Prinsloo 'was actively pursuing a conspiracy of his own concerned with deconstructing the relationship between the Trust and the company and the Union and replacing it with a relationship in which the Union was largely freed of the supervision and control of the company and, by extension, the Trust'. In simpler terms, Prinsloo was trying to free the Golden Lions Rugby Union from the clutches of the Ellis Park Stadium company and the Golden Lions Rugby Sports Trust, both of which were headed by Luyt.

This meant, Luyt said, that Prinsloo wanted to create a situation where 'the Union and the players would determine the basis of remuneration for players without interference or participation by the (Ellis Park) company in the belief that the Trust would then be compelled to honour such obligations willy-nilly.'

According to the transcripts, Prinsloo told Augustyn (whom he called *Oom* or Uncle) on 3 August 2000: 'This thing of the fight with Ellis Park will cost us a lot in the end. There are many people, people like Corrie Pypers, I understand, who are getting sick and tired. We are going to have big problems soon.' Augustyn replied: 'Well, it is the only way how I can see it resolved – there will have to be a bit of an explosion.'

Later on, Prinsloo said: 'I think what has to happen is that Laurie has to ask the Executive Committee at some point what is going on

... When the teams were transferred to Ellis Park, it was only done for income tax purposes. The letter was slightly adjusted so that the Receiver of Revenue shouldn't think they are being done in, and that was all. I mentioned it again yesterday to the Doc. I was at a meeting. Look, he nearly took my head off.'

> AUGUSTYN: 'I think the Executive Committee should get to a point.'
>
> PRINSLOO: 'Look, you have to (see) Jomo at some point. I spoke to Jomo King last night, you must ring him some time and ask: Jomo, I don't know. I hear from the clubs, I hear from other people. What the hell is going on?'
>
> AUGUSTYN: 'No, I thought, for example, Hugh Bladen [a union executive committee member and trustee] sits there, but I don't know how he and Jomo communicate with each other.'
>
> PRINSLOO: 'They communicate, but you have to remember, Hugh is very thankful about the job his child got that was organised by the Luyts with certain people. They have looked after Hugh's kid. So I don't know if that affects it at all.'
>
> AUGUSTYN: 'And then I don't know where Jannie Ferreira stands. Doc mentioned the other day that Jannie said the clubs were not a problem. Because I tried to find out from the clubs, but they didn't talk about it.'
>
> PRINSLOO: 'No, I don't understand either. One will never know with him. That is the problem. Most people only want the problem solved. At the end of the day you have to manage, then the Executive Committee has to go back and tell him [Luyt]: we are taking the team back and that is it. [Take the] professional teams back and then everybody has to stand up and say that is the way it is going to be.'

The next day, 4 August, Prinsloo told Augustyn on the phone: 'Look, the ex-players, there are many people who are causing big trouble and at the end of the day it is not what we want. But it is perhaps time for the Executive Committee to go and tell Ellis Park that this thing with the teams isn't working. They want the teams back, finish and *klaar*.'

Prinsloo also had a phone conversation with union executive member Sampie Pienaar on 3 August. Prinsloo asked him: 'Do you think the Executive Committee will have enough guts to tell Ellis Park: look, this thing isn't working, we want the professional teams back?' Pienaar responded that some of them would, others not.

On the same day Prinsloo spoke to Hennie le Roux, player and player representative (he referred to Le Roux as 'luscious Hennie' at one point). Prinsloo said: 'I have an idea that if you as the team and the coach ask the Executive Committee ... tell the Executive Committee that the relationship between Transvaal and Ellis Park isn't working, you want the team to go back to the control of the Executive Committee. Then it has to go to the Executive Committee and they have to decide, and you have to talk to Sampie beforehand. I have already spoken to Sampie. Talk to a few guys there so that they can push this thing through, so that Jomo will be forced to tell Luyt: we want to cancel that agreement.'

And then there was Luyt's transcript of his conversation with hooker James Dalton. Luyt described how he came to tape that conversation: 'On the morning of 24 August 2000, James Dalton, who plays for the professional division of the Golden Lions, came to see me unsolicited, after having made various attempts to do so. He told me that he had remorse at what transpired. When I realised what he was saying I believed it was essential to have a record of this conversation and I recorded it without disclosure. I believed Dalton was likely to be subjected to strong pressure to retract or deny the conversation and I wished to be in a position to have some irrefutable evidence of what he wanted to say and also I did not wish to frighten him off from making the disclosures that he was apparently then ready to make.'

Dalton was reporting on a meeting of players and some officials at Sun City, and another meeting at a team practice.

LUYT: 'What were Hennie's [le Roux's] words?'

DALTON: 'OK, basically that things have gone on long enough, that we have been fighting for years, the players and the Union, and the unpleasant work environment and that there is also, what do you call it, friction between the players and the Union.'

LUYT: 'That's what Hennie said.'

DALTON: 'Yes, but I'll get Doc a copy of that thing presented to the ...'

LUYT: 'What was the reaction of these men?'

DALTON: 'Well, no, they said, basically they only said they hear what we are saying, they will take it up. They will sit down and discuss it and give us feedback on a regular basis after the tour. And we also, in that thing it was said that they want feedback for the players within seven days, they want answers on all these things.'

LUYT: 'And what was Mains's input?'

DALTON: 'He just said Doc refused to take his calls and Doc was tapping his phone and that he is now getting legal advice and he is not prepared to be part of an institution which taps people's phones and he never said ...'

LUYT: 'But at Sun City, what did he say at Sun City?'

DALTON: 'Oh, at Sun City, basically that things have to change. That the time had come for Doc and Doc's son to go. And you know, he said he had nothing to gain. He would get his money in any case, so he is not going to allow Doc to beat him. So if he says now he gives up, then Doc had won basically, and then he said he would not. What else did he say? I'll have to go and think and write it down.'

Luyt said of Hennie le Roux: 'I don't care about him at all [*gee nie 'n duit vir hom om nie*]. I have never cared about him.' What did bother him, Luyt indicated, was that senior players like Rassie Erasmus, Thinus Delport, Grant Esterhuizen and Leon Boshoff were also against him. 'I want little Louis' resignation,' Dalton reported. 'Who wants it?' Luyt asked. 'No, that's what these players said,' replied Dalton.

Dalton later told Luyt that he wanted their conversation to remain confidential. When Luyt said it could not, it had to come out, Dalton said if it did become known that he had talked to Luyt, 'I would prefer it if Doc could look after me'. Luyt replied: 'I won't drop you, James.' Dalton said if Mains were to stay on as coach and it became known that he (Dalton) had talked to Luyt, 'then he will work me out of the team and then I'll sit with nothing, where will I play rugby, where do I get a contract?'

> LUYT: 'Mains is not your future. Mains is a New Zealander who is here for a short time, that is all. But that he does these sort of things against me ... That is why he can't get a job in New Zealand, James.'
>
> DALTON: 'Yes, they say he is a coach who has never won a trophy.'
>
> LUYT: 'Well, at least he won the Currie Cup, but with a group of very good guys around him. No, that is so ... So they said they are unhappy with me and Louis junior and that some of the trust money was missing?'
>
> DALTON: 'Yes, and the trust money was not used for the players and some of the trust money was missing and the trustees should be changed, and they are unhappy that Doc has control over the trustees, about the handling of the medical aid ...'

The 'misuse' of trust funds later came up in a letter from GLRU president Jomo King to Luyt on 29 August. King wrote: 'At my meeting with yourself at 5 pm on Wednesday 23 August, you informed me that an unnamed player had stated that "someone" whom you did not identify, had publicly stated that "Trust Funds had been misused". At the time, I automatically believed that this was with reference to the GLRU Sport Trust Fund. It was naturally of great concern to myself if such a statement had been publicly made. I have investigated this matter and believe the following to be the correct facts. As I believe you are aware, the Players' Committee organised a golf day and a dinner during 1999 to raise funds on behalf of the players, and this was known as the Players' Fund, although sometimes it is mistakenly referred to as the Players' Trust. During July 2000 when the Players' Committee endeavoured to establish how much money was in this fund, it was established that these monies had all been paid into the GLRU/Ellis Park Stadium accounts and that no accurate record of the amounts had been kept of a separate and identifiable amount.'

Hennie le Roux, chairman of the Golden Lions Union players' committee, told the newspaper *Beeld* that 'in the ranks of the players there is a very deep disappointment' in James Dalton after it was revealed that he was Luyt's source of information.

In Luyt's application for an urgent interdict against Johan Prinsloo, three other trustees of the Golden Lions Rugby Sports Trust were also listed as respondents: Jomo King, president of the GLRU, Hugh Bladen and Professor Johan Gouws, vice-president of the GLRU.

Prinsloo's counsel, Advocate Edmund Wessels, argued that Luyt's application was malicious, outrageous and groundless and that there was not a shred of evidence that there was a conspiracy against him. Judge Ivor Schwartzman said he would give his ruling in a few days' time.

But if Luyt's 'conspiracy' accusations and his court application came as a shock to the administrators and players at the Golden Lions Rugby Union, Luyt came with a bigger one: he suddenly and inexplicably announced that he was withdrawing the lawsuit against Prinsloo.

Lawyers were stunned at Luyt's sudden cold feet. 'You can't throw in the towel more than this,' one said, pointing out that Luyt had even offered to pay all Prinsloo's legal costs on a scale of 'attorney and client'. This is described as a 'penal cost order' and is only awarded in highly exceptional cases. The fact that Luyt had offered to pay these costs even before the court had given its findings in his appeal against Prinsloo showed 'at the least that Dr Luyt really got cold feet', law professor Marinus Wiechers was quoted as saying.

In fact, Luyt's move was so unexpected and surprising that the GLRU executive and the Sports Trust trustees nervously waited for days afterwards for the 'catch'. 'Something is not right here. Doctor Luyt is not a person to throw in the towel so easily. The bomb is still going to burst, just watch,' a senior official said.

There was no catch. Luyt had made two huge mistakes in his court application – mistakes pointed out by Prinsloo's counsel, Edmund Wessels. The first mistake was that he implied that the remaining trustees of the Sports Trust were supporting him in his application, when they were not. The second mistake was that he said that he had tapped only Prinsloo's phone, but Wessels and his team had seized some of his records and discovered that he had tapped virtually all the phones of TRFU and Ellis Park officials working from the Ellis Park offices. If he had persisted in the case, these untruths, declared under oath, would have come to light.

In the period after his withdrawal, Luyt's friend Henry Vorster acted as 'mediator' between Prinsloo, Luyt and the GLRU executive. He indicated to the executive at one meeting that Prinsloo had agreed to resign, which was not true. When the executive discovered this attempt at misleading them, they were angry and decided to finally confront Luyt.

From this point, things started happening quickly. On 25 October 2000 Laurie Mains announced his resignation as coach of the Golden

Lions with a year left of his contract. He blamed the 'management style of Ellis Park and their constant interference and undermining of the team' for his decision. Mains did not mention Luyt by name in his statement, but said: 'It has been impossible to maintain the focus, commitment and motivation to function effectively. Sadly, 2000 has been a traumatic experience for all of us at the Lions.' Mains stayed on as coach of the Super 12 team the Cats, and had a very successful 2001 season.

On 26 October 2000 Luyt announced his resignation from all his positions at the Golden Lions Rugby Football Union and Ellis Park, and Louis junior resigned from his positions at Ellis Park Stadium.

In a statement announcing his resignation, Luyt said he was withdrawing from rugby completely: 'I am severing all ties with the GLRU and Ellis Park Stadium. I have given a great deal of my life to rugby and to Golden Lions, sometimes at great personal cost, and am therefore not prepared to be involved or associated with individuals who use petty personal vendettas and ambitions to further their rugby careers.

'These happenings at the GLRU will no doubt reflect negatively on the Golden Lions Rugby Union, its management, its financial status, Ellis Park Stadium and the Sports Trust.'

Luyt added: 'The time is now prudent to announce that on 26 September I informed the board of directors of Ellis Park Stadium (Pty) Ltd as well as some of the A trustees of the Golden Lions Sports Trust that I had decided to sever all ties at the end of December. I was also going to resign as an honorary lifelong member of the Golden Lions [union]. That I have done two weeks ago. From individual quarters, I was asked to reconsider my decision, but the continued problems, internal strife and the absence of trust between EPS, the Trust, myself and the GLRU necessitated this decision.'

The decision to sever all ties, Luyt went on, had been made 'a long time ago': he had sold his house in Saxonwold, Johannesburg, and had already moved to Ballito on the KwaZulu-Natal north coast.

'Other business interests require my attention and I have also indicated in June that I will retire from politics at the end of the year. In severing my ties with the Golden Lions it will also be necessary to call in a loan which I made to EPS, which amounts to several millions, to protect the foreign investment, that is, not to realise the overseas investment to fund the GLRU and the other entities.'

Referring to his son, Louis junior, and his old friend Willie Kruger, he said: 'The premature public announcement of the GLRU officials, who have no standing in this matter whatsoever, on individuals at Ellis Park terminating their services complicated this matter even further. Negotiations were on their way with these individual personnel with regards to severance packages and this premature announcement could add to a protracted process which could include legal action by the parties concerned.'

Luyt gave the impression that he was simply sick and tired of the drama at Ellis Park and that was why he quit, but GLRU insiders tell another version. Two days before his resignation, they said, the executive committee of the GLRU met to discuss a motion that Luyt be asked to resign from all his positions at the union, Ellis Park and the trust. Five out of the six members voted for the motion, the other one abstained from voting. Immediately after this meeting the same motion was put to a meeting of all the chairmen of the Golden Lions Rugby Union rugby clubs. Eighteen of the twenty-one delegates voted in favour of it.

That was the Monday evening. On Tuesday morning Luyt was officially informed of the vote at the two meetings. The next day he announced his resignation. He had no option.

The most controversial and tumultuous era in South African rugby, the 'Luyt era', was over. At the end of 2000, Luyt was living in Ballito Bay with no ties to South African rugby or politics.

CONCLUSION

'Yet each man must kill the thing he loves.' The words of Oscar Wilde might have been written exclusively for Louis Luyt.
— *François Pienaar, 1999*

When Luyt phoned me the week before I finished writing the book, he sounded much more relaxed and at peace than I had ever heard him before. Apart from controlling a few business interests, it seemed as if he has at last decided to slacken the pace of his hectic life. I could hear children in the background, and he said he was really enjoying his grandchildren.

He has retired to his hotel-like mansion on the beachfront of Ballito Bay on the KwaZulu-Natal north coast. The house is very much like Luyt's life: eighteen bedrooms, a lobby, two studies, dining room, lounge, a balcony which can accommodate 126 people for dinner, a bar, snooker room, TV room, gymnasium, sauna, pool, squash court, and fourteen bathrooms. The main bedroom is two hundred square metres in size. The air-conditioning, woodwork and finishing were all imported from the United States. When Luyt built the house in the early 1980s, it cost him US$6 million, he says.

He told the *Sharks Magazine* in May 2001: 'I'm actually ashamed to admit it, but here at Ballito I'm the laziest person to get up in the morning. Four hours sleep a night used to be more than enough for me. And if I didn't take sleeping tablets it would be two hours. But nowadays I walk around in shorts and sometimes only take a shower around 9:30 in the morning. And you know what, it's fabulous. I really enjoy it because I can relax.'

I wonder what he thinks when he looks over the Indian Ocean from his balcony and reflects over his achievements and failures.

Luyt's rise from poor Karoo kid to one of the richest men in South Africa is truly the stuff Hollywood movies are made of. It must give him tremendous satisfaction, because he did it all on his own, and in the face of adversity. It wasn't easy for a young Afrikaner to make it in the financial world of the 1950s and 1960s – although it is true that some of his transactions and business practices were frowned upon.

But what did he do for rugby? There is little doubt in my mind that Luyt did more to change the face of rugby in South Africa than anyone else. In the second half of the 1980s South African rugby was showing signs of being isolated from the world and of being a cultural tool of Afrikaner nationalists. In New Zealand, Australia, Britain and France the game had progressed – not only the style of rugby, but rugby management and its relationship with commercial sponsorship and television broadcast rights. Danie Craven was perhaps a wonderful old chap, but he was a man living in the past. He clung to a puritanical, nostalgic notion of rugby that the other major rugby-playing countries had already outgrown. It is unlikely that any one of the other rugby administrators around in the late 1980s and early 1990s would have had the instinct, guts, knowledge and energy to take South African rugby management into the new era as swiftly and effectively as Luyt did – first at Transvaal and then at SARFU.

But I also think Luyt did a lot of damage to South African rugby. I'm not even referring to his rudeness and lack of diplomacy or the petty squabbles with players and other administrators that brought the sport into disrepute. He was the head of SARFU when South Africa won the World Cup in 1995. It is now a cliché to say that Nelson Mandela and François Pienaar together on the winners' podium made one of the magic moments in our nation's history. But clichés are often true. Millions of black South Africans looked at this *Boere se sport* with new eyes for the first time. Luyt and his fellow rugby executives squandered a once-in-a-lifetime opportunity to capitalise on this – to build rugby into a truly national sport in South Africa. It would have been good not only for rugby; it could also have helped bridge the deep racial divide in South African society.

Instead, Luyt and his men spent all their energies on the commercial and financial side of the sport. He had inspired and resourceful men like Edward Griffiths and Morné du Plessis in his employ, who saw it as their vision to popularise rugby in all communities and to stimulate and develop young black players, and in François Pienaar he had a charismatic man who could have served as a symbol of this new unity.

Instead, he fired Griffiths because he 'became too important', and he alienated Du Plessis and Pienaar, allowing Pienaar to be driven out of the country. At the time Luyt retreated from rugby, the sport was still suffering from a bad image among the majority of South Africa's people.

Part of Luyt's obsession with rugby as a multi-million rand business was his decision to give the pay channel M-Net virtually exclusive television broadcast rights. To this day the vast majority of the people in the country have no exposure to rugby. This only perpetuates the image of rugby as a 'white' sport.

It is possible that Luyt, like so many others, still feels deep down that rugby is a white domain. His remark after he had the old apartheid anthem played at Ellis Park in 1992 – that if it was acceptable to play *Nkosi Sikelel' iAfrika* at soccer matches, why not *Die Stem* at rugby matches? – could be an indication of this, as is his outburst against 'spineless whites' who don't want to fight for what they own after he was kicked out of SARFU.

I asked Jannie Engelbrecht, a Springbok hero of the 1960s who has been deeply involved in rugby all his life, what he thought Luyt's contribution to South African rugby was. 'I think in the early stages Louis was very good for South African rugby,' Engelbrecht said. 'There was a vacuum after Doc's death. The unification process was very difficult. Louis got off to a good start. His business acumen meant that rugby became financially strong again. But it slowly deteriorated. Internationally we became worse polecats than we were during isolation.

'And internally he was very destructive. He hired and fired people, some of them top people, at will. He never built people up. It became so clear, the minute someone became strong, Louis got rid of him. It is the characteristic of a dictator that he always wants weak people around him. To a degree Doc Craven had the same problem, he also did not like strong people around him. But Louis was more ruthless. The moment someone became popular and successful, he saw that man as a threat. Perhaps it is a feeling of inferiority that made him like that, that made him feel he had to be totally in control at all times.'

In his autobiography, François Pienaar writes about Luyt's ousting from SARFU: 'I felt sad that this man who had contributed so much to the game over two decades, from his dynamic leadership of Transvaal to his legendary business acumen, should have suffered such a humiliating and undignified exit. He had created everything with great skill, and yet then appeared to preside over its destruction. He created a truly great Transvaal team, and appeared to preside over its destruction; he had created the world champion Springboks and then appeared to preside over its destruction. "Yet each man must kill the thing he loves." The words of Oscar Wilde might have been written exclusively for Louis Luyt.'

Former Transvaal scrumhalf and nowadays popular talk show host John Robbie (probably the only man ever to tell Luyt to his face 'fuck you') has a serious soft spot for Luyt. He has fond memories

230

of Luyt's first years at Transvaal and recalls that during those years all the players thought Luyt had been sent to Transvaal from heaven. 'At his best, he had a rare ability to see a problem in its simplest form. He went for the problem with an energy and enthusiasm that swept all along with him and swept away all who couldn't stand the pace. Identify, plan and execute. Simple as that.' Robbie believes Luyt is a highly intelligent man 'who wants to do well and wants desperately to be loved by everyone. However, as with so many, his strength is his weakness, and his career has seen a succession of highs and lows, triumphs and disasters that are extraordinary by any standards.'

Senior rugby writer and erstwhile Luyt confidante Dan Retief (of whom Luyt later said: 'I know him, I don't like him, I don't trust him') expressed his sadness when Luyt finally quit rugby. Retief wrote in an opinion piece on the Internet website *www.superrug-by.co.za*: 'We used to talk a lot in that big office of his. I admired his intellect and his ability to get things done. There was a bust to the right of his desk and I once enquired at its relevance. Luyt recited the Latin phrase that I have subsequently seen attributed to the Roman poet Juvenal: *Quis custodiet custodes ipsos?* Who will guard the guards themselves? To me it provided an insight into the enigma that is Louis Luyt. He needs to be in total control. He trusts no man. He loves the law, but he is suspicious if he does not draw up the rules himself.'

Retief explains why Luyt's retirement made him sad: 'Perhaps because Luyt failed to be what he could have been. He righted a list-ing SARFU ship and he ran the best World Cup there has ever been, but unlike Doc Craven his motivation was not for the greater good of rugby and his ego got in the way.'

Towards the end of writing this book, many friends and colleagues asked me what Louis Luyt was really like. After researching his life intensively for three months, I should probably have been able to give an insightful and snappy answer. But I can't.

Luyt is the most complex person I have ever come across. Every time I thought I had an idea of how he thought or what his personality was like, he surprised me by acting in a way I least expected. A more classic case of Dr Jekyll and Mr Hyde will be hard to find. He is more than utterly unpredictable; he is a walking contradiction. Almost every person I spoke to who knew Luyt well, talked about his unpredictability, although some called it impulsiveness. There are so many clear examples of his speaking or acting without forethought – like his disastrous speech at the 1995 World Cup dinner.

Probably connected to this trait are his infamous mood swings. An old associate of Luyt's, who actually still calls himself a friend and admirer, told me: 'Whenever I see Louis, all my antennas are up to test his mood. If he is in a good mood, he is excellent, intelligent company, really good to be with. When I sense he is in a dark mood, I always try to get away quickly, because you never know what could happen next. The problem is he sometimes switches moods unexpectedly. But if you stay on Louis' right side, he is a great and loyal friend, a really special guy.'

Perhaps it is inevitable that a person with Luyt's extraordinary energy and drive would be at least a little mercurial. If he had been a stable, controlled person he probably would not have been so powerful and dynamic.

I have gained the impression from all my research and interviews that Luyt is a highly intelligent, streetwise and resourceful man. But he has serious control issues: he simply cannot stand not being in charge of a situation. This makes him manipulative, even callous. Stories abound of Luyt using money or threats to get people to do what he wanted. Because his life had been hard and lonely, he is prone to vengefulness, intolerance and even pettiness. You are either his friend or his enemy. He doesn't tolerate opposition or criticism.

Former Springbok and Transvaal flyhalf Hennie le Roux, a successful businessman in his own right, has a telling story about Luyt. Le Roux was one of the most outspoken men when it came to players' rights, and at one point during the unhappiness in the Golden Lions camp he proposed that a players' representative serve on the union's executive committee. A few days later he bumped into Luyt who snarled at him: 'Oh, so you want to be on the executive? It will never happen in my lifetime!' He did not even greet Le Roux for two years after that.

Luyt was also known as someone with an explosive temper. In the middle of his battle with Sports Minister Steve Tshwete about the commission of inquiry in March 1997, a photographer from *The Star*, Rian Horn, waited outside Luyt's Ellis Park offices to take a picture of him. Luyt lunged at him, grabbed his camera and smashed the flash. He took Horn by the shoulders and started shaking him. 'When he heard I was from *The Star*,' Horn said, 'he went pale with anger and tried to break the flash even further.'

I asked Jannie Engelbrecht to explain Luyt's extraordinary behaviour. 'I wish I understood,' he mused. 'Perhaps people with deeper psychological knowledge should try to analyse his personality. There is a side of him that I liked, but his actions were inexplicable. I wasn't the only one to experience Louis like that. Let me put it to you like this: it was far from normal behaviour, far from what one expects from a normal person.

'Normally people know what the consequences of their actions are going to be. You have to take responsibility for your own actions. I know that if I drive a car at 250 km/h and the tyre bursts, I'm going to see my backside. I know it. Somehow Louis never knew that. *En kyk hoe lyk hy nou* (And look at him now).'

Perhaps South African rugby is better off without Louis Luyt. He was a divisive figure and because of his volatility and authoritarianism too much time and energy was spent on rugby politics instead of rugby development. He did not fit in with the new culture of transparency and democracy in South African society. His unashamed nepotism and his controversial business dealings cast a shadow over the respectability of the sport.

When Luyt phoned me in the days before this book went to print, he tried to justify some of the things he had done. He told me out of the blue that he had personally contributed R4 million to the *Citizen* project; that he thought that newspaper was a purely commercial project until he found out at the last moment when it was too late to pull back that it was a government project; that he and Sanlam's Andreas Wassenaar had financed the referendum PW Botha held to get approval for the constitutional changes that added coloured and Indian houses to the white Parliament.

I thought that was quite sad. Clearly Luyt can still not face the mistakes he has made in his life. His denial of reality cost him dearly towards the end of his public life. It is a pity that in retirement he cannot confront that denial and admit his mistakes, at least to himself.

Now Louis Luyt is standing on his balcony, a lonely and ostracised sixty-nine-year-old man. He was the architect of his own demise: too much greed, too much hunger for power, too much dishonesty, too many people humiliated and stepped on.

The one thing he has not lost is his money. He is still one of the richest people in South Africa – for what that's worth.

SELECT BIBLIOGRAPHY

I want to thank my fellow journalists who have written about Louis Luyt over the last three decades. I relied heavily on newspapers and magazines to form a picture of Luyt, especially *Die Burger, The Star, Cape Times, Beeld, Rapport, Sunday Times, Sunday Tribune, Huisgenoot, Leadership, Financial Mail, Finansies en Tegniek, Cape Argus, Mail & Guardian, Die Volksblad* and *The Citizen.*
I also consulted the following books for information and insights:

Keith Clayton and Chris Greyvenstein, *The Craven Tapes – Doc Tells All.* Cape Town: Human & Rousseau, 1995.
Paul Dobson, *Doc – The Life of Danie Craven.* Cape Town: Human & Rousseau, 1994.
Paul Dobson, *Nick Mallet – The Story So Far.* Cape Town: Struik, 1999.
George Gerber, *Dok Craven – Agter die Kap van die Byl.* Stellenbosch: Stellenbosch Rugbyvoetbalklub, 2000.
Edward Griffiths, *One Team, One Country – The Greatest Year of Springbok Rugby.* Johannesburg: Penguin, 1996.
Albert Grundlingh, André Odendaal and Burridge Spies, *Beyond the Tryline – Rugby and South African Society.* Johannesburg: Ravan, 1995.

Ian McIntosh, with John Bishop. *Mac – the Face of Rugby. The Ian McIntosh Story.* Cape Town: Don Nelson, 2000.

François Pienaar, *Rainbow Warrior.* Jeppestown: Jonathan Ball, 1999.

Rory Steyn, *One Step Behind Mandela – The Story of Rory Steyn, Nelson Mandela's Chief Bodyguard, as Told to Debora Patta.* Rivonia: Zebra, 2000.

Gary Teichmann, with Edward Griffiths. *For the Record.* Jeppestown: Jonathan Ball, 2000.

Derek Wyatt, *Rugby DisUnion – The Making of Three World Cups.* London: Victor Gollancz, 1995.

GLOSSARY

amaBokoboko : Africanised term for Springbok rugby team

Afrikanerleier : Afrikaner leader

armblankes : poor whites

bakkie : small van or truck with a cabin and open back

braai, braaivleis : barbecue

Boertjie : young Afrikaner

Boks, Bokke : Springbok rugby team

Broeder : member of the Afrikaner Broederbond

Broederbond : secret brotherhood of influential Afrikaner males

dominee : minister of the Dutch Reformed Church

dorp : small town

gatvol : sick and tired

goeie : good

kaffirs : derogatory term for blacks

korrelkop : crusty, ill-tempered

Nat : member of the National Party

oom : uncle

shebeen : tavern

volk : the Afrikaner people

volksbyeenkoms : gathering of the *volk*

volksfees : festival of the *volk*